DAVID AND THE
DEUTERONOMIST

Indiana Studies in Biblical Literature
Herbert Marks and Robert Polzin,
general editors

DAVID AND THE DEUTERONOMIST

A Literary Study of the
Deuteronomic History

Part Three
2 SAMUEL

ROBERT
POLZIN

INDIANA UNIVERSITY PRESS
BLOOMINGTON & INDIANAPOLIS

The paper used in this publication meets the minimum
requirements of American
National Standard for Information Sciences—Permanence of Paper for Printed
Library Materials, ANSI Z39.48-1984.

Manufactured in the United States of America

Library of Congress Cataloging-in-Publication Data

Polzin, Robert.
    David and the Deuteronomist : 2 Samuel / Robert Polzin.
        p. cm. — (A literary study of the Deuteronomic history ; pt.
  3) (Indiana studies in biblical literature)
    Includes bibliographical references and indexes.
    ISBN 0-253-34553-7 (cloth : alk. paper)
    1. Bible. O.T. Samuel, 2nd—Criticism, interpretation, etc.
I. Title. II. Series. III. Series: Polzin, Robert. Literary study
of the Deuteronomic history ; pt. 3.
BS1325.2.P649   1993
222′.44066—dc20   93-22056

1 2 3 4 5 99 98 97 96 95 94 93

For Joan, Jonathan, and David

CONTENTS

PREFACE

In this third volume of a projected four-part study of the Deuteronomic History (Deuteronomy through 2 Kings), little remains to be said by way of prologue. Like its predecessors, this book is a contemporary reading of an ancient text and is addressed to specialists and laypersons alike.

As this series has progressed, I have tried more and more to keep matters of methodological or theoretical interest in the background. My emphasis has been on the reading itself rather than on arguing for such a reading. This is not to claim that the focus of these three volumes has not varied: *Moses and the Deuteronomist* does address methodological and hermeneutic issues more insistently than its successors, and *Samuel and the Deuteronomist* indeed makes a serious attempt, in its scholarly apparatus, to compare its readings with those of many previous studies. In the present volume I have decided to keep such evidence of dialogue with contemporary scholarship to a minimum, not in order to ignore or deny the importance of such dialogue, but rather to allow my version of the story in 2 Samuel to speak for itself. Nevertheless, the philosophy of language and the love of literature that are associated with Mikhail Bakhtin and his school continue to provide the major contemporary inspiration for my retelling of an ancient classic.

By the time that 2 Samuel reached a stable enough shape to enable the kind of reading this book offers, countless individuals—all those ancients whom we know existed but about whom we scarcely know anything—had contributed to the final product in ways so important we assign the terms authorial or editorial to them, or so insignificant we talk of glosses, scribal lapses, or the like. To this anonymous host, who helped create what Frank Kermode has called "a collection of books produced without thought of literary value, yet possessing it to a unique degree," I offer a commemorative word of admiration and gratitude.

In a more contemporary vein, I am grateful to those who have helped me at various stages in the preparation of these volumes on the Deuteronomic History. At an especially critical period in my research, Naomi Griffiths, then Dean of Arts at Carleton University, was instrumental in helping me keep this project alive. Edgar and Dorothy Davidson, through their establishment of a fund in Religious Studies at Carleton, but especially through their constant encouragement and friendship, did more for the completion of my research than they can imagine. The superb critical judgment and constant support of Herbert Marks has been evident in every volume of Indiana Studies in Biblical Literature. His advice about how to improve the lot of readers of this volume was once again on target. Also my thanks to the staff at Indiana University Press for its invaluable assistance in maintaining the quality of offerings in this series. I hope that the present volume measures up to these standards.

Finally, during the past three years, while I labored to understand how members of David's household helped to shape the story in 2 Samuel, Joan, Jonathan, and David continued to provide strength and love within my own family.

Ottawa
September 1992

DAVID AND THE
DEUTERONOMIST

· 1 ·

HEROES
(1:1–27)

For they have not rejected you, but they have rejected me from being king over them . . . forsaking me and serving other gods, so they are also doing to you. (The LORD to Samuel, 1 Sam. 8:7–8)

With the death of Saul the Deuteronomic History turns its full attention to David, who will dominate the story until his own death in 1 Kings 2. The division of the original Book of Samuel into two books seems to have occurred relatively late, yet a close reading of 2 Samuel 1 indicates how appropriately placed the break in the story appears to be. Although the entire chapter looks backward through a second account of Saul's death (1–16) and through a rehearsal of the meaning of that death in David's moving elegy about the fall of the mighty (17–27), much in the chapter also looks forward. Like the opening chapter of 1 Samuel that began an intricately structured overture to the entire monarchic history, 2 Samuel 1 will prove to be a nuanced introduction to the life and career of David now beginning in earnest after the death of his rival. And like 1 Samuel 1, this introduction will weave various narrative threads into a multitextured tapestry of king and kingdom, private life and public event, all profoundly integrated in Israelite ideology.

Another feature of the beginning of 2 Samuel that calls to mind the beginning of 1 Samuel is the combination of prose and poetry; in both introductions the particular resources of each form of language are used to produce an especially persuasive and moving summary of the detailed history to follow.

Doubling the Account of Saul's Death (1:1–16)

Most immediately calling for interpretation in chapter 1 is the discrepant account that the Amalekite lad gives of the death of Saul. Saul is described

in 1 Samuel 31 as having committed suicide; the lad claims to have killed
him himself. Is he lying or telling the truth? On one hand, the omniscient
narrator has already told us at the end of 1 Samuel "what really happened." On the other hand, what if there is some truth in what the lad
says? What if his very lie addresses a narrow or simplistic view of how Saul
came to die and, more importantly, of what his death *means*? What if the
twofold explanation of Saul's death is precisely what this fractured account
in 1 Samuel 31 and 2 Samuel 1 means to emphasize? And how does one go
about piecing together such a splintered view of things?

David's Double

Chapter 1 brings David his first intelligence about Saul's death. For the
reader this chapter doubles back on the events recounted in 1 Samuel 31,
and such a repetition means something different to scholars of different
bent. A source-oriented scholar will want to turn literary historical skills to
the fashioning of a plausible theory, say, about a twofold tradition concerning the death of Saul. A discourse-oriented reader, on the other hand,
might concentrate on the obvious duplicity of the Amalekite messenger in
order to use this feature of the story to reinforce the ironic dimensions of
a theme that began in 1 Samuel 1–7 and continues on in the entire History. David himself expresses the theme in 4:10, where he looks back on
the events of 2 Samuel 1: "When one told me, 'Behold, Saul is dead,' and
thought he was bringing good news, I seized him and slew him at Ziklag,
which was the reward I gave him for his good news."

There is a conventional punchline that begins, "I have some good news
and some bad news." The second book of Samuel is far from an ancient
joke, yet there are enough indications within it, as this literary reading will
suggest, either that good news and bad news are two sides of the same
narrative coin, or else that one is not always able to make heads or tails out
of the distinction itself.

Whether the strong or weak version of a skeptical attitude toward "what
really happened" is truer to this narrative unfolding of David's life may be
difficult to establish in the postmodern atmosphere of contemporary
scholarship. Nevertheless, it may be possible at least to suggest how profoundly saturated 2 Samuel is with what Bakhtin called *internally persuasive
speech* (as distinguished from the authoritative word). In this respect and as
a particularly apt example of ancient Israelite narrative, 2 Samuel—and
the entire History for that matter—appears in its literary stylistics to be
much closer to the modern novel than most scholars would ever have
dared to suggest. The paradox, of course, is that biblical literature has

always rightly been seen as the epitome of the authoritative word within western civilization and culture. That supremely authoritative speech and internally persuasive speech can be thoroughly integrated within the same utterance—as I have been suggesting for the Deuteronomic History—was, in my opinion, one of Bakhtin's more profound insights.[1] The second version of Saul's death, here in 2 Samuel 1, is a striking illustration of the History's stylistic and ideological resources that have gone unnoticed within, and perhaps because of, the obviously authoritative convention of biblical narrative.

Is Saul supposed to have killed himself by falling on his sword (1 Samuel 31) or did the Amalekite dispatch him at his own request (2 Samuel 1)? Despite the speculative possibility of alternate traditions having been combined rather awkwardly into the Books of Samuel, a modern poetics of narrative might rather see in this second account an obvious lie that brings to the one who utters it a quick death. Whether David kills the youth for lying to one king or for killing another or, if the latter is the case, in a principled defense of the LORD's anointed or for the sake of appearances—none of this is especially clear from repeated readings of the story. What is clear is how the convention of the narrator's omniscience and reliability, in 1 Samuel 31 as elsewhere, helps to underscore the duplicity of the Amalekite's version. What still needs to be described in some detail, however, is how the character's duplicity and the narrator's doubling coalesce to form an apt introduction to the account of the Davidic dynasty now beginning.

We know that the Amalekite is lying, but the story does not allow us to know for sure whether David knows also. This gap in the story is another reminder of how well the narrator has shielded from us the inner life of David; we continue to know little of David's motivation in this and other important matters. It is not a simple matter within the narrative to see Saul's death—and the deaths that will follow it—from David's perspective. Perhaps the Deuteronomist has invested the story with other means to help us characterize David.

The first words of the Amalekite immediately indicate that more is at stake in this chapter than a duplicitous attempt to win favor with the one thought most likely to take Saul's place as king. The messenger responds to David's initial query by saying "I have escaped (*nimlaṭṭî*) from the camp of Israel" (v. 3), that is, "from the camp of Saul" (v. 2). Just as Saul in the later chapters of 1 Samuel was continually described as the one who sought after (*biqqēš*) David,[2] so also, from 1 Samuel 19 on, David is par excellence the one who escapes from the murderous Saul.[3] In fact, apart from David, the only other escapees (*nimlāṭ*) in 1 Samuel are Abiathar, who escapes to David from Saul in 22:20, and the Amalekites, who escape from David in 30:17. It appears, then, that the narrator introduces the Amalekite messenger as a figure who doubles for David according to a narrative purpose that still needs to be described.

David is characterized in 1 Samuel as the one who continually escapes from Saul; in its concluding chapters he manages to escape to the Philistines. In a rare glimpse into the inner life of David the narrator tells us, "David said in his heart, 'I shall now perish one day by the hand of Saul; there is nothing better than that I should certainly escape (*himmālēṭ 'immālēṭ*) to the land of the Philistines; then Saul will despair of seeking me any longer within the borders of Israel and I shall escape (*wᵉnimlaṭṭî*) out of his hand'" (1 Sam. 27:1). David's "I shall escape from Saul's hand" and the Amalekite's "I have escaped from Saul's camp" unite these characters as doubles for one another within the larger story line.[4]

The characterization of David as the preeminent escapee in 1 Samuel has an ideological dimension that explains his double's function here in 2 Samuel 1. The controlled manner in which the Deuteronomist implicates David in the death of Saul from 1 Samuel 24 on, even as the narrative seeks continually to exonerate him from such a charge, is surely a powerful example of the History's artistic and ideological complexity. The History is profoundly double-voiced on the subject of David's own efforts to take possession of the crown that follows upon the LORD's anointing in 1 Samuel 16.

Perhaps nothing illustrates how effectively the History gets this double message across than the account of the spoils of David in 1 Samuel 30. Here David, having been left behind by the Philistines as they were preparing to do battle with Saul, is made to formulate a statute and an ordinance that suggests, in a marvelously effective way "to this day," David's unavoidable involvement in the death of Saul and in the coming fall of his house: "As his share is who goes down into battle, so shall his share be who stays by the baggage; they shall share alike" (1 Sam. 30:24). That is to say, the Deuteronomist uses David's own words to implicate him in the death of the king whom he had twice refused to kill in 1 Samuel 24 and 26.[5]

By the time we arrive at the events of 2 Samuel 1, we are already prepared to see David not only as the one whose successful escapes from Saul's clutches beautifully complement David's own narrative escape from responsibility for Saul's downfall, but also as the chief spokesperson for a less idealized picture of his own, that is, David's, rise to power. In the narrator's refusal, so far, to give the reader more than a few glimpses into the inner life of David, the Amalekite youth comes to us as he came to David, as a personification of David's own motivations, and perhaps even as an anticipatory suggestion of David's hidden role in the fall of the house of

Saul. The narrator confronts David with his alter ego, and the reader with David's double.

Notice that the Amalekite obviously did not kill Saul, yet just as obviously claims that he has. At this turning point the appearance of a character who claims to have killed Saul, but clearly has not, is both an apt conclusion to a story in which David has had no obvious part in the death of Saul and a fitting introduction to one in which David will appear to have had no part in the deaths of those loyal to Saul—but perhaps did. The duplicitous Amalekite in 2 Samuel 1 is a wonderful vehicle for the story of David throughout both books of Samuel.

Is there any narrative significance in the designation of this self-proclaimed murderer of Saul as an Amalekite sojourning in Israel? The end of 1 Samuel had David, an Israelite, sojourning in Philistia; the beginning of 2 Samuel describes David's counterpart as an Amalekite sojourning in Israel. Given the preeminent place Amalek occupies in the list of Israel's enemies (Deut. 25:17–19) and its central role in the downfall of Saul (1 Samuel 15; 28:18) and in the spoils of David (1 Samuel 30), the characterization of Saul's self-confessed killer as the son of an Amalekite sojourner (2 Sam. 1:13) positions him very close to Saul's character zone—but to David's also. The "Amalekizing" of this Davidic figure would be an appropriate way to characterize David as somehow both cause and beneficiary of Saul's downfall.

Another detail of the narrator's story—and of the Amalekite's story within it—helps us to see the Amalekite as a narrative stand-in for David. When the Amalekite recalls the battle scene at Gilboa, he describes Saul as looking behind him and asking, "Who are you?" This questioning of the identity of the lad is immediately repeated by David himself, who has just heard the lad quote his answer to Saul, "I am an Amalekite" (1:8): David repetitiously asks, " 'Where do you hail from?' And the young man answered, 'I am the son of a sojourner, an Amalekite' " (1:13). Why this doubled questioning of the young man's identity?

One of the most persistent themes in the last half of 1 Samuel is Saul's seeking after David, and this quest for the life of David mirrors the reader's quest for the identity of David and for a key that will unlock the mystery surrounding God's favorite. The narrator establishes this elusive characterization of David not only by concealing David's inner life most of the time but also by reporting numerous questions about David almost from the beginning of his appearance in chapter 16.[6] Saul's triple question about David after the death of Goliath opens us up to a puzzlement over David that will continue throughout the rest of the book: "Whose son is this youth? Inquire whose son this stripling is. Whose son are you, young man?" (17:55, 56, 58). David responds to Saul's offer of his daughter in marriage by asking rhetorically, "Who am I, and who are my kinsfolk?" (18:18). When Saul accuses Ahimelech of conspiracy with David against the king, Ahimelech responds, "Who of all your servants is so faithful and honored in your house as David?" (22:14). When David confronts Saul outside the cave, his questions to the king echo the narrator's continuing questions to the reader about David, "After whom has the king of Israel come out? After whom do you pursue?" (24:14). When David's servants ask Nabal for food, this Saul-figure responds with his own questions about David, "Who is David and who is the son of Jesse?" And even David's servants share in his ability to provoke questions: Nabal asks, "Shall I take my bread and water and my meat and give it to men who come from I do not know where?" (25:10–11). When David calls to Abner about his failure to watch over Saul, Abner responds, "Who are you that calls to the king?" (26:15).

We see from all this that just as Saul, the loser, was a center of dubiety in the first half of 1 Samuel,[7] so David, the winner, has become the book's dubious center within the second half. By the time we hear David ask the Amalekite, "Where do you come from?" (v. 3), "How did it go?" (v. 4), "How do you know?" (v. 5), and "Where do you hail from?" (v. 13), and as Saul had supposedly asked him earlier, "Who are you?" (v. 8), we are already conditioned to see in the Amalekite a stand-in for the enigma that is David.

By such means, the narrator introduces the Amalekite as a Davidic double who represents a set of complex human factors surrounding the fall of Saul and of his house. On one hand, the narrator reliably stated that Saul committed suicide in 1 Samuel 31; on the other hand, the Amalekite's competing claim is close to the narrator's indirect suggestions in 1 Samuel that David somehow shares in the killing of Saul and in the deaths of his descendants and supporters—however distanced David appears to be from all this slaughter. Whether the narrator's indirection in this regard is guided either by the clear and present danger accruing to one who would lay such responsibilities at David's feet or by other considerations no longer available to us, I cannot say. Nevertheless, it is a small step from the Amalekite's obviously lying claim that he was directly responsible for Saul's death to an indirect suggestion that David might himself be lying in denying either responsibility for, or at least satisfaction over, Saul's death.

The young man who claims to have killed Saul comes to David with his clothes rent. No sooner does David hear the news of Saul's death than he and his followers also rend their clothes (v. 11); David immediately puts on the garb of his double. Just as one who portrays himself as Saul's killer can mourn the dead king, so also David, who is portrayed as mourning for Saul, may also be a secret sharer in the crime. The Amalekite's verbal lie is that he killed Saul. His behavioral lie, so to speak, is that all his signs of mourning—torn clothes and earth on head—clash with his equally obvious anticipation of being rewarded for his alleged contribution to the royal succession.

Might not David's behavior be similarly duplicitous? How can he not rejoice, finally, at the death of the murderous Saul, an event that clears David's path to the throne of Israel? When David speaks to the dead Amalekite, "Your blood be upon your head, for your own mouth has testified against you, saying, 'I have slain the LORD's anointed'" (1:16), we may perhaps hear the narrator's unspoken words to David concerning the young king's complicity in the death of Saul and his coming involvement in the fall of Saul's house: "Your blood be upon your head, for your own mouth has testified against you, saying, 'I have *not* slain the LORD's anointed.'" The Amalekite lad, therefore, may very well be a counterbalance to the story's open defense of David as having had nothing to do with the downfall of Saul's house.

The lad explains how he stripped the fallen Saul of his crown and royal armlet and has brought them to David, "For I knew that he could not live after he had fallen." Such certainty over the death of Saul reminds us of David's equally certain statement to Abishai in defense of his own decision not to kill Saul, "As the LORD lives, the LORD will smite him; or his day will come to die; or he shall go down into battle and perish; the LORD forbid that I should put forth my hand against the LORD's anointed" (1 Sam. 26:10–11). Both David and his double outwardly mourn the death of Saul, but perhaps both secretly rejoice over it. *Neither actually kills Saul but both look forward to profiting from his death.* As the Amalekite strips Saul of his emblems of royalty, so David has done with the cutting off of Saul's royal robe in 1 Samuel 24. As an effective narrative embodiment that suggests duplicity in profiting from the death of Saul while publicly bemoaning his demise, the lying Amalekite is a fitting narrative emblem for a complicated story of the rise and fall of Israel's first two kings. The Amalekite is an anticipatory figure of the David who will speak and act in 2 Samuel.

If there is any basis in the narrative for seeing this lad as David's double, then we have in David's command to have the lad killed a kind of narrative doubling of the royal suicide in 1 Samuel 31. Just as the wounded Saul asks his armorbearer to kill him but finally has to do the job himself, so the narrator has David command the killing of his own double. David has his double killed at the beginning of 2 Samuel just as Saul kills himself at the end of 1 Samuel. The one suicide is literal, the other metaphoric. At one and the same time, David is Saul's narrative successor and paradigmatic replacement. As a parable of the life and death of every king to come after him, Saul's suicidal story is also David's.

Thus does the Deuteronomist infuse the narrative with a dramatic irony that has been replayed over and over again in the stories of leaders who publicly mourn the passing of the individual whose crown they wear and in whose fate they privately rejoice. Concerning such transfers of power, it is often impossible to establish how often and to what extent public grief masks secret conspiracies or unexpressed joy.

The Deuteronomist's Double

If the Amalekite is a narrative double for David, this messenger is also a double for the one who dares to raise a narrative hand against "the anointed of the LORD" (v. 16). The Deuteronomic History condemns royal Israel and documents kingship's demise, so that David's words over the corpse of the Amalekite lad whom he has had killed may be the Deuteronomist's articulation of a royalist response to the anti-royalist history that began in 1 Samuel. The narrative uses the Amalekite even to do double duty as a double: the lad is a stand-in not just for the character David but also for his author, the Deuteronomist.

For a start, consider David's command to one of his men to fall upon (*pāgaᶜ bᵉ*) and kill the Amalekite (2 Sam. 1:15). Apart from its geographic meaning, to touch or border on, *pāgaᶜ bᵉ* is almost always used in the History to signify a hostile encounter or attack.[8] More to the point, the use of this phrase here in 2 Samuel 1 looks backward to the account of Saul's murder of the priests of Nob (1 Sam. 22:17, 18 [twice]) and forward to Solomon's murderous elimination of those who threaten his throne (1 Kings 2:25, 29, 31, 32, 34, 46). Both accounts—Saul's murder of the priests of Nob and Solomon's killing of Adonijah, Joab, and especially Shimei—are saturated with the Deuteronomist's negatively charged evaluations of the manner in which "the throne of David is established before the LORD forever" (1 Kings 2:45). That throne was first made possible by the disastrous reign of Saul, who tried to retain, at whatever cost, what was already lost to him; David's throne is finally established by the ruthless actions of Solomon immediately following David's death in 1 Kings 2.

No matter that Saul, David, and Solomon justify their commands to attack and kill by appeal to just punishment for crimes committed (even as they distance themselves from the killing by having others do it): in each case *opposition to the throne of David is the central issue.* Each king who commands these murderous attacks justifies his action as retaliation for conspiracy against the throne: Saul has Doeg kill eighty-five priests and Solomon will have Benaiah kill Adonijah, Joab, and Shimei. Between his "father" Saul and his son Solomon stands David, whose initial act here in 2 Samuel 1 is to command one of his men to fall upon the Amalekite for claiming to have raised his hand against the LORD's anointed, and whose final words in 1 Kings 2 will command Solomon to eliminate Joab and Shimei for past disloyalty to the Davidic throne.

If the priests of Nob, the Amalekite lad, Adonijah, Joab, and Shimei all die for alleged disloyalty to the LORD's anointed, how much more deserving of attack are the creators of this history of royal Israel, whose profoundly negative characterization of the Israelite monarchy in general and the Davidic throne in particular causes David to exclaim, "How is it you were not afraid to put forth your hand to spoil (or bring to ruin: *saḥēt*) the LORD's anointed?" (v. 14). The Amalekite may very well be an apt stand-in for the Deuteronomist as well as for David, and an appropriate personification of the History's main ideological stance.

Seeing the Amalekite as a double for the History's author—in Bakhtin's terms, for the text's ultimate conceptual authority—allows us to recognize the ideological function of a number of details in the present story. Both the narrator and David designate the Amalekite as a messenger.[9] We can see from David's words to the sons of Rimmon in 4:10 ("When the messenger said to me, 'Saul is dead' and thought he was bringing me good news [*kimbaśśēr*], I seized him and slew him at Ziklag, which was the reward I gave him for his news [*bᵉśorāh*]") that the messenger (*hammaggîd*) who brings news to David about the death of Saul (1:5, 6, 13; 4:10) or about Absalom's popularity within Israel (15:13) is connected closely to the bearer of news (*mᵉbaśśēr*) about kingship that is both good and bad.[10] And all these instances are narrative reenactments of the parabolic end to kingship announced to Eli by the Benjaminite, who, like the Amalekite in 2 Samuel, has his clothes rent and earth upon his head (1 Samuel 4).

As the Deuteronomist's double, the Amalekite tells a story about the death of Saul that is, after all, fundamentally accurate. It is the History's task to kill Saul off so that David's succession to the throne may be accomplished. Also, as 2 Kings 11:12 illustrates, the giving of the crown symbolizes the conferral of kingship, so that here in 2 Sam. 1:10 the Amalekite's taking the crown from Saul and bringing it to David represents the transition of royal authority from Saul to David effected by the narrative itself. When the Deuteronomist's double says, " 'I knew that he would not live after his fall, so I took the crown and armlet and have brought them to my Lord here' " (v. 10), he expresses perfectly the text's function at this point in the History. Saul is dead, that is to say, the narrator has just killed him off, and he who tells of his death transfers the physical symbols of royalty to the one who now dominates the royal history.

Besides these thematic and functional similarities between the messenger as character and as author, the text embraces more formal compositional means for the same purpose. If we compare the scene between David and the Amalekite recounted by the narrator with the scene (within this scene) between Saul and the Amalekite recounted by the latter, it is easy to see that the second is patterned on the first. Both narrators introduce their scenes with a synchronic perspective established by *wᵉhinnēh* plus participle:

> Narrator: "And, behold, a man coming from Saul's camp" (v. 2).
> Amalekite: "And, behold, Saul leaning upon his spear" (v. 6).

Also, the narrator presents David asking the Amalekite a series of questions just as the Amalekite presents Saul asking him a question with a similar answer (Saul: "Who are you?" "I am an Amalekite" [v. 8]; David: "Where do you hail from?" "I am the son of a sojourner, an Amalekite" [v. 13]). Finally, the narrator has the Amalekite killed off in the main story, just as the Amalekite has Saul killed off in the imbricated story. This formal mirroring of the narrator's story by the Amalekite's story within it is a central compositional technique whereby the doubling of the story reflects the doubling of the storyteller.

The Deuteronomist, then, fashions a continuing message about the evils of kingship, but also includes the response that such a message might engender within an audience schooled to exalt the everlasting throne of David. In a fitting climax to this opening scene of the history of David's rule, David stands over a corpse that represents both himself and his biographer and utters an ironic curse: " 'Your blood be upon your head; for your own mouth has testified against you saying, 'I have slain the LORD's anointed' " (2 Sam. 1:16). The disastrous history of monarchic Israel can now continue.

David's Elegy (1:17–27): Themes and Issues

Here is one way to describe the thematic progression in David's lament. David begins by stating the heart of the matter in general terms that will echo throughout the poem: "How the mighty have fallen" (v. 19). Thinking of the joy Israel's enemies must feel, he forbids publishing news of Israel's defeat in Philistia (v. 20) and then pronounces a curse on

Mount Gilboa (v. 21a), because hatred and abhorrence of the shield of Saul occurred there (v. 21b). Verse 22 not only begins David's move from elegy to eulogy but also employs a striking image to express the Deuteronomist's appropriation of David's words for larger historiographic and ideological purposes.[11]

Eulogistic emphases begun in verse 22 continue throughout the rest of the poem. What unifies this perspective are the two epithets David uses for Saul and Jonathan in verse 23: they are indeed *beloved* (*'āhēb* in the *nifal*) and *lovely* (*nā^cîm*, that is, pleasant or satisfying). As to why the daughters of Israel should weep, David appeals to their gratitude: Saul lavished riches upon them (v. 24). Then the poem applies its refrain to Jonathan alone ("Jonathan lies slain upon thy high places," v. 25), enabling us to see that what David says about Jonathan in verse 26 ought somehow to connect up with earlier statements in the lament. Both of the deceased were lovely (v. 23), but Jonathan indeed "was very lovely to me" (v. 26a). And if Saul himself ought to be loved (v. 23) by the daughters of Israel, then Jonathan's love for David is more to be marveled at than either the love of women (that is, the daughters of Israel) for Saul or else the love of men for women (v. 26b). The poem ends as it began, by intoning the fall of the mighty (v. 27).

Who speaks this elegy over Saul and Jonathan? As with every instance of a narrator's reported speech, there are two utterances here, David's address to Israel within the story on one hand, and (part of) the Deuteronomist's discourse to an audience on the other. Another way to describe the same thing is to say that two voices can be heard in the elegy, David's and the Deuteronomist's, and that our primary responsibility as readers is to try to understand how these voices interact with one another. To decide what David is "really" saying to his audience is a first step in determining what the Deuteronomist is also saying to an audience.

Second, as Bakhtin has emphasized, when we reflect upon our experience of how speakers or writers manage so often and so successfully to communicate their intentions, few aspects of utterances are as important as *speech genres*.[12] That David and the Deuteronomist speak here through poetry, that is, through heightened language in lamentation of the dead, has important implications for the function of this speech within its literary context. This song sets itself off from its prosaic setting as something special, a signal part of David's story and the Deuteronomist's history.

Finally, the importance of the elegy is underlined not only by its heightened language but also by its compositional placement within the Deuteronomic History itself. Here its structural relationships and thematic similarities and differences with the Song of Hannah at the start of the Books of Samuel (1 Samuel 2) and with the Song of David near their end

(2 Samuel 22) testify to its central importance. David's elegy will turn out to be a particularly powerful illustration of what Bakhtin called *speech interference:* two voices sounding within a single utterance, voices that are at profound odds with one another.

David's Lament: From Elegy to Eulogy

The narrative itself elevates the importance of the elegy by introducing it as a composition which David "commanded be taught to the Sons of Judah" and which already "is written in the Book of the Upright" (1:18). Having commanded that Israel learn this song by heart so that its message may be repeated time and time again, David also addresses Israel within the song itself. It is as important a statement for our understanding of the story to come as was the Song of Hannah. The elegy follows immediately upon the complex account of David's encounter with the Amalekite, and we cannot avoid feeling that this poem will reveal a profoundly divided David. We still do not know whether David has discovered how Saul really died, nor have we gotten any direct entrée into the thoughts and feelings of 2 Samuel's protagonist. Once again, we are forced to puzzle over David and to construct our characterization of him without the direct guidance of the narrator. Earlier, Saul puzzled over the David whom we thought he already knew (1 Sam. 17:55–58); yet even now the reader continues to struggle over the enigmatic figure of David.

David's magnanimity toward Saul in the elegy is usually explained by a presumed apologetic stance or strand first encountered toward the end of 1 Samuel and continuing into the introductory chapters of 2 Samuel.[13] Indeed, given the elegy's antecedents, the obvious manner in which David eulogizes Saul can scarcely be denied. Nothing in the poem appears to reflect negatively upon Saul; there are no references in it to Saul's previous attacks against David or to his serious failures as king of Israel. Obviously, what David *does* say in the elegy will set the tone for the lament and perhaps help us get to the heart of the man after God's own heart.

Framed by a chiastic *inclusio* formed by verses 19 and 25, David's elegy is a hyperbolic glorification of Saul and his son.[14] As Talmon has recognized, this *inclusio* integrates and focuses David's elegy both structurally and thematically:[15]

Verse 19
The splendor, O Israel, is slain upon thy high places!
How the mighty have fallen!

Verse 25
How the mighty have fallen in the midst of the battle!
Jonathan is slain upon thy high places!

David literally glorifies the deceased king and his son. The glory ($ṣ^ebî$) that is slain in verse 19 specifically stands for Saul and Jonathan in the poem. That $ṣ^ebî$ in verse 19, whatever its meaning, refers to the fallen king and his son is clear both from its parallel term in the verse, *gibbôrîm*, "the mighty," epithets for Saul and Jonathan elsewhere in the poem, and from the substitution of "Jonathan" for "glory" in verse 25, which repeats the parallelism of verse 19 but in reverse order.

The poem favors its fallen subjects by also speaking of them in terms that sometimes appear to be at odds with the story in which it is imbedded. For example, when David says of Saul and Jonathan "in life and in death they were not separated" (v. 23), this scarcely fits the story in 1 Samuel, where Jonathan so often acts in behalf of David against the interests of his own father. Yet given the poem's elegiac genre, even this discordant feature is not especially bothersome.

Other details in the poem also help to turn David's elegy into a eulogy. Facing the unavoidable, David acknowledges the joy that Saul's and Jonathan's death will bring to Philistia (v. 20), curses the mountains where such a tragedy took place (v. 21), and concentrates on the bravery of the fallen heroes: "From the blood of the slain, from the fat of the mighty, the bow of Jonathan turned not back, the sword of Saul returned not empty" (v. 22). Father and son courageously killed many of the enemy before they themselves were killed. Then David describes Saul and Jonathan as beloved and lovely, swifter than eagles and stronger than lions (v. 23), and laments the death both of Saul, who clothed his subjects so sumptuously (v. 24), and of Jonathan, who was so pleasing to David, "Your love for me is more wonderful than the love of women" (v. 26). To ignore the negative and to concentrate on the positive by magnification and even invention belongs to the nature of the elegiac beast: *nil nisi bonum de mortuis.*

In terms, then, of how the words of David help us characterize him, our task is not so much to rehearse the specific features of the lament whereby David romanticizes a fallen enemy, but to ask why he would be portrayed as eulogizing him in the first place. Later, "on the day when the LORD delivered him from the hand of all his enemies, and from the hand of Saul" (2 Sam. 22:1), David has no time for magnanimity: "I pursued my enemies and destroyed them. I beat them fine as the dust of the earth, I crushed them and stamped them down like the mire of the streets" (2 Sam. 22:38, 43).

David's magnanimity toward Saul in the lament, I would suggest, is as politically motivated as his magnanimity toward Saul was in cave (1 Samuel 24) and camp (1 Samuel 26). There, David refused to raise his hand against the LORD's anointed (1 Sam. 24:7, 11; 26:9, 11, 16, 23); here he refuses to open his mouth against the same. In both cases David is portrayed as establishing a model of behavior toward kingship that exemplifies the obligations of a nation toward its own royal house. David certainly recognized how fortunate he was to have had Jonathan's loving loyalty, and may very well have admired Saul in many respects. Yet what David's eulogy finally expresses is proper respect for those who will sit upon the throne, even when their "weapons of war do perish" (v. 27).

Such motivation helps to explain why David "commanded that the sons of Judah be taught the words of this lament" and why indeed "it is written in the Book of the Upright" (1:18). *Nil nisi bonum de regibus* is the teaching of David's eulogy. It appears that the Deuteronomist did not take David's lesson to heart.

A final feature of the lament helps us glimpse part of the narrator's characterization of David. Following on 1 Samuel's almost complete concealment of David's inner life, of his inner thoughts and feelings, David here is shown finally revealing something of what Jonathan's love and loyalty has meant to him. What is significant for our understanding of David's character is how self-centered it appears to be. Why, counsels David, should the daughters of Israel weep over Saul? Because of the riches Saul lavished upon them (v. 24). Why is David distressed over Jonathan's death? Because Jonathan was so pleasing to him and his love for David so wonderful (v. 26). David refrains from speaking directly of his own love for Jonathan, just as the Deuteronomist continues to shield us from a direct view of the heart of David.[16]

The Deuteronomist's Voice: From Eulogy to Elegy

Bakhtin has described with force and clarity how individual utterances—whether written or oral, simple or complex—can be profoundly saturated with someone else's speech. This common phenomenon of speech communication is ultimately connected with what Bakhtin understood to be the central problem of speech genres. He writes: "When we select words in the process of constructing an utterance, we by no means always take them from the system of language in their neutral, dictionary form. We usually take them from other utterances that are kindred to ours in genre, that is, in theme, composition, or style. Consequently, we choose words according to their generic specifications. A speech genre is not a form of language, but a typical form of utterance."[17]

As material for a poetic elegy, many of the words and phrases of this poem are emotionally charged and filled with expressive and evaluative intonations. If we examine the vocabulary, themes, and style of the elegy from the point of view of authorial composition and expressive intonation, what stand out most clearly are those generic qualities within it that belong to impassioned prophetic and cultic speech. The following interpretation makes no claim about direct borrowing of words, phrases, or statements from specific prophetic or cultic texts of the Bible. Reference to such texts serves simply to illustrate the generic features that constitute the basis for an interpretation.

One way to get at the intention behind the Deuteronomic voice, as it interferes with David's voice in the elegy, is to describe the style infusing the expressions found therein. Specific details will allow us to see how and why the elegy is more than just a personal or communal lamentation of a character in the story. It is also a prophetic lamentation, spoken by the Deuteronomist over fallen Israel. In a previous volume I suggested some ways in which the elegy looks backward to the Song of Hannah and forward to 2 Samuel 22. I now want to enlarge this picture by describing the cultic and prophetic accents that specify not only the elegy's rehearsal of the deaths of Saul and his son, but even its uncanny preview of the story to come.

The High Places

The clearest indication that something central to the overall vision of the Deuteronomic History is at work here is David's description of Saul's and Jonathan's deaths as having taken place "upon your high places" (*bāmôtêkā*, vv. 19, 25).[18] The importance of this phrase is underlined in two ways: by its use in the *inclusio* that frames a major portion of the elegy (vv. 19–25), and by its direct address to Israel, "It was upon *your* high places, O Israel, that the mighty were slain."

The coming use, throughout the History, of "the high places" as a frequent expression for the idolatrous worship that caused the LORD to punish Israel and send it into exile invests David's lament with unavoidably cultic and prophetic accents: the high places not only recall the particular circumstances of Saul's death (upon the heights of Gilboa) but also foreshadow the Deuteronomist's devastating critique of the idolatry that will characterize Israel's monarchic history after the temple is built.

Evaluative accents surrounding the use of "the high places" within the History extend from the very positive to the very negative. Before the temple is built, reference to the high places carries no necessarily negative accents.[19] After Solomon's building of the temple, however, *all* references to the high places are negatively charged; the phrase is intoned in condemnatory statements at least twenty-eight times in the two books of Kings.[20]

The evaluative and emotional aura surrounding specific Deuteronomic references to high places, therefore, ranges from positive exaltation, as in Deut. 32:13, to respectability, as in 1 Sam. 9:19, to outright condemnation, as throughout 1 and 2 Kings. Here in 2 Samuel 1, its use in a lament surely pushes the phrase toward negative connotations, but not entirely so. David does invoke the courage and bravery of Saul and Jonathan in verse 22 as a eulogistic motif. Before they were killed, Saul and Jonathan were responsible for the deaths of many Philistines on these high places, so that David at least manages to highlight the heroism of Saul and Jonathan even in their defeat. Still, the authorial accents surrounding "the high places" in this poem remain mostly negative. To see why this is so, we need to examine the specific language the poem uses to describe what happened on those heights.

More is involved in David's double invocation of "the high places" than personal tragedy or communal respect for tragic heroes, for David is made to lament the death of Saul and Jonathan in terms that foreshadow Israel's fate and the causes of its downfall. As Hannah's multivoiced song rehearses not only her own circumstances but also the triumphs and tragedy of the history to follow, so the present poem not only looks back on the tragically heroic life and death of Israel's first king but also sees them as rehearsing the fate of a nation and of its greatest royal dynasty. Central to the account of that national fate will be the idolatrous high places instituted and fostered by Israel's kings.

Death and Pollution upon the High Places

What language does the Deuteronomist use to describe the lamentable event that took place "upon your high places, O Israel"? There, we are immediately told, someone or something (*haṣṣebî*, whatever this term means in verse 19) was mortally wounded, and there Jonathan was slain (*ḥālal*, vv. 19 and 25): how the mighty are fallen (*nāpal*, vv. 19, 25, 27). The use of the roots *ḥālal*, "to pierce," and *nāpal*, "to fall," certainly looks backward to the account of the battle itself in 1 Samuel 31 when "the men of Israel fell slain (*wayyippᵉlû ḥᵃlālîm*) on Mount Gilboa" (v. 1) and when "the Philistines came to strip the slain (*ḥᵃlālîm*) and found Saul and his three sons fallen (*nopᵉlîm*) on Mount Gilboa" (v. 8).[21] Nevertheless, what also strikes the ear here are unavoidably prophetic accents that reverberate around these two structurally and semantically important verses in the elegy. Listen, for example, to Ezekiel as he rails against the high places: "Thus says the LORD God to the mountains and the hills, to the ravines and the valley: 'Behold, I, even I, will bring a sword upon you, and I will destroy your high places (*bāmôt*). And I will cast down (*nāpal*) your slain (*ḥālal*) before your idols. . . . Your high places shall be ruined and the slain (*ḥālal*) shall fall (*nāpal*) in the midst of you' " (Ezek. 6:3–4, 6–7). In a fit of ironic retribution God will sacrifice upon the high places those who themselves offered idolatrous sacrifices thereon. Let the punishment fit the crime.

What takes place upon the high places of the poem is even more complex than this, for other cultic and prophetic accents reverberate around these heights. If *ḥālal*, "fallen, slain," in verses 19 and 25 clearly denotes the piercing that results in death, it may also connote that cultic pollution that is both caused by and results in death. The root, *hll*, occurs in the Bible in two rather separate semantic fields: it may mean to *pierce* or *wound* and just as frequently may mean to *pollute, profane,* or *defile.* As we would expect, the context of the first meaning is often military, that of the second mostly cultic.

The military context of the elegy is obvious, but its cultic associations need emphasizing. For example, the substantive, *ḥālāl*, meaning someone or something that is unclean, occurs in the context either of cultic pollution (Lev. 21:7, 14), where a semantically related word is *ṭāmē',* or of prophetic condemnation, where the prophet addresses Judah's king— probably Zedekiah—as "you profane (*ḥālāl*) wicked one" and warns him of the sword of the king of Babylon (Ezek. 21:30, 34).

I will be suggesting in what follows that cultic and prophetic vocabulary, themes, and accents systematically permeate the largely military context surrounding the deaths of Saul and Jonathan. In other words, the language that David is reported using as he laments the death of fallen heroes is chosen precisely for its *prophetic* and *cultic* power to foreshadow the fall of Israel and the idolatrous role of its kings in bringing about this disaster.

There is another way to describe this aspect of the poem. Some of the vocabulary within it that has most puzzled commentators is strikingly not found elsewhere in the History. Whatever this may mean for the literary historian, an important feature of the poem, considered as an utterance reported by the Deuteronomic narrator, is its cultic picture of death and pollution sketched with somber prophetic strokes that nevertheless foreshadow the Deuteronomist's explicit ideological explanation for Israel's exile and also look backward to the causes of Saul's downfall: "For I desire obedience rather than sacrifice," God said to Saul in 1 Samuel 15.

The Gazelle and the Glory upon the High Places

Scholars disagree about whether the first word of the elegy, *ṣ^ebî*, means "gazelle" or "glory," whether the letter *he* that precedes it represents the definite article, *ha-*, or the particle *ho*, "Alas!" and whether, finally, this *ṣ^ebî* or Israel itself is addressed directly by David. I will assume that Israel is the addressee and that the choice of *ha-* or *ho* is relatively insignificant beside the larger questions about gazelle and glory. Yet even here, the choice itself may be unnecessary if we look at the poem as both David's and the Deuteronomist's. Actually, the play between various meanings of *ṣ^ebî* may help us understand the extent of the *speech interference* operating in this verse and in the rest of the poem. Just as there seems to be wordplay here between death and pollution (*ḥālal*), corresponding respectively to the personal accents of David and the prophetic stance of the Deuteronomist, so also the first word of the elegy appears to oscillate in meaning between *gazelle* and *glory.*[22]

As is clear from all the occurrences in the Bible of *ṣ^ebî* clearly meaning gazelle, the animal is an exemplar both of swiftness[23] and of what is ritually clean (*ṭāhôr*, that is, what is not *ṭāmē'*).[24] The passages 2 Sam. 2:18 and 1 Chron. 12:9 even liken the swiftness of specific fighting men to that of gazelles, and help to show how appropriate is the application of this epithet to Saul in the martial context of the elegy. However, it is the cultic or ritual aspect of gazelles as represented by the legislation of Deuteronomy 12, 14, and 15 that helps us understand how extensive may be the wordplay surrounding *ṣ^ebî* here. Combining the cultic connotations of *ḥālal* (profaned, defiled, polluted), as discussed above, with those of *ṣ^ebî* as exemplar of what is ritually clean, and then combining these cultic associations with the attested military associations of the gazelle as swift, we begin to get a sense of the poetic polyvalence at play in this opening line of the elegy.

The poem may begin by saying, "Saul, though swift as a gazelle, was overtaken and now lies slain." After all, David calls Saul and Jonathan swifter than eagles later in the elegy (v. 23). On the other hand, David may be saying, "Saul, though pure and clean as a gazelle, now lies defiled." Or we may understand the poem even from the outset to be invoking both the military and the cultic associations of *gazelle:* "Swift Saul has been overtaken and killed; pure Saul lies defiled."

Yet the wordplay involving *ṣ^ebî* is not finished, for *ṣ^ebî*, understood as glory, splendor, beauty, also finds support within the verse itself as well as in the rest of the poem. After all, if David were somehow to call Saul the beauty of Israel in its opening line, this would only find an echo in his later statement that Saul and Jonathan are beloved and lovely (*neˁîmim,* v. 23).

What makes the use of *ṣeˀbî,* understood as beauty or glory, so problematic and yet so attractive here in 2 Samuel 1 is its use everywhere else in the Bible. The sublime rather than the zoological meaning of *ṣeˀbî* occurs only in prophetic discourse where the context is a national prophecy of doom or salvation and where, when it does not refer to the LORD's glory (Isa. 24:16; 28:5), it properly describes particular lands, peoples, nations, or specific groups thereof. *Ṣeˀbî* construed as glory has a context that is properly geographic and communal: the most frequent substantive to which it refers is the land, *'ereṣ.*[25]

Listen to God through Jeremiah bemoan the beauty of the land he gave Israel: "'I thought how I would set you among my sons and give you a pleasant land, an inheritance most glorious (*ṣeˀbî ṣibˀôt*) of all nations; so have you been faithless to me, O house of Israel,' says the LORD" (Jer. 3:19, 20). Listen also to Isaiah rail against the glory of Tyre and prophesy its defilement: "The LORD of hosts (*ṣeˀbāˀôt*) has decided to defile (*ḥālal*) the pride of all glory (*ṣeˀbî*), to dishonor all the honored (*nikbād*) of the earth" (Isa. 23:9). Listen again to the way Isaiah repeats the wordplay in chapter 23 by connecting up the military hosts of the LORD with the national glory which he is about to restore and which he equates with power: "In that day the LORD of hosts will be a crown of glory (*ṣeˀbî*), and strength (*geˀbûrāh*) to those who turn back the battle at the gate" (Isa. 28:5). Listen finally to *all* the utterances in which *ṣeˀbî* as glory appears in the Bible; whether the glory is affirmed or denied, promised or threatened, it is almost always a communal matter with geographic emphasis. And like its semantic twin, *kābôd,* the glory that nations or lands possess or lose is but a shadow of the LORD's glory: "Therefore in the east give glory (*kabbeˀdû*) to the LORD, songs of glory (*ṣeˀbî*) to the Righteous One" (Isa. 24:15–16).[26]

Considering the semantic openness of verse 19, we should realize, as Bakhtin has emphasized, that "the first and last sentences of an utterance are unique and have an additional quality. For they are, so to speak, sentences of the 'front line' that stand right at the boundary of the change of speech subjects."[27] When therefore the first statement of the elegy is as open to wordplay as we have been suggesting, then readers or hearers need to allow the further words of the elegy to lead them along toward a coherent and retrospective understanding of the wordplay that begins the poem.

If wordplay involving *ṣeˀbî* as glory or beauty does exist in the elegy, it would seem to pertain to the Deuteronomist's voice rather than to David's. Only a voice that could invoke the particular circumstances of Saul's death

in order to create an image of his cultic failures and of the related fate of
the land of Israel would be able to evoke these circumstances in terms that
are at one and the same time personal and communal, heroic and disastrous, military and cultic, eulogistic and elegiac, prospective as well as
retrospective. When we hear David intone the first line of the poem, and
when we concentrate on its sublime (glorious) rather than its zoological
(gazelle-like) associations, we hear the Deuteronomist saying something
like, "Alas, the glory of thy land, O Israel, has been both destroyed and
defiled upon your high places." Such a message looks forward to a story
that will end in pollution of the land and exile from it; it also looks backward to the deaths of another father and son, Eli and Phinehas. *That* military disaster caused Phinehas's wife, like David, to utter a statement
mysteriously foreshadowing the fate of a nation: "Glory (*kābôd*) has gone
into exile from Israel" (1 Sam. 4:21). In both statements we hear the voice
of the Deuteronomist speaking through the voice of a character.

The Heart of the Matter

Once the opening line of the poem allows us to hear cultic and prophetic
accents, it is a relatively easy matter to find an interpretive focus for the
lines that follow. Verses 20 and 21 culminate in verse 22, a statement providing us with a graphic image as suggestive and powerful as any we have
so far encountered in the Books of Samuel:

> From the blood of the slain/profaned,
>   From the fat of the mighty,
> the bow of Jonathan turned not back,
>   the sword of Saul returned not empty. (v. 22)

The most striking aspect of this appeal to blood (*dām*) and fat (*ḥēleb*) is
the almost exclusive use of this verbal pair in biblical contexts of cultic
ritual or sacrifice.[28] This verse of the elegy can be seen to inject sacrificial
language of blood and fat into a transparently martial context, thus providing us with a pointed confirmation of the authorial accents we have
been hearing within David's lament.

Joining the semantic fields of military and ritual slaughter is a particularly appropriate metaphoric move here, one that finds forceful expression elsewhere in prophetic contexts. Isaiah, for example, proclaims the
fate of God's enemies (here Edom) in this way:

> The LORD has a sword; it is sated with blood,
> it is gorged with fat,

with the blood of lambs and goats,
with the fat of the kidneys of rams.
For the LORD has a sacrifice in Bozrah,
a great slaughter in the land of Edom.
Their land will be soaked with blood,
and their soil made rich with fat. (Isa. 34:6–7)[29]

In Isaiah, the LORD wields his sword with sacrificial intensity. Similarly, the elegy employs the military bow and sword as ritual instruments which Saul and Jonathan wield to shed the blood of the unclean and impale the flesh of the mighty.

As an implement of death, the bow of Jonathan "did not turn back" (*lo' nāśôg 'āḥôr*), that is to say, it was admirably successful in achieving the purpose for which it was fashioned. Throughout the Bible, this "turning back" always denotes a reprehensible action associated with disobedience, rebellion, dishonor, shame, disloyalty, or defeat.[30] The expression from David's lips here in verse 22 elegiacally denotes Jonathan's avoidance of such embarrassments. In like manner, the sword of Saul "returned not empty" (*lo' tāšûb rêqām*), denoting the effectiveness with which Saul killed Philistines before he died.[31] Both verbal expressions emphasize *success:* David refers here to the slaughter of the Philistines which Saul and Jonathan accomplished before they themselves fell to sword and bow. Heard as coming from David's voice, the military image simply reverses the polarity of the lament. Up to this point in the poem, the slain warriors referred to by David were Saul and Jonathan, who are now in turn described as those who themselves slaughtered the mighty upon the hills of Gilboa that day. As David's discourse, then, verse 22 is a signal that the elegy has become a eulogy.

Yet the striking language of verse 22 is more than a poetic trope designed to soften the ultimate pain of defeat. Once one has begun to hear an authorial voice transforming David's perspectives, the image in v. 22 describes not just the valor of Israel's first royal house but the ritual slaughter of Israel itself. The defiled slain, whose blood and fat the implements of Saul and Jonathan spill and spear, begin to merge retrospectively with the animals of Saul's actual or contemplated sacrifices in 1 Samuel 13, 14, and 15, as well as prospectively with the polluting animals royal Israel will continually slaughter upon its high places throughout the coming history. In such idolatrous rituals, the glory (*ṣᵉbî*) of the land that the LORD gave to Israel is profaned and the mighty that make up Israel's fighting force are defeated. The Song of Hannah has already foreshadowed such a reversal of fortune—just as the account in 2 Kings 24 and 25 will describe it in climactic detail.

It is appropriate, therefore, that the military slaughter of Israel's first king and dynastic heir be conjoined in the poem with the image of cultic retribution upon Israel's high places—a nice example of poetic justice. In the striking image of verse 22, Saul and Jonathan are not only like sacrificing priests, they are also like the sacrificial animals that Isaiah speaks of in his prophetic vision (34:6–7). In terms of the story, the reader ought not to forget whose blood the sword of Saul did not hesitate finally to spill and whose mighty flesh it pierced at the last: the Deuteronomist describes both the personal death of Saul and the national fate of Israel in terms of cultic suicide.

If there is any value in the thematic and stylistic associations that we are suggesting for the language used in the elegy, one can still only guess at the feelings such sacrificial images would have evoked within those Israelites who were supposed to have recited the lament at David's command. The power of a phrase like "to return empty" (*šûb rêqām*), for example, has no necessary military or cultic connotations, yet such connections are well attested within the History as well as outside it. The similarities between verse 22 of the elegy and the statement of Jeremiah quoted above ("For behold I am stirring up and bringing against Babylon a company of great nations; their arrows are like a skilled warrior [*gibbôr*] who does not return empty handed" [50:9]) depend not only on the military metaphor employed but also on the prophetic context in which the victorious nation's weapons, like Saul's and Jonathan's, belong to a warrior who does not "return empty." As for the cultic associations surrounding the language of not returning empty (-handed), one thinks immediately of the Philistines' compliance with the advice which their priests and diviners gave for returning the plague-filled ark to the Israelites, "If you send away the ark of the God of Israel, do not send it empty (*šālaḥ rêqām*), but by all means return (*šûb* in *hifíl*) to him a guilt offering. Then you shall be healed" (1 Sam. 6:3). One also thinks of the Israelite abhorrence of appearing before the LORD empty-handed: "Three times a year all your males shall appear before the LORD your God. They shall not appear before the LORD empty handed" (Deut. 16:16).[32]

The Deuteronomist employs a powerful image of a king and his son successfully wielding their weapons upon the idolatrous high places like priests employing sacrificial implements against the unclean. The merging of military defeat and cultic defilement possesses an ironic force very much like the image that merges the priestly seat and the royal throne from which the blind Eli fell over backwards and broke his neck, "for he was an old man, and heavy/honored (*kābôd*)" (1 Sam. 4:15).[33] Both images, I think, combine the priestly and royal themes of the Deuteronomist's story with unequaled suggestive power. It is no accident that references to the deaths of Eli in 1 Samuel 4 and of Saul and Jonathan in 1 Samuel 31 and in 2 Samuel 1 and 4 are explicitly connected with the bringing of news that is both bad and good.[34] Priest and king will participate each in his own way in the idolatrous slaughter upon the high places.[35]

Shielding God

When verse 22 is read along the lines just suggested, the curse on the mountains of Gilboa in verse 21a and its motivation in 21b take on added significance. The drought is called for because "the shield of the mighty was abhorred" (v. 21b). But what does this line mean by calling this shield "the shield of Saul *not* anointed with oil"? Considered as part of David's utterance, 21b expresses the situation accurately and McCarter's comment is apposite: "The point of the present bicolon [21b], then, is that Saul's shield is not oiled and ready for action, as befits a hero's shield; rather, it lies neglected and covered with grime on Mount Gilboa."[36]

Yet when we ask how verse 21b fits in with the rest of the poem considered as the Deuteronomist's utterance as well as David's, the matter is rather more complex. Consider that the poetic use of *māgēn*, "shield," as an epithet for the LORD is especially frequent both within the History and outside it. In contrast to its literal meaning, nearly two-thirds of the word's poetic occurrences have it standing for the LORD.[37]

Could David himself be understood here as referring to abhorrence of the LORD? Elsewhere in the History (2 Sam. 22:3, 31, 36 = Ps. 18:3, 31, 36) and even outside it—most notably in the psalms explicitly attributed to David (Ps. 3:4; 7:11; 28:7; 59:12; 144:2)—God as referent for "shield" is a particularly Davidic turn of phrase. As such, the Deuteronomist may be using David's characteristic discourse as a vehicle for an authorial expression of what is superabundantly true about the events commemorated in the elegy. We have already seen a number of examples of such authorial manipulation in 1 Samuel.

If then we construe verse 21b as equating "the shield of the mighty" and "the shield of Saul" with the LORD, we here (as elsewhere in the poem) find evidence to counter a common view that the poem is "purely secular."[38] Granting that the phrase, "not anointed with oil," may be appropriate for Saul's actual shield, as McCarter suggests and as we would construe David's utterance to be saying, the phrase also implies a divine reference for *māgēn* and thus continues to emphasize the wider aspects of the events on Mount Gilboa. The Deuteronomist here explains that Israel's high places are cursed because the shield of the mighty, the shield

of Saul, was made abhorrent upon them.[39] Which shield was reviled upon
the high places of Gilboa? The king's physical shield, like the king himself,
may be anointed with oil, but the mighty possess another shield that can
not be anointed with oil, for that shield is the LORD himself.

The Role of Jonathan in the Elegy

"How are the mighty fallen in the midst of battle: Jonathan is slain/pro-
faned upon your high places" (v. 25). This verse forms a chiastic *inclusio*
with verse 19 so that Jonathan now becomes the emotional focus of the
poem. David not only rounds off the elegy in its more public social aspects
but also chooses a more personal tone with which to end the lament, a
tone heard most clearly in verse 26. Verses 25 and 26, then, express the
personal significance of Jonathan's death for David. Verse 23a had already
set up the terms that David now uses to characterize this personal relationship: Jonathan and Saul are loved (*'āhēb*) and pleasing or satisfactory
(*nāᶜîm*). David now repeats these key words in his tribute to Jonathan:
"You have been so pleasing (*nāᶜîm*) to me, your love (*'ahᵃbāh*) for me
more wonderful than the love of women" (v. 26).[40]

All this is obvious when we read the poem as David's utterance, but
when we look at it as the Deuteronomist's statement as well, it also, like the
rest of the History, expresses fundamental social realities. As 1 Sam. 8:8
emphasized, Israel's political adulation of kings is comparable to its cultic
adoration of gods. I have been suggesting that an authorial voice with prophetic accents uses David's elegy to mourn a fallen Israel exiled for its
abominable practices of idolatry upon the high places. The prophetic and
cultic language in the poem that has been condemning a nation now gives
way to a more directly personal expression of the grief felt over the sins of
monarchic Israel.

As the heir apparent of the Saulide dynasty, Jonathan, the son of Saul,
the rejected one, is exemplar of all Israel's kings, good as well as bad.
Indeed Jonathan is exemplar of Israel itself. The words in verses 25–26 are
addressed by David to "Jonathan, my brother." This is the first time David
calls Jonathan his brother, and we shall soon see how the coming chapters
of 2 Samuel revolve around *brothers* as a focus for the History's ultimate
conceptual authority.

I have suggested elsewhere that the emotional undertones of God's
words to Samuel in 1 Sam. 8:8 ("For they have not rejected you [Samuel]
but they have rejected me from being king over them") are very close to
those of Elkanah to Hannah: "Hannah, why do you weep? And why do you
not eat? And why is your heart sad? Am I not worth more to you than ten

sons?" Given the equation of sons and kings in the introduction to the history of royal Israel in 1 Samuel 1–7, Elkanah's voice dissolves into God's, who can be heard chiding Israel in similar terms: God asks Israel throughout the History, "Am I not worth more to you, O Israel, than ten kings?"[41]

Once more the words of God to Samuel in 1 Samuel 8 form an emotional linchpin that helps us understand the character zones of analogous individuals in the story. Just as Elkanah in 1 Samuel 1 sounds like God in 1 Samuel 8, and just as Hannah's rejoicing in 1 Samuel 2 has melancholic overtones that prefigure the Deuteronomist's story to come, so also David's words of grief for his brother Jonathan form the climax of a poem that has important structural and compositional significance for the History itself. "I am distressed over you, O Israel," God plaintively intones in verse 26, "you have been so pleasing to me and your love more wonderful than the love of (men for) women."[42] Following upon the Deuteronomist's evocation of Israel's disobedient idolatry upon the high places, these personalized words in verses 25–26 take on the disappointed tones of unrequited love. Central to the complexities of the pathos here are the History's previous characterizations not only of a disastrously disobedient Saul but of a patently loyal Jonathan as well. That Jonathan has been portrayed in the story in largely positive terms should help us remember that kingship itself, as described in the History, is the paradoxical result of both disobedience and obedience to the LORD.

We have seen in some detail how the elegy reflects the voices of David and the Deuteronomist. David's eulogy looks back on the death of Saul in order to prescribe a "correct" attitude toward Israel's kings, especially those who go down to defeat. The Deuteronomist's lament, on the other hand, looks backward to the ritualistic and sacrificial obsessions of Saul and forward to the idolatrous practices of Israel—in both cases with a view to placing the audience, now in exile, in a proper attitude toward the institution of kingship itself. In the beginning Israel had insisted: "No! We will have a king over us that we also may be like all the nations, and that our king may govern us and go out before us and fight our wars (*milḥāmôt*)" (1 Sam. 8:19–20). Israel in exile now hears the Deuteronomist, midway through the History, intone God's elegiac response: "How are the mighty kings fallen, and their weapons of war (*milḥāmāh*) perished!"

We still need to see how the Deuteronomist's coming characterization of David will measure up both to a lovingly loyal Jonathan, who so satisfied David, and to an impatiently disobedient Saul, who may have pleased the daughters of Israel, but finally displeased God. Will David fare any better than his two royal heroes?

·2·

BROTHERS
(2:1–4:12)

That brother should not war with brother, and worry and devour each other. (William Cowper, *The Nightingale and Glow-Worm*)

How long before you bid your people turn from pursuing their brothers? (Abner, 2 Sam. 2)

Variations on a Theme: Ritualized Murder in Chapter 2

Here is a summary of chapter 2. Expository material in verses 1–11 describes David's move to Hebron, his anointing as king of Judah, his blessing of the men of Jabesh-Gilead, and his rivalry with Ishbosheth. The battle between the two forces at Gibeon is succinctly recounted in verse 17, which is preceded by a curious tournament that provides the catalyst for the battle and followed by an equally curious pursuit of Abner that explains how the battle ended. The chapter concludes with the return of both forces to their homes and with the tally of their casualties. David and Ishbosheth are conspicuously absent from the tournament and battle.

Despite this straightforward recitation, an air of unreality pervades the entire account. Consider the performance at the pool of Gibeon in verses 12–16. Joab and Abner, the agents of David and Ishbosheth, sit with their men on either side of the pool and choose twelve men from each side to perform before their brethren. What apparently starts out in jest ends in earnest as "each caught his opponent by the head and thrust his sword in his opponent's side and they fell together" (v. 16). Observant characters and readers alike are meant to view this activity as distanced from the "reality" according to which the generally mimetic story in 1–2 Samuel is composed.

With respect to the spectators within the story, the actions of twelve pairs of combatants whereby all simultaneously seize their opponents by the head and finish them off by the sword are so choreographed that they could hardly have been perceived as "really" happening: the players were all dead before the spectators would have had a chance to realize it. Attention may have been sustained, but shock is delayed; had any soldier present at the ceremony ever witnessed a real battle ending in such a manner? Twenty-four men enter combat and each simultaneously kills his opponent, leaving twenty-four corpses upon Flint's Field.[1] We almost get a picture of Abner's and Joab's men waiting in puzzlement for their colleagues to arise after whatever the ancient version of applause had died down. The choreography of the joust at the beginning may very well have temporarily masked the absence of jest at the end.

Readers should be as puzzled by the death scene as the story's spectators would have been. Why is the narrator's performance as little influenced by verisimilitude as that of the characters?

Consider also the implausibility of the battle's end in verses 18–28. The crisply efficient conversation between a fleeing Abner and a fleet Asahel is scarcely credible in such breathless circumstances. Afterwards, Abner will impale Asahel with what seems to be the handle of his spear (*'ah^{a}rê hah^{a}nît*) so that it sticks out Asahel's back (2:23): the end result provides a strange image of Asahel having been the one pursued and mortally struck from behind. This death scene appears mimetically backward. Then, when Joab and the Judahites manage to catch up with him, Abner pleads for mercy by appealing to fraternal loyalty in verse 26 ("How long before you bid your people turn from pursuing their brothers?")—an incredible argument for a cornered, even if reluctant—killer to address to his victim's brother. Nevertheless, Joab is immediately convinced by it: Abner and his men return to Mahanaim, Joab's forces to Hebron, and readers are struck by the unreality of it all. Ought not such imaginative details disturb readers as much as the twenty-four dead jousters are meant, perhaps, to shock those who sat around the pool at Gibeon foolishly waiting for their fallen brethren to stand up?

What follows is a sampling of the chapter's extended ritualization of action as it is described through extensive stylization of language. Such details support my suggestions concerning what this narrative event is about within its literary context. At the very least, I want to explore how characterization leads to, and is defined by, authorial motivations lying behind these highly ritualized actions.

The Sport of Kings: Ritualized Action

The tournament preceding the battle and the pursuit of Abner concluding it remind us of Israel's ritualized crossing of the Jordan in Josh. 3:1–5:1 as well as the similarly plotted battle scenes in 1 Samuel 14 and 17. Josh. 3:1–5:1 recounted a liturgical exercise while 1 Samuel 14 and 17 described military action; the latter events are obviously closer to home from the point of view of story and theme. Yet whether the pronounced choreography is sacral or martial, its effect upon narrative is to lessen the mimetic qualities of the story even as it increases the narrator's opportunities to use highly stylized language.

Scholarly arguments usually attempt to ground the account of the tournament in ancient gladiatorial practices. But the stylized and ritualized features of the narrative must have been as obvious to ancient readers as they are to us.[2] There simply are too many correlations between ritualized action and stylized language to allow the denial of careful choreography employed for larger ideological and narrative purposes. That there may lie behind the account of chapter 2 ancient gladiatorial practices remains a proper subject for scholarly speculation. Nevertheless, an aura of unreality impinging upon reality—and mysteriously commingling with it—is surely a good part of the function of this tournament within the larger story line. For onlooking characters and readers alike, the action of play here constitutes a means for constructing a story—and even for interpreting it from within.

Notice the spatial dimensions of actions that have been choreographed into both tournament and battle. In chapter 2's play-within-a-play, the observers and players are both ritually positioned: spectators sit "one on one side of the pool and the other on the other side of the pool" (v. 13). Asahel's pursuit of Abner contains two references to "swerving to the right and left" (vv. 19, 21). If some combatants cross over ($^{c}\bar{a}bar$, v. 15) into ritual to fight in the tournament, so also Abner's men cross over ($^{c}\bar{a}bar$) the Jordan after the "real" battle has ended (v. 29).[3] In the tournament, the spectators sit while the players rise and fall; in the battle account, the narrator discloses that mourners come and stand at the place where Asahel had fallen (v. 23). During the chase, Abner's men line up behind him "and became one band, and took their stand on the top of a hill" (v. 25). Near the end of the chapter, Joab's blowing of the trumpet causes the Judahites to stand or stop from pursuing Israel (v. 28). Both armies then march through the night (vv. 29, 32) and return to home base.

Two other aspects of the battle scene and its setting reinforce the feeling that we are observing a ritual performance even in the events that succeed the tournament. First, numbers appear to perform symbolic functions within the story. In the tournament, "twelve versus twelve" probably has a tribal significance mirroring the conflict between north and south that constituted "the long war between the house of Saul and the house of David" (3:1). And in the battle itself, when we finally read the tally of those killed, we find that Abner's casualties are 360 men versus 20 men on Abner's side. The lopsided outcome of the initial battle foreshadows the climax of the war itself between competing royal houses. Second, the reader who has already recognized the narrative implications for Israel of Saul's suicide, recounted in 1 Samuel 31 and reviewed in 2 Samuel 1, cannot now ignore the meaning for Israel of a ritual performance in which all twenty-four Hebrews kill their fellows (*rēᶜēhû*) before their armies ever meet one another in formal battle.

The Play of Authors: Stylized Language

In addition to these examples of a narrative staging of action, the chapter's frequent recourse to *stylized language* also tends to work against the mimetic features of the story. Perhaps nothing better illustrates the Deuteronomist's ability to communicate important ideological truths in an elegantly persuasive manner than the unusually frequent and variable use of *'aḥᵃrê*, "after or behind," throughout chapter 2. If we want to suggest why the narrator uses certain details with which to fashion this beginning account of civil war in Israel, we need only look behind the many ways in which *'aḥᵃrê* integrates themes within chapter 2 and elsewhere in the History.

Some form of *'aḥᵃrê* (including a related form, *'aḥᵃrôn*) appears fifteen times in chapter 2. Apart from Nehemiah 3, where a formulaic *'aḥᵃrâyw*, "after him," is used sixteen times in mechanical enumeration of those who worked on the wall, and from 1 Kings 2, a passage whose frequent use of this form is related to its use here in 2 Samuel 2, nowhere else in the History, or in the Bible for that matter, do we have such a piling up of occurrences of, and various meanings for, *'aḥᵃrê* and its related forms. To understand the importance of *'aḥᵃrê* in chapter 2 is to begin to understand how the chapter functions within its literary context.

The use of *'aḥᵃrê* opens up a variety of perspectives on the idea of *succession* in a chapter which begins the story of who will rule after Saul. The thematic and semantic opportunities that the stylized use of this form allows are especially numerous. What does it mean to be or act *behind* Saul, David, their successors, or their supporters? Of what value for Israel is royal succession and the pursuit of kings? Chapter 2 gives us an inventory of possible answers to such questions.

As in all stories, the basic kind of succession indicated by constructions using *'aḥar* is *narrative:* "after this" (v. 1) and "in the end" (v. 26). In addition, "to be behind someone" is to support or obey them (v. 10); similarly, "to gather behind someone" is to fight on their side (v. 25). On the other hand, "to pursue after" is to follow after someone with harmful intent (vv. 19, 24, 28). Such pursuits can end when one "takes oneself away from after" (v. 27) or "turns aside from after" (vv. 21, 22, 26, 30) one's quarry. The proper sequence involved in such pursuits is indicated by someone "turning (to look) behind oneself" at the pursuer (v. 20). Finally, we find in chapter 2 the end of such pursuits in the "end" of Abner's spear (*'aḥᵃrê haḥᵃnît*) which sticks out "the back of" Asahel (*mē'aḥᵃrāyw*) (v. 23). What is *behind* such obviously stylized language?

It is no coincidence that the only other passage in the Bible where the use of *'aḥᵃrê* is both thematically functional and unusually frequent is 1 Kings 1, a chapter addressing the question, "Who will rule after David?"—the very question following the one about which 2 Samuel 2 is concerned, "Who will rule after Saul?" A look at 1 Kings 1, therefore, should give us some perspective on what is at stake here in 2 Samuel 2.

The story in 1 Kings 1 revolves around the person who will "reign after" (*mālak 'aḥᵃrê*) David (1:13, 17, 24, 30) or "sit upon the throne after" him (1:20, 27). Questions of royal succession involve the support of influential Israelites like the priest, Abiathar, and the commander, Joab, who "help after" pretenders to the throne such as Adonijah (1:7), who, for all his pretensions, was unfortunately "born after" (*yālad 'aḥᵃrê*) Absalom (v. 6). Nathan, however, will support Bathsheba's claims to David in behalf of Solomon by conspiring to "come after" her into the king's presence to confirm her words (v. 14). Finally, royal pursuits demand that priest and people "ascend after" (*ᶜālāh 'aḥᵃrê*) the king (vv. 35, 40).

I am suggesting that various expressions concerning who follows after whom in 1 Kings 1 are deliberately chosen to support and focus the main theme of the chapter. In similar fashion, the extensive use of *'aḥᵃrê* in 2 Samuel 2 is a stylized counterpart to highly ritualized actions. Both techniques (the ritualization of action and the stylization of language) sharpen the thematic focus of the chapter. The Deuteronomist uses both semantic and ritual sequencing to reinforce an ongoing theme concerning royal succession: the pursuit of kings and the pursuit of one's brethren are to be intimately connected in Israel's coming history. Both are tantamount to turning aside from (following) after the LORD.

This brings us to another example of stylized language through which the Deuteronomist choreographs Asahel's pursuit of Abner to great ideological effect. We read twice about "swerving (*nāṭāh* or *sûr*) to the right and left": Asahel refuses to do so even after Abner pleads with him (vv. 19, 21) This language seems ideologically innocent, until one considers that almost everywhere else in the History the use of similar phrases indicates obedience, mostly to the LORD.[4] Such language transforms the chase into a legal matter involving royal pursuits. Given that the royal dispute between David and Ishbosheth has already caused bloodshed between them, and that Abner and Joab finally agree *to turn aside* from brother pursuing brother (vv. 26, 27), it is not difficult to view Asahel's unswerving pursuit of Abner as a stylized comment on the legalities of royal pursuits.

If we look backward, Deuteronomic legislation specifically commands that the king's heart "not be lifted up above his brothers nor turn aside from the commandment either to the right hand or to the left" (Deut. 17:20). If we look forward, we encounter King Josiah who "did what was right in the LORD and walked in all the way of David, his father, and did not turn aside to the right hand or to the left" (2 Kings 22:2). In whichever direction we look in the History, the ideological accents heard in the phrase, "to swerve to the left or the right," are unavoidable. On one hand, to swerve neither to the left nor to the right connotes action obedient to God's law; on the other hand, here in 2 Samuel 2, it embodies the homicidal pursuit of one's brethren because of competing claims to the throne. In the History, we are never far away from the Deuteronomist's central stance concerning kingship: it came about through both obedience and disobedience to God's law. Like Josiah after him, Asahel indeed swerved neither to right nor left. Nevertheless, Asahel's life was lost just as Josiah's reform would fail. Both represent royal pursuits that fail, one at the rise of the house of David, the other near its fall.

Through these examples of "after or behind" and "swerving to the left or the right," I have sought to illustrate how the Deuteronomist chooses words and describes actions with the same kind of craft apparent in a finely choreographed performance. I have suggested also that 2 Samuel 2 is an excellent example of narrative events ritualized both in the story itself and through the generous use of stylized language. The tournament in verses 12–16 is narrated as a ritual performance; the account of how the battle ends in verses 18–28 is transformed into one. The Deuteronomist uses highly stylized language in 2 Samuel 2 either to reinforce what is already presented as a ritual event or to invest apparently realistic action with ideologically loaded detail.

When we come to discuss 2 Samuel 3, we will give a name to these miniaturized images by which the Deuteronomist constantly mirrors the larger story line.

The Deuteronomist's Voice

In terms of the outcome of "the long war between the house of Saul and the house of David" now beginning (3:1), the initial battle between them in chapter 2 clearly foreshadows the coming victory of David: his forces slay 360 of Abner's men while only losing 19 men plus Asahel (vv. 30–31). Indeed, "Abner and the men of Israel were beaten before the servants of David" (v. 17). Moreover, the narrator signals the rise of David at the beginning of the chapter through David's inquiring of God about where to take up residence. In scarcely more than one verse, we read of David's ascent four times: "Shall I ascend?"; "Ascend!"; "To where shall I ascend?"; "So David ascended." Chapter 3 will begin in more direct fashion: "David grew stronger and stronger and the house of Saul became weaker and weaker" (v. 1).

Moreover, with respect to the chapter's structure, we are now in a position to see how inner and outer play interact. Joab's blowing of the trumpet and each army's return to their home base by marching throughout the night into a new day—Abner and his men crossing the Jordan to Mahanaim and Joab back to Hebron—signal the end of the initial skirmish. One cannot avoid the impression that this opening battle has been as carefully staged for readers as the tournament was for its immediate spectators. The entire battle account is like a dress rehearsal for the tribal conflict that follows.

Thus, whereas the play-within-the-play can show the reader the ultimate fate of a nation bent on royal pursuits, the play-outside-the-play is now only beginning. The play must go on. Joab and Abner will have a continuing role in the story as David's victories, foreshadowed by the battle, unfold. Such narrative necessities may account for Joab's unexpected acceptance of Abner's desperate pleading and for the temporary cessation of hostilities. The very implausibility of the details outlining how the battle ends— artificially contrived speech and action alike—looks like a narrative convention that allows even ancient readers, I would suggest, to recognize the battle account for what it is, a clearly marked narrative designed to foreshadow the outcome of the war between the house of Saul and the house of David. Joab's trumpet blast brings down the curtain, so that the story's characters may now act in a more "realistic" manner.

Yet in chapter 2 there are other important indications of the author's perspective on the coming career of David within the history of royal Israel. Having suggested that the events of chapter 2 make sense especially when narrative mimesis is downplayed and stylized language emphasized, I now want to return to the tournament in order to show how *its* ritualized action and stylized language illustrate the ideological power of play.

Much ink has already been spilled in attempts to establish a gladiatorial event in 2 Samuel 2. Two points are relevant to such admittedly plausible historical reconstructions. First, when Abner and Joab agree to have some of their men "play" (*śāḥaq*) before them at the pool of Gibeon, it is not likely that they envision a contest to the death, since this verb and its related word, *ṣāḥaq,* are only used in the History to initiate less deadly instances of entertainment. When the Philistines have Samson play before them (Judges 16) or when the women of Israel play their song of praise for David (1 Samuel 18) or, finally, when David himself plays before the LORD (2 Samuel 6), those who initiate the play do not contemplate a performance to the death.

Nevertheless, "to play" does have serious, sometimes deadly, consequences in the History. As in 2 Samuel 2, Samson's playing before the Philistines starts off in fun but finally spells death—in this case for all "who looked on while Samson played" (Judg. 16:27). After David kills Goliath, the women make merry by singing a song that voices the end of Saul's popularity and thus provokes his angry displeasure (1 Sam. 18:7–9). And in 2 Samuel 6 we will soon see how David's naked playing before the LORD causes Michal to despise him in her heart. Always full of conflict, the Deuteronomist's references to play only involve death by surprise.

But we are basing such remarks on only three Deuteronomic passages besides 2 Samuel 2, so that a serious gladiatorial contest as historical background for our present account remains a possibility. Even so, assuming that Joab and Abner agree to such a deadly contest from the beginning, a second point needs emphasizing: the narrator's description of the tournament in verses 15–16 involves so much ritual action and stylized language that it appears to preclude serious mimetic interpretation. No pictorial or textual account from the past that may be relevant to such combat disposes us to imagine how twelve pairs of combatants could seriously grab each other by the head and thrust their swords into each other, either simultaneously or *seriatim.* This would appear implausible from a historiographic point of view, so that conclusions about the account of the tournament based upon verisimilitude seem to me to miss the point. However we try to imagine things *after* the soldiers cross over (v. 15) into performance, we are led away from a realistic account by the Deuteronomist's ritualized and stylized version of the performance itself.

Having already seen the forceful use the Deuteronomist makes of supposedly modern techniques like *the double and double-voiced language* in chapter 1, we should not be surprised in chapter 2 by our encounter of a play-within-a-play. Whatever may be the historical background of such gladiatorial contests, the performance described in verses 12–16 looks like a ritual enactment of the narrative situation in which Israel will conduct its affairs from now on. Like the Deuteronomist's graphic images of the death of royal Eli in 1 Samuel 4, and of the ritual slaughter of royal Israel in David's lament (2 Samuel 1), the tournament in 2 Samuel 2 is the Deuteronomist's graphic picture both of the exultant period of Israel's history—from the rise of the house of David, when "David grew stronger and stronger" (2 Sam. 3:1), to the succession of Solomon, when finally "the throne of David is established before the LORD forever" (1 Kings 2:45)— and of the wider, but more tragic, period from the rise of David to the fall of Israel. The pursuit of kings within the house of David ultimately will be an exercise in self-annihilation on both a personal and national level.

Notice first the symbolism, already mentioned, of the twelve pairs of Hebrews "crossing over" (v. 15) into ritual and narrative performance. These pairs of combatants represent, I have suggested, the twelve tribes for which David and Ishbosheth contend. That royal hegemony over the twelve tribes is at issue here is indicated by each man seizing the "head" (*ro'š*) of his "neighbor or opponent" (*rē'ēhû*). Tribal brother battles against tribal brother over who will be their king. We recall Samuel's words to Saul, "Are you not the head (*ro'š*) of the tribes of Israel? The LORD anointed you king over Israel" (1 Sam. 15:17). This contest is about seizing headship over the tribes of Israel. By the time 2 Samuel draws to a close, Saul's successor as head of the tribes of Israel will be referring to himself as "the head even of nations" (2 Sam. 22:44).

However clearly we see this *seizing of the head* as stylized imagery for the grasping of kingship, the semantic fullness of "head" here is scarcely exhausted. For from the beginning of his career to the end, David's character zone is intimately connected with the head as a locus of guilt and death. For one thing, David, either wittingly or unwittingly, is constantly associated with the contemplated or actual beheading of his enemies, whether Goliath (1 Sam. 17:46, 54, 57), Saul (1 Sam. 31:9), Ishbosheth (2 Sam. 4:7, 8, 12), Shimei (2 Sam. 16:9, where David rejects a suggestion to behead Shimei), or Sheba (2 Sam. 20:21). Even David's enemy and son, Absalom, is killed by Joab's armor-bearer after "his head was seized by the oak tree" (2 Sam. 18:9). We notice, finally, how the head functions as the locus of the guilt and sin of David's enemies (e.g., 1 Sam. 25:39; 2 Kings 2:44), often expressed in bloody terms (2 Sam. 1:16; 3:29; 1 Kings 2:32, 33, 37).

In the varied instances of bloody death or bloody guilt involving the heads of David's enemies, the narrative will now implicate him, now exonerate him. Nevertheless, blood flows upon and from the heads of David's enemies more often than with any other character in the Bible. Even granting the relatively extensive narrative that describes his life and career, the heady bloodshed surrounding David still remains a significant means by which he rose to become "head of the tribes of Israel" (1 Sam. 15:17) and "heads of nations" (2 Sam. 22:44). Even after David's death, Joab and Shimei are executed by Solomon because of their bloodied, that is, guilt-ridden, heads in accordance with David's dying wishes in the previous chapter (1 Kings 2).

Besides providing an indelible image of grasping kings and abundant bloodshed, the performance at the pool of Gibeon also portrays what monarchy will mean for the king's subjects: seizing the head of "one's neighbor" (*rē'ēhû*) and killing him (*rē'ēhû*) by the sword brings guilt upon one's own head and recalls Solomon's prayer at the dedication of the temple: "If a man sins against his neighbor (*rē'ēhû*), condemn the guilty by bringing his conduct *upon his own head*" (1 Kings 8:31–32). The ritual at Gibeon's pool enacts what Abner will soon ask Joab to terminate: "Shall the sword devour forever? How long before you bid your people turn from the pursuit of their brethren?" (2 Sam. 2:26). Tribal grasping of kings will pit brother against brother, neighbor against neighbor. Abner's reference to the sword that devours "forever" is bound up in the History with Solomon's establishment of the throne of David "forever" (1 Kings 2:45). Between both *forevers* we find the sword of David, whether wielded by him or handed over to others by him or the narrator. Like most of the History's *forevers,* David's will end with the exile.

Variations *en-Abyme:* The Seduction of David in Chapter 3

An air of seduction permeates chapter 3, which details the incidents leading up to the murder of Abner without the knowledge of David, whose public mourning convinces Israel that he was not implicated in such a crime. Before concentrating on those aspects of the story that seem to me to reflect authorial intentions most clearly, I want to describe some of the chapter's features that my own interpretation seeks to explain.

First, the narrator describes events with almost a frenzy of activity. People go, come, go out, send (away), and return more often than anywhere else in 2 Samuel: there are at least forty-two references to such activity in chapter 3, so that the reader is bound to wonder what the narrator's concentration on the comings and goings of characters means. This question is especially relevant since the story itself thematizes the problem through Joab's recrimination of David, "You know that Abner the son of Ner came to deceive you, and to know *your going out and your coming in*" (v. 25). Moreover, Joab's statement occurs between the narrator's statements that Joab and his army "came in" (*bā'û*) and that Joab "went out" (*wayyēṣē'*) from David. What has the alleged attempts of Abner to learn about David's comings and goings to do with the comings and goings of Abner and the other characters of the chapter?

Second, throughout 2 Samuel 3 issues of knowledge (*yādaᶜ*) or its lack are central to the statements of both narrator and characters. The narrator makes it clear that David did not know beforehand of Joab's intention to kill Abner (v. 26) and that the people came to know David's innocence in this matter through his public actions and statements (v. 37). The characters in the story also speak of knowledge as crucial to their affairs. When Joab accuses David of not being aware of Abner's evil intentions he does so with proper decorum: Joab's affirmation to David, "you know that," means just the opposite, "you obviously do not know that Abner came to deceive you." Moreover, Joab's characterization of Abner's actions twice mentions a desire for intelligence: Abner wants to know David's comings and goings and to know what David is doing (v. 25). And David himself ends the chapter by affirming the people's knowledge of Abner's greatness (v. 38). What does all this emphasis on the presence or absence of knowledge have to do with the Deuteronomist's main concerns here in the History?

Third, the narrator is conspicuously generous with inside views of characters in chapter 3. We learn that Ishbosheth's speechlessness is caused by his fear of Abner (v. 11), that David did not know of Joab's plans (v. 26), that revenge for Asahel's death was the motive for Abner's murder (vv. 27, 30), and that the people knew of David's innocence and took great pleasure in all that he did (vv. 36–37). We may be used to the narrator's sharing of such privileged information at various points throughout the History, yet we are aware also that the narrator has rarely allowed us to enter the inner life of David. Why does the narrator now make sure that readers know that David is innocent of Abner's death? This question is especially important, since the narrator at the same time conceals from us crucial information about Abner's turnabout in behalf of David: we simply do not know whether Abner was falsely accused by Ishbosheth. Not knowing this, we find it difficult to evaluate Abner's move to the side of David. Does he conspire to bring Israel to David in an understandable response to Ishbosheth's false accusations or rather in angry retaliation over being found out by Saul's son? However we judged his reluctant killing of Asahel in chapter 2, Abner's inner motivation and Joab's consequent characterization of him in chapter 3 remain a permanent gap in the story.

Fourth, just as Joab's words mean the opposite of a formal affirmation that David knew what he was doing in letting Abner go in peace (v. 25), so the narrator's voice in vv. 36–37 clearly distances itself from its reference both to the people's wholesale pleasure in David and to their knowledge of David's innocence in the death of Abner. How can the narrator be so intent on making sure that readers know of David's innocence in this crime, only then to sound a note of caution about how easily the people of Israel were won over to David's side by his funerary deportment? How are David's seductive power over all Israel and Israel's knowledge of David's innocence bound up with the Deuteronomist's presentation of David in the History?

Fifth, the Deuteronomist's presentation of David in chapter 3 associates him with other characters in the story according to narrative purposes that require explanation. For example, the issues of knowledge and seduction mentioned above serve to unite David to Joab in a manner that appears central to the story. If Joab succeeds in seducing David immediately after accusing Abner of the same in verse 25 ("You know that Abner came to deceive you [*lᵉpattotkā*]"), so also David continues to entice or seduce the people even as he condemns Joab for the murder of Abner. Also, David curses Joab's house in terms that anticipate his mourning fast over Abner's death: "May the house of Joab never be without one who lacks bread" (v. 29); "then all the people came to persuade David to eat bread, but David swore, 'I shall not taste bread until the sun goes down'" (v. 35). Is there something of a self-curse in David's curse of Joab?

Finally, the manner in which Joab and Abishai kill Abner is clearly a narrative mirroring of Abner's killing of their brother Asahel in chapter 2. Abner tells Asahel to turn aside (*nāṭāh*), but Asahel would not turn aside (*sûr*), so Abner smote him in the belly (2:22–23). Similarly in chapter 3, "When Abner returned to Hebron, Joab took him aside (*nāṭāh*) and there he smote him in the belly" (v. 27). What functions does this narrative patterning of murder serve in the story?

Mise-en-Abyme

Some of the questions just raised may find an answer through recognition of the continued use, in this and previous chapters, of a literary device that effectively mirrors authorial intentions. This phenomenon, which some scholars suggest "may be found in all periods, in all genres and literary modes," is called *mise-en-abyme*.[5]

Apologetic accounts in behalf of David continue to motivate the narrative in chapter 3 and have been emphasized by scholars in recent years.[6] What has not been sufficiently recognized, here as elsewhere in the History, is the abundance of narrative details that serve to mirror the History's main concerns and, thus, to provide the reader with a variety of authorial signposts that point to what these individual events are *about*. The History's prodigality in individual mirrorings is simply amazing. Literature, like language, communicates through redundant features, and when such communicative functions are abundant rather than infrequent in a narrative, contemporary critics call such texts "readerly." Among the techniques whereby authors of all ages strive to make their narratives more readerly, one of the most interesting is what André Gide first called *mise-en-abyme*. (We have no commonly accepted designation in English for this literary phenomenon, so I will continue to use the customary term for it.)

I want to suggest that 2 Samuel 3 is eminently readable because of the instances of *mise-en-abyme* that integrate the events narrated therein and that reflect other instances of this phenomenon in the text. How 2 Samuel 3 succeeds in mirroring its own message will help us understand something of the nature and narrative power of the Deuteronomic History.

Here is a description of *mise-en-abyme* by Brian McHale:

> A true *mise-en-abyme* is determined by three criteria: first it is a nested or embedded representation, occupying a narrative level inferior to that of the primary, diegetic narrative world; secondly, this nested representation resembles (copies, says Hofstadter) something at the level of the primary, diegetic world; and thirdly, this "something" that it resembles must constitute some salient and continuous aspect of the primary world, salient and continuous enough that we are willing to say the nested representation *reproduces* or *duplicates* the primary representation as a whole.[7]

McHale goes on to explain that the aspects of the primary world reproduced by *mise-en-abyme* might be the narrative story line, its situation, or its style and poetics. We shall see with what frequency the History exploits these possibilities, especially since embedded representations do not always have to be at a narrational level below the primary narrative world.[8]

The Death of Abner and David's Comings and Goings

When Joab returns to Hebron and discovers that David has just sent Abner away in peace, he warns the king, "You know that Abner the son of Ner came to deceive you, and to know your going out and your coming in, and to know all that you are doing" (3:25). What makes Joab's statement so relevant to the larger implications of the story is its focus on the interconnections between Abner's knowledge, his supposed seduction of David, and David's comings and goings. Joab's claim is that Abner's reason for making a treaty with David is seduction for the purpose of intelligence: Abner intends to entice, attract, or even deceive David so that he might find out what David is doing. This charge is much more than a simple reflection of Joab's position in the story before his murder of Abner; it reflects larger concerns in two important ways. First, it illuminates the same issues surrounding the treaty between Abner and David before

Abner's death as those surrounding the treaty to be enacted between Israel and David after it. Second, Joab's characterization of Abner is a perfect description of the reader, who constantly desires to find out what David is doing and what are his comings and goings, so as to understand why all his enemies are being so conveniently and violently removed from his path as he approaches the throne of all Israel.

Let's look at these points in some detail. The volatile mixture of seduction and knowledge that unites Abner and David in the first part of the chapter also unites Israel and David in the second part. Whatever insight there is in Joab's words to David, the force of David's personality over those he encounters and his ability, from the beginning, to win them over to his side cannot fail to provoke the reader to wonder whether the seduction or enticement that effects their treaty is not as much David's as Abner's. Perhaps Abner is as much seduced by David as seducer of him.

What makes it especially difficult to sort out the issues involved in the negotiations between Abner and David is the reader's inability to construct an adequate characterization of Abner in the story: from first to last Abner remains an enigmatic and artificial figure. Partly because his role in 2 Samuel 2, as we have seen, was largely non-mimetic and partly because of a permanent gap about him in 2 Samuel 3, Abner departs the scene without having established himself as a full-fledged character in the story. Earlier, we could not tell how his reluctant killing of Asahel and his impassioned pleas for an end to fratricide in Israel functioned from a characterological point of view. The words and actions of narrator and characters alike in 2 Samuel 2 were too stylized for Abner to emerge as anything but an artificial vehicle for the foreboding purposes of the Deuteronomist.

Even here in chapter 3 we are unable to pin down the significance of Abner's conversion to David's side, because the narrator never clarifies Abner's actions as he does David's. We know for certain that David had no knowledge of Joab's plans to kill Abner, because the narrator tells us this in v. 26. But what are we to make of Ishbosheth's accusations about Abner's going in to Saul's concubine? Since we are unable to find out whether Abner has done what Ishbosheth accuses him of, we are hard pressed to obtain a sufficiently clear picture of Abner's abrupt about-face. Does he begin negotiations with David and use his influence to further David's cause within Israel as Ishbosheth's loyal commander, who is now falsely accused, or as a disloyal culprit who, having been caught out by his king, now makes the best of a bad situation by changing sides? Does the narrator's initial statement that "Abner was making himself strong in the house of Saul" (v. 6) incline us to interpret Ishbosheth's accusations concerning Saul's concubine as a rather weak attempt to inhibit Abner's growing influence over Israel or rather as an accurate representation of one of the means Abner employs to consolidate his power and publicize his aspirations to Saul's throne? We cannot tell, nor will subsequent details in the story clarify these ambiguities.

Another indication of the artificial nature of this character, Abner, is the narrator's use of him twice to report the words of the LORD that authenticate transference of royal power to David (v. 10) and prophesy David's coming victories over the Philistines and all Israel's enemies (v. 18). Nothing we have learned about Abner so far prepares us to understand why the narrator here uses him as the mouthpiece of the LORD. In contrast both to the complex yet opaque presentation of David from 1 Samuel 16 onwards, and to the clear presentation of Abner's enemies, the sons of Zeruiah, throughout their careers, Abner speaks and acts only as a two-dimensional figure employed by the Deuteronomist primarily as an agent for plot movement or as an obvious vehicle for the narrative's more obvious ideological statements. When Abner quotes God in chapter 3 and when he nobly asks Joab in chapter 2, "Shall the sword devour forever? Do you not know that the end will be bitter? How long will it be before you bid your people turn from the pursuit of their brethren?" (v. 26), Abner's utterances are all but drowned out. The Deuteronomist's takes them over to address a set of central questions to a nation contemplating defeat in exile and wondering what it means.[9]

Since, therefore, David's enticement of Abner is at least as much a possibility as Abner's seduction of David, the ability of Joab's words to mirror the situation in which Israel finds itself in the second part of the chapter is considerable. Abner's deceptive, and perhaps even deceived, attempts to find out "what [David] is doing" (v. 25) end in his death. What then are we to make of the narrator's words concerning David and Israel: "And *all the people* took notice of it [David's public acts of mourning] and it pleased them; as *everything* that the king did pleased the people. So *all the people* and *all Israel* knew that day that it had not been the king's will to slay Abner the son of Ner" (vv. 36–37)?

What is the basis for the people's acceptance of David's acts of mourning as authentic signs of his innocence in the death of Abner? The narrator makes the claim that this is merely an instance of what the people *habitually* think and feel about David. However, the narrator's words are much more than a statement of the people's thoughts and feelings about David. What sounds loud and clear through the piling up of universals ("all the people," "everything that the king did," "so all the people and all Israel") is the narrator's distance from the people's wholesale acceptance of David, even in this instance when such confidence in him, as the reader well knows, turns out incidentally to be justified. However innocent

David is in this instance, the narrator is saying, the people appear foolish in their wholesale acceptance of the king.

Verses 36–37, therefore, form a *hybrid expression* that reverberates with the inner words and feelings of all Israel and with the critical accents of the Deuteronomist. The people's attitudes toward David are not only reported but also critically evaluated through words that unmask the seductive and dangerous power David exercised over all the people. One is reminded here of the ironic overtones in Josh. 21:43–45, through which the Deuteronomist unmasked the seductive but erroneous beliefs of Israelites that their forebears had completely devastated the nations in the first stages of the occupation. As Joshua 13–21 provides a narrative context in which the nationalistic beliefs expressed in Josh. 21:43–45 are clearly shown to be misguided,[10] so here in 2 Sam. 3:36–37, preceding and future events in David's career help to transform the people's confidence in David into their seduction by him.

Joab criticizes David by claiming that Abner came in order to know what *David is doing* (v. 25); the narrator criticizes the people for being pleased in everything that *David did* (v. 36); and we shall soon see how the Deuteronomist uses David's own words condemning Joab against their own speaker: "the LORD repay him *who is doing evil* according to his wickedness" (v. 39).

How does Joab's statement in verse 25 provide the reader with a miniaturized model of a continuous and salient aspect of the larger story line of which it is a part? How, in other words, does verse 25 function as a *mise-en-abyme* of the larger story of David? There are at least three different ways in which Joab's statement to David can be seen as a nested reproduction of the primary story world. On a limited scale, verse 25 mirrors the very language and style that the narrator uses to recount the events of chapter 3. More importantly, however, this verse both duplicates the Deuteronomist's representation of David's entire life and career and also reveals something of the situation between implied author and audience that motivates such a representation in the first place.

We can start by remarking on the least important but most obvious aspect of the embedded statement of Joab. When Joab charges David, "You know that Abner the son of Ner came to deceive [seduce, entice (*pātāh*)] you and *to know your going out and coming in* and to know all that you are doing" (v. 25), Joab's (and perhaps Abner's) emphasis on David's comings and goings mirrors the narrator's unusual emphasis on the comings and goings of all the characters in this chapter. As I mentioned at the beginning of this section, the frenzy of activity expressed by the narrator (at least forty-two instances of characters going, coming, going out, sending [away], and returning) finds a miniature reflection in Abner's alleged attempt to find out about David's "going out and coming in." A central theme of Joab's statement thus mirrors a superficial but obvious aspect of the narrative style of the chapter.

Much more importantly, however, Joab's statement of Abner's intentions is an embedded representation of a major theme of the History concerning the life and career of David. Like Abner, the reader wants to know David's going out and coming in, that is, what David is doing. Moreover, the reader needs to integrate Abner's alleged intentions in the first part of the chapter with all Israel's acceptance of David in the second part. What is the relationship between the people's traditional pleasure in everything that David did (v. 36) and their knowledge that David had nothing to do with the death of Abner (v. 37)? Abner's success in deceiving David (implied by Joab in v. 25), Joab's success in deceiving David by hiding his intention to murder Abner (attested by the narrator in v. 26), and David's success in publicizing his own innocence throughout all Israel (seen in 31–39)—all revolve around the seductive knowledge of David's comings and goings as he "seizes the head" (*ḥāzaq bᵉroʾš* in the *mise-en-abyme* of 2:16) of all Israel.

In order to see how Joab's statement is clearly a miniaturized version of the Deuteronomist's larger story line, we need only recall how the Deuteronomist employs references to "going out and coming in" (*yāṣāʾ* and *bôʾ*). In general, the combination of these two verbs serves as a shorthand expression for the totality of one's actions (Deut. 28:6, 19), and the phrase is especially appropriate for individuals in authority. Moses tells his people, "I am a hundred and twenty years old this day; I am no longer able to go out and come in" (Deut. 31:2); conversely, Caleb tells Joshua, "My strength now is as my strength then, for war and for going out and coming in" (Josh. 14:11). The comings and goings of kings like Joash or even Sennacherib are referred to in the History by this paired expression (2 Kings 11:8; 19:27). Also, when a city is besieged, it is not able to engage in conduct necessary for its existence: Israel besieged Jericho so that "none went out and none came in" (Josh. 6:1) and Baasha, king of Israel, built Ramah "that he might permit no one to go out or come in to Asa, king of Judah" (1 Kings 15:17).

More to the point, the way in which the History uses this expression to focus upon the problematic actions of David is especially important for our understanding of what is at stake here in 2 Samuel 3. Whereas Joab claims that Abner came in order to deceive David, to find out his going out and coming in, the Deuteronomist, almost from the appearance of David in the story even to events subsequent to his death, is intent upon showing the seductive power of *David's* actions. From 1 Samuel 16 to

1 Kings 2—that is, while David is alive in the story —the Deuteronomist states a concern for no one else's going out and coming in except David's. They are always met with a positive response from other characters. And there is usually a seductive quality to David's comings and goings throughout the story.

Thus, Saul's fear of David moved the king to make him a commander who "went out and came in before the people. But all Israel and Judah loved David; for he went out and came in before them" (1 Sam. 18:13, 16). Indeed, when Israel comes finally to anoint David king over them, they appeal to his successful comings and goings: "In times past when Saul was king over us, it was you who led out (*yāṣā'* in the *hifil*) and brought in (*bā'* in the *hifil*) in Israel" (2 Sam. 5:2). If David pleased the people, he also impressed Achish, who tells him, "As the LORD lives, you have been honest, and to me it seems right that you should go out and come in with me in the campaign; for I have found nothing wrong in you from the day of your coming to me to this day" (1 Sam. 29:6).

If David succeeds in deceiving the enemy by his actions, does his "going out and coming in" ever deceive his fellow Israelites? This is precisely the question that the Deuteronomist has been raising—and raises once again in 2 Samuel 3. Such a question even looks forward to the request Solomon later makes to the LORD to be like his father: "O LORD, my God, thou hast made thy servant king in place of David my father, although I am but a little child; I do not know how to go out or come in" (1 Kings 3:7). How does Solomon's awe of David's actions compare to the Deuteronomist's presentation of these same deeds? Are the people as seduced by David's comings and goings in 2 Samuel 3 as David was allegedly seduced (*pātāh*) by Abner or actually seduced by Joab after the coming in (v. 24) and going out (v. 26) of Joab? And does the Deuteronomist intend the reader to be as seduced by David's comings and goings as Achish was?

In the light of all this, it may be possible to make sense of the narrative's explicit exoneration of David concerning Abner's death on one hand and its obvious criticism of all the people for being so pleased in all that David did on the other. On a formal level, Joab's statement to David in v. 25, "you know," means, in context, "you do not know." Similarly, the narrator's "so all the people and all Israel knew" emphasizes the seductive and precarious basis for the people's generalized acceptance of David's innocence, which in the particular case of Abner just happened to be correct. In other instances, however, David's seductive power, by which "everything that *the king* did pleased all the people," (v. 36) will lead to disaster. Just as Abner's presumed pleasure in finding out David's comings and goings is simply prelude to personal disaster, so the people's pleasure in (thinking they know) all that David does precedes their own downfall.

"Does Abner die as a fool dies?" laments David (v. 34). Will Israel fall
before the wicked as Abner fell, that is, as one thinking he knows his king's
going out and coming in, what David is doing?

In my suggestion that verse 25 is a wonderful encapsulation of the larger
story's account of the comings and goings of David—a *mise-en-abyme* of the
History's primary narrative world—I am also saying something about the
historical background against which this communication between anonymous author(s) and hidden audience is to be understood: I am calling
v. 25 a *mise-en-abyme* of the History's situation of discourse. What my
reading of the history of royal Israel has emphasized, time and again, is its
desire to teach an audience in exile that cherished traditions about the
royal throne of David have a seductive air about them.

So there is an important respect in which the situation of discourse
between David and Joab in 2 Samuel 3 mirrors the situation of discourse
that exists between the History's implied author and audience. Again, in
Joab's statement to David, "you know" means "you do not know," just as
later in the chapter the narrator's statement about the people's knowledge
of David implicitly questions the justification for their beliefs. What Joab
says about David's knowledge of Abner and what the narrator says about
all the people's knowledge of David may be very close to what the Deuteronomist is saying about an exiled audience's knowledge of and pleasure in
its royal traditions—especially those concerning the house of David.

The communicative situation between Joab and David in verses 24–25
mirrors so well the one between the History's author and audience
because the omniscient narrator shields the reader from crucial information concerning the inner motivations of Abner in the *mise-en-abyme* of
verse 25 and of David throughout much of the primary story world of
1–2 Samuel. Given the gap in the story about the truth or falsehood of
Ishbosheth's accusations of Abner, and given the narrator's habitual
shielding of the inner life of David from the reader, the "real" reason for
Abner's actions remains hidden from characters and readers alike just as
the "real" reasons for David's actions up to this point typically remain
hidden from characters ("all Israel") and readers alike.

Nor, finally, should we fail to consider Joab's deception of David immediately after he purports to enlighten David about Abner's. If Joab, the
speaker, deceives David, his audience, immediately after accusing Abner of
deception, what might this communicational model tell us about the relationship between the History's implied author and audience? Those who
might object to associating enticement or seduction (*pātāh*) with an omniscient narrator should recall that the omniscient LORD more than once is
said to deceive or entice his human subjects (1 Kings 22:20, 21, 22;
Jer. 20:7).

When, therefore, verse 25 is seen as a reflection of the narrative's situation of discourse, the Deuteronomist may be heard claiming to enlighten an exiled audience about the limitations of its cherished royal traditions. Such a construal implies another level of seduction within the chapter: it is only through a kind of narrative persuasion or seduction that the Deuteronomist will achieve whatever purposes lay at the heart of the narrative. This type of seduction lies at the heart of all persuasive narratives and ought to be no more mysterious or distasteful to readers of the Bible than the seductive attractiveness either of David or of the mysterious LORD who was himself attracted to him. Like Joab's statement to David in verse 25, the narrator's implicit statement to the audience at the end of the History, "Now *you know,*" will be true only to the extent that the audience is persuaded by the History to also hear, "Now *you don't know.*"

The Deuteronomist's Use of *Mise-en-Abyme*

It may be helpful to pause here in our interpretation of 2 Samuel in order to suggest how often the narrative mirrors its larger concerns through images that are closely related to *mise-en-abyme.*

Look first at the varied ways in which 2 Samuel seeks to insure that aspects of its situation are constantly before the reader's eyes. In chapter 1, the Amalekite's story within the narrator's story is a wonderful example of a *mise-en-abyme* expressing the Deuteronomist's intentions with a beauty and power that direct authorial statements might only achieve with great difficulty. Through formal expression and thematic development, the Amalekite lad and the story he tells marvelously reflect an authorial voice and the story it tells. A particular character as a deliberate figuring forth of its author is an example of *mise-en-abyme* well attested in world literature. We also saw how the Amalekite lad does double duty as a double, so that as a double for David also, he bodies forth hesitant questions about the apologetic stories exonerating David—stories which the Deuteronomist may be responding to in the very act of incorporating them into the History.

When we came to David's lament over Saul and Jonathan (1:19–27), we found another example of *mise-en-abyme.* This poem is at once David's review of the meaning of Saul's life and death and the Deuteronomist's preview of the rest of the history of royal Israel. The stark image of Saul and Jonathan upon the high places wielding bow and sword like the sacrificial implements of Israel's idolatrous priests surely rivals the more majestic sayings of Israel's prophets.

We then came to 2 Samuel 2 with its performative (as opposed to narrated) *mise-en-abyme* at the pool of Gibeon (2:12–16). Twelve pairs of Israel-

ites seizing each other by the head and killing him by the sword forms
another remarkable image of the coming war between the houses of Saul
and David, on one hand, and of the coming history of monarchy on the
other. Then the finely choreographed story of how the battle between
Saul's and David's forces ends (2:18–32) can be seen as a highly stylized
account of the pursuit of brother by brother that will constitute a central
theme of the coming history. The climax of this *mise-en-abyme* has Abner
appealing to Joab, and the Deuteronomist to an exilic audience, for an
end to the fratricide involved in Israel's pursuit of kings and its kings'
pursuit of their Israelite brethren.

By the time we arrive at chapter 3, the multifaceted employment of
embedded reflections of larger narrative concerns should come as no surprise.

Nor should any of the instances of *mise-en-abyme* in 2 Samuel surprise the
reader who has seriously thought about the literary crafting of 1 Samuel.
When one stands before the first seven chapters of this book, there opens
up an expanse within which the Deuteronomist has incorporated a multi-
layered *mise-en-abyme* of the coming history of royal Israel. The rise and fall
of the priestly house of Eli and the loss of the ark beautifully mirror the
larger story. This opening section even formalizes the author's situation of
discourse in chapter 7 by providing a program for reversing the History's
disastrous conclusion.

The careful detail with which this extensive introductory *mise-en-abyme*
constitutes a proleptic model of the larger story cannot be overempha-
sized. The weaning of Samuel as an image of the false start and providential delay embodied in Saul's abortive kingship; the events of chapter 4
culminating in the death of Eli falling off his throne as a stark image of the
coming fate of kingship; the tragicomic loss and recovery of the ark in
chapters 4–6 as a figuring forth of the exile and its end; and the idealized
repentance of Israel under a judicial Samuel in chapter 7 as the Deuteronomist's call for an exilic Israel to cease clinging to royal robes—all these
features of 1 Samuel 1–7 make of it a masterful ancient example of the
ability of *mise-en-abyme* to reflect authorial intentions in an effective way.

1 Samuel 8–31 contains further reflections of the larger story. Consider
the vision of a resurrected Samuel seen through the eyes of the woman of
Endor as "one rising up like a god from the earth" (28:13). Here is a
powerful expression for the idolatry that kingship entails in 1 Samuel: in
his death as in his birth Samuel represents kingship. Consider also the
story in chapter 30 about the spoils of David. Not only is it a story that
previews David's future manner of consolidating all Israel, it is also an
authorial comment upon apologetic traditions exonerating David from
complicity in the death of Saul: the account concerning the statute and

ordinance David made "that day forward" (30:25) is a concise *mise-en-abyme* expressing an authorial view implicating David in the fall of the house of Saul. The entire story in chapter 30 may even reflect the inability of the LORD's anointed to rescue Israel from exile: all David achieves here is to rescue exiled Israelites and restore them to an original exile in Ziklag.

My reading of 1–2 Samuel has so far suggested many instances of *mise-en-abyme* that serve as narrative indicators either of the larger story, of the communicative situation of author and audience, or of the poetic and stylistic features that characterize its composition. The literary imagination and ideological perspectives everywhere apparent within and behind the Deuteronomic History through the use of these devices involve ontological and epistemological principles without which such phenomena would be unthinkable: a confidence that historiography can capture some of the reality or meaning of historical events; the ontological and epistemological claim that reality is somehow structured, stable, and at least partially knowable; and finally the reluctant acceptance of knowledge and ignorance as useful reflections of one another, so that, in story as in history, part can mysteriously reflect whole in a long sequence of limited insights forming an abyss like the various *mise-en-abyme*'s within it.

Variations on *'aḥîm:* Murdering Brothers in Chapter 4

By the time one finishes reading the account of Ishbosheth's murder and the execution of his murderers in 2 Samuel 4, there can be little doubt that the Deuteronomist's constant introduction of brothers (*'aḥîm*) into events following Saul's death has central significance in this phase of the History. Despite their long association in the second half of 1 Samuel, David for the first time calls Jonathan "my brother" only at the beginning of 2 Samuel (1:26). As emphasized above, Abner is reluctant to kill Asahel because of fraternal considerations: "How could I then lift up my face to your brother Joab?" (2:22). Abner then invokes fraternity in pleading for his life before Asahel's brother Joab, "How long will it be before you bid your people turn from the pursuit of their brethren?" (2:26). Joab is grateful for these words because they move him to cut short this "pursuit of their brethren" (2:27). In chapter 3, Abner angrily defends his loyalty to "[Saul's] brothers" (3:8) and at the end dies "for the blood of Asahel [Joab's] brother" (3:27). Finally, the narrator repeats this charge with further fraternal references, "So Joab and Abishai, his brother, slew Abner, because he had killed their brother Asahel in the battle of Gibeon" (3:30).

Here in chapter 4, we read about "Rechab and his brother Baanah," who escape after killing Ishbosheth (v. 6). The brothers flee to David, who "answered Rechab and Baanah his brother" (v. 9), before having them executed for the murder of Ishbosheth. These explicit references ought not to distract us from fraternal considerations that go without saying in the chapter: the blood brother of Ishbosheth is Jonathan, who is, as David stated in 1:26, "my brother." There is fraternal symmetry to this chapter, for brothers kill brothers for the murder of a brother.

When we think about the narrative significance of this emphasis on brotherhood in 2 Samuel, two matters need to be correlated. On one hand, in contrast, say, to Deuteronomy or 1–2 Kings, 2 Samuel uses the word "brother(s)" predominantly in its familial rather than national or tribal meanings (twenty-seven out of thirty-four occurrences).[11] On the other hand, as we have already seen, 2 Samuel 2 juxtaposes "brother" and "fellow or neighbor" ($r\bar{e}^{ac}$) in two scenes (the gladiatorial contest in vv. 12–16 and the pursuit of Abner in vv. 18–27) in order to refer proleptically to *tribal* or *national* fratricide as a central theme of the coming story. How does one deal with these apparently divergent emphases within 2 Samuel?

Chapter 2's equation of '$\bar{a}h$, "brother," and $r\bar{e}^{ac}$, "neighbor," in reference to tribal or national fraternity clearly accords with the Deuteronomist's practice elsewhere in the History. Because both '$\bar{a}h$ and $r\bar{e}^{ac}$ are used throughout the History, in both legislative and narrative contexts, to designate a fellow Hebrew or Israelite (that is, one who is not a foreigner [$n\bar{a}kr\hat{\imath}$]), the two words are used synonymously and can even be employed interchangeably within the same literary context. Thus in 2 Kings 7:3–9, the statement, "they spoke each man to his brother" (v. 6) alternates with "they spoke each man to his neighbor" (vv. 3, 9). Moreover, specific texts have $r\bar{e}^{ac}$ (or $m\bar{e}r\bar{e}^{ac}$), "neighbor," following '$\bar{a}h$, "brother," to indicate that "brother" in these instances has a tribal or national rather than familial reference—for example, in 2 Sam. 3:8—just as "brother" can immediately follow "neighbor" to clarify that the neighbor referred to in context is precisely a Hebrew, that is, a non-foreigner—for example, in Deut. 15:2. It is clear, therefore, that Abner's and Joab's references to "brothers" in 2:26–27 and the narrator's double reference to "neighbor" in 2:16 are appropriately synonymous with respect both to the language of the History and to the interpretation of chapter 2 that I outlined above. The stylistic and ritualistic account of the events of 2 Samuel 2 indicates that the establishment of the throne of David will be accomplished and maintained through a bloodbath of tribal and national fratricide.

Given this narrative purpose, why then does 2 Samuel introduce so many literal "brothers" into its stories? My suggestion, fairly simple yet wide-ranging in its implications, is this: during the life and career of David and beyond, stories of murder and mayhem that are based upon fraternal considerations of a familial nature are frequent vehicles for reinforcing the History's larger tribal and national concerns. The bloody chaos that envelops brothers (and sisters) within a single royal house or between fraternal defenders of one royal house and those of another is simply 2 Samuel's reflection, in personal terms, of the History's central social message about the institution of kingship as a major cause of frequent fratricide on a tribal or national level.[12]

Thus, Abner's hesitancy in killing Asahel because of his brother Joab, Joab's and Abishai's murder of Abner because of his prior murder of their brother Asahel, and the fraternal cooperation of Rechab and Baanah in killing Ishbosheth, the brother of Jonathan, are each a microcosmic reflection of the pervasive shedding of blood that will continue to surround the throne of Israel to the end. The fraternal trio, Joab, Abishai, and Asahel, and the fraternal pair, Rechab and Baanah, are all easy killers.

Later in the story, brothers will not so much band together for murder and mayhem as be in conflict with one another because of unbrotherly activity. The events in chapters 13–14 surrounding the rape of Tamar by Amnon her brother begin when Jonadab, Amnon's friend ($r\bar{e}^{ac}$) and cousin—he is the son of Shimei, David's brother ('$\bar{a}h$)—suggests a scenario for the rape (13:4–5), and end with Absalom killing his brother Amnon. Then Absalom ends his exile only after the widow of Tekoa tells David her story about the injustice of exacting the life of one brother for the murder of another brother (2 Sam. 14). From the moment David calls Jonathan "my brother" in 2 Sam. 1:26 until Solomon has "my brother Adonijah" killed in 1 Kings 2:22, brothers tend either to band together for violence in defense of, or against, the throne of David or to act in murderous or criminal conflict with one another within David's own house in pursuit of the throne.

So what transpires in 2 Samuel in behalf of or within the house of David reflects the Deuteronomist's larger conception of affairs within the house of Israel. Familial fratricide coalesces thematically with tribal or national fratricide in this part of the Deuteronomist's History. In precisely this way, Abner's words to Joab reverberate with the Deuteronomist's questions to an audience that appears to be in exile, "Shall the sword devour forever? You know, don't you ($h^{a}l\hat{o}$') that the end is finally bitter? How long before you tell the people to turn from pursuing their brethren?" (2:26). If the guiding metaphor for kingship in 1 Samuel is a request for sons, in 2 Samuel the metaphor switches to the pursuit of brethren.

Murder and Dialogue

The account of the murder of Ishbosheth by two of his own men, the Benjaminite brothers, Baanah and Rechab, in the first part of the chapter

(vv. 1–8a) is prelude to the dialogue between the two brothers and David in the second part (vv. 8b–11), just before David has the two brothers executed (v. 12).

Vv. 1–8a provide the context for both the characters' and the author's dialogues with their audience. It is important for the narrator to establish that Baanah and Rechab are themselves Benjaminites (v. 2) so that, in light of the above discussion of how familial and tribal/national meanings of "brother(s)" coalesce in 2 Samuel, readers clearly understand that the murder of Ishbosheth involves the killing of a tribal brother by a pair of familial brothers. After the reference to Mephibosheth in v. 4, which commentators usually consider out of place,[13] the account of the murder appears in rather ragged form in vv. 5–8a.[14]

The description of Ishbosheth's death in verse 6 is crucial for an understanding of the following dialogue between David and the murderers: Baanah and Rechab "smote [Ishbosheth] in the belly." This manner of murder, smiting (*nākāh*) in the belly (*ḥomeš*), looks backwards to Abner's killing of Asahel in 2:23 and Joab's and Abishai's reciprocal killing of Abner in 3:27. Moreover, it looks forward to Joab's murder of Amasa in 20:10. What is important here is that "smiting in the belly" appears in the Bible only in these four passages and always in the context of an explicit reference to "brother":[15]

> And Abner said again to Asahel, "Turn aside from following me; why should I smite you to the ground? How then could I lift up my face to *your brother* Joab? But he refused to turn aside; therefore Abner smote him in the belly with the butt of his spear. (2 Sam. 2:22–23)

> And there [Joab] smote him in the belly, so that he died, for the blood of Asahel *his brother*. . . . So Joab and Abishai *his brother* slew Abner, because he had killed *their brother* Asahel in the battle of Gibeon. (2 Sam. 3:27, 30)

> They smote him in the belly; and Rechab and Baanah *his brother* escaped. (2 Sam. 4:6)

> And Joab said to Amasa, "Is it well with you, *my brother?*" So Joab struck him with [the sword] in the belly. (2 Sam. 20:9–10)

These four occurrences of smiting in the belly are variations on the theme of fraternal murder within and between the houses of Saul and David. In three of the cases (2:23; 3:27; 20:10), the *familial* brothers of Saul or David are involved: Joab, Abishai, and Asahel are Amasa's cousins according to 2 Sam. 17:25; they are David's nephews according to 1 Chron. 2:13–17;

and Abner is Saul's cousin according to 1 Sam. 14:50. In the fourth case, here in chapter 4, Saul's *tribal* brothers are involved in the murder of his son.

From another point of view, 2:23 and 3:27 involve retributive murder *between* Saul's house and David's house while 4:6 and 20:10 describe analogous murders first *within* the house of Saul and then *within* the house of David. The familial brother of Saul, his cousin Abner, kills (according to 1 Chronicles) the familial brother of David, his nephew Asahel in 2:23; and 3:27 has the familial brother of David (according to 1 Chronicles), his nephew Joab, killing the familial brother of Saul, his cousin Abner. Then 4:6 narrates how, within the house of Saul, the Benjaminites Rechab and Baanah kill their tribal brother Ishbosheth; and 20:10 describes how, within the house of David, Joab kills a familial brother, his cousin Amasa.

The contrastive patterning in these fraternal variations is twofold. On one hand, we have fraternal murder between royal houses (2:23 and 3:27) or within royal houses (4:6 and 20:10). On the other hand we have fraternal murder involving familial brothers either as both the killer and the killed (20:10) or else as only the killers (3:27 and 4:6) or the one killed (2:23).

In all these cases of smiting in the belly or belt, the war between the house of Saul and the house of David (3:1) involves the murder of one's fellow Israelite, that is, one's covenantal or national brother, so that the words of Abner to Joab are applicable, "How long before you bid your people turn from the pursuit of their brethren?" (2:26). Nevertheless, David's dialogue with the two brothers Rechab and Baanah emphasizes fratricide in its *tribal* dimensions within one royal house; David does so by referring back to the events of 2 Samuel 1.

In the dialogue of 4:8b–11, the brothers describe their killing of Saul's son in terms that are similar to those of David's companions when they tried unsuccessfully to provoke him to kill Saul in 1 Samuel 24 and 26: killing David's enemies, those who have sought his life, is God's will. David responds by recalling his meeting with the Amalekite lad: as David had the lad slain at Ziklag, so will he have the brothers killed at Hebron. David's explanation of his execution of the Amalekite at Ziklag is that the supposed good news to the king involves bad news to the messenger.

Similarities between the messengers in chapters 1 and 4 are relevant. Both declarers of good news are sojourners: the lad in chapter 1 is an Amalekite sojourning in Israel (1:13); Rechab and Baanah are Benjaminites sojourning in Gittaim (4:3). Each brings news that is good for the house of David but bad for the house of Saul. Each is executed by David in response to their real or alleged action against the house of Saul.

If David emphasizes the similarities between the two incidents in 4:10, in

4:11 he emphasizes their differences as well: "How much more (*'ap kî*), when wicked men have slain a righteous man *in his own house* upon his bed." David's "how much more" invokes a contrast between the two events that is worth exploring. Saul was killed in battle, supposedly at his own request; his son was murdered in the heat of the day and in his own house. How much more a crime is the second than the first. David's characterization of Ishbosheth as "righteous" may be meant to contrast the good son with the evil father.

However, David's *'ap kî*, "how much more!" also contains contrastive accents that look forward as well as backward concerning the royal pursuit of brothers. On one hand, the lad's claim in 2 Samuel 1 only involved an Amalekite killing an Israelite; Rechab's and Baanah's deed involves Benjaminites killing a brother Benjaminite. That is to say, Ishbosheth's murder was an affair *within his own house,* a murderous event amongst tribal brothers. Here we have regicide that is also fratricide, an action helping to explain how "the house of Saul grew weaker and weaker" (3:1). On the other hand, this actual beheading of a Benjaminite contrastively looks forward to Abishai's proposed beheading of Shimei, which proposal will provoke David again to exclaim "how much more": "Behold, my own son seeks my life; how much more (*'ap kî*) now may this Benjaminite!" (2 Sam. 16:11). Murder and mayhem caused by the pursuit of kings not only include intra-tribal killing within the house of Saul but will even involve intra-familial murder within the house of David. Thus we have a variegated series of capital crimes revolving around matters of royal succession, with each instance in the narrative series progressing toward an ever more narrow meaning for *fratricide:* (1) *Inter-national* and *Inter-tribal:* a non-Israelite, who also doubles for David, claims to have killed Saul (2 Sam. 1); (2) *Intra-tribal:* Benjaminites kill a Benjaminite (2 Sam. 4); (3) *Intra-familial:* David's own son seeks to kill him (2 Sam. 16:11); and (4) *Fraternal* (in the most literal of senses): Solomon kills his older brother, Adonijah (1 Kings 2). The first two instances concern who will succeed to the throne of Saul; the last two concern who will succeed to the throne of David.

David's reference to the good/bad news of the Amalekite once more recalls the paradox about kingship inaugurated by 1 Samuel's opening *mise-en-abyme* concerning the rise and fall of the house of Eli in chapters 1–7. To announce (*bāśar*) the death of Hophni and Phinehas in 1 Samuel 4, of Saul and Jonathan in 2 Samuel 1, of Ishbosheth in 2 Samuel 4, and of Absalom in 2 Samuel 18 is joyfully to declare God's choice of David as successor to the house of Saul. At the same time, such declarations of divine will concerning royal succession need always to be balanced by the Deuteronomist's continuing view of kingship, David's included, as idolatry. The pursuit of royalty needs to be reversed. The back of Abner's spear comes out of Asahel's back (2 Sam. 3:23) just as Eli falls over backward and dies (1 Sam. 4:18). That is to say, the Deuteronomist writes this history for a pro-Davidic audience because, at least in the matter of kingship, they had got things all backward.

·3·

HOUSES
(5:1–7:29)

When we build, let us think that we build forever. (John Ruskin, *The Lamp of Memory*)

Unless the LORD builds the house, those who build it labor in vain. (Psalm 127)

From Brotherhood to Household

In 2 Samuel 1 the narrator used language of military defeat to signal the disastrous cultic idolatry associated with Israelite kingship. Then 2 Samuel 2–4 employed images of fraternal murder and mayhem to underscore Israel's decline through a fratricidal pursuit of kings. Now 2 Samuel 5–7 will describe Israel's and David's rising fortunes, and also suggest their failures, in terms of housebuilding. That is to say, as the Deuteronomist traces Israel's path along the corridors of history, royal influences on cult, brotherhood, and household help to explain this nation's unquestioned successes—but its eventual collapse as well.

One way to see how the story shifts from fraternal to domestic emphases in an effort to underscore similar ideological issues is to examine Israel's statement immediately before anointing David king. All the tribes of Israel say to David, "Behold we are your bone and flesh" (ʿeṣem and bāśār: 5:1). The phrase, "bone and flesh," acts here like a narrative bridge that spans the many meanings of "brother" on one hand and "house" on the other. We have already seen how "brother" can be used in familial, tribal, and national contexts, and it is especially significant that the History uses "bone and flesh" as a synonym for both "brother" and "house" else-where in the History. For example, in Judg. 9:2–3 "bone and flesh" and "brother" are synonymous in a familial sense: Abimelech tells his mother's brothers, "I am your bone and your flesh" (v. 2) and they respond amongst themselves, "He is our brother" (v. 3). In 2 Sam.

54

19:12–13 David speaks to his fellow Judahites and explicitly combines "house," "bone and flesh," and "brother," all in reference to tribal affinities: "Why should you be the last to bring the king back to his *house.* You are *my brothers,* you are *my bone and my flesh.*" And here in 5:1, all the tribes of Israel call themselves flesh and bone of the Judahite David, thus invoking a national relationship: anointing David king reinforces the national fraternity that already exists between Israel and Judah, essential components of the community of Hebrews.

As 19:12–13 indicates, "house" (*bayit*) can be construed in the History very much like the terms, "brother" and "bone and flesh." We encounter "house" in its familial usages when we read about the house or household, say of Obed-edom (6:11) or of David (6:20). When such a house belongs to a king, its familial aspects take on dynastic overtones as well. David says, "Is there anyone left of the house of Saul, that I may show him kindness for Jonathan's sake?" (9:1). "House" is frequently used to refer also to tribal unities, as when we read about the house of Judah (2:10) or the house of Benjamin (3:19). Finally, "house," like "bone and flesh" and "brother," has its national references as well: "David and all the house of Israel were making merry before the LORD" (6:5).

All these uses of "house" are figures of speech operating on the scaffold of that physical building which houses occupants related to one another either familially, tribally, or nationally. And it is this *material house,* understood as a literal locus of habitation, that enables the Deuteronomist to explore issues that transcend merely human concerns about national fratricide or suicide. In the history of Israel, traditions about the institution of kingship and the construction of the temple are so intimately bound up that any statement about the role of kingship tends to have important implications for the status of the temple—and vice versa. We shall see how the image of building or making a house for someone helps the Deuteronomist explore the complex historiographic and ideological connections between the royal palace and the divine temple. If the History relates the ultimate tragedy of a nation that made room for David's house, it also raises serious questions about that nation's building of God's temple.

Simplistic condemnation of king or temple is not the issue here. In the History we frequently hear a voice exalting both the house of David and the temple of God. Yet at the same time, another voice continues to sound, in an effort to neutralize Israel's nationalistic pride in palace and temple. When God tells David, "Your house shall be made sure forever" (7:10), and when Solomon tells God, "I have built for thee an exalted house, a place for thee to dwell in forever" (1 Kings 8:13), both *forevers* end with the end of the History. If, as I have been suggesting, a purpose of this history is to turn an exilic Israel away from a centuries-old glorification of kingship, a related purpose may very well have been to speak against Israel's understandable desire to rebuild the temple. If dismantling the house of David might help to end the exile one day, perhaps a step toward recovering the lost ark, the Deuteronomist may be saying, is to resolve never again "to build a house for the name of the LORD."

David's Domicile: Chapter 5

In chapter 5, the narrator uses quick, deft strokes to detail the rise of David over all Israel. Israel anoints David king (vv. 1–5); David then takes over Jerusalem and transforms it into "the city of David" (vv. 6–16); and a double victory of David over the Philistines ends the chapter (vv. 17–25). Characters and readers alike know that David's swift success has God as its cause: the narrator directs readers to God's support in verse 10 and then notes David's awareness of this support in verse 12.

Still, a number of textual details in chapter 5 continue to puzzle readers, and it is questionable whether these difficulties can ever be resolved satisfactorily. What precisely the Jebusites are saying to David in verse 6b, what David responds in verse 8a, and what the narrator means in verses 8b and 9b are questions as difficult to answer as any found elsewhere in the History. This is not to deny that we can lessen some of our confusion over the meaning of these statements by reference to what is clearly emphasized in the context surrounding them. Here again, the text's artful composition provides guidance that may aid the reader's comprehension even when much of the apperceptive background against which the chapter sounds apparently has been lost. Fortunately, both clear and confusing portions of the chapter hover around questions of domicile that look toward the Deuteronomist's profound meditation on royal house and divine temple in chapter 7: chapter 5 describes David's shift in domicile from Hebron to Jerusalem, chapter 6 relates the ark's move from Abinadab's house in Baale-judah to David's tent, and chapter 7 explores the precise relationship between the house of David and the temple of the LORD.

Look first at the puzzling references of the Jebusites and David to the blind and lame in 5:6b and 8a: the narrator explains these verses with an equally puzzling etymology in verse 8b: "Therefore it is said, 'The blind and the lame shall not come *into the house.*'" Whatever verses 6 and 8 mean, that meaning involves a house, whether David's, the LORD's, or anyone else's, specifically or generally. Look also at the narrator's opaque statement in verse 9b; it too revolves around the construal of *bayit*, "house." Does *wābāytāh* mean "inward" or "homeward" or something else? Whatever the case, the word *bayit* is once more part of the problem.

We may not know what the text specifically means by these puzzling statements, yet some kind of *house-bound* construal is involved. This is perhaps as much as we can say about them.

When we turn to the less confusing sections of the chapter, we find indications that David's domestic situation is starting to take center stage in the story. Nothing in the chapter indicates the ideological complexities of David's rise as directly as the narrator's notice in verse 11, "And Hiram king of Tyre sent messengers to David, and cedar trees, also carpenters and masons *who built a house for David.*"[1] The observation here of Hiram's workers building a house for David introduces into David's story the royal theme of divine predestination and punishment already foreshadowed, within 1 Samuel 1–7's opening *mise-en-abyme,* in the anonymous man of God's forecast of the fall of Eli's house and the LORD's establishment of a new priestly house: "I shall build for him a sure house," God promises in 1 Sam. 2:35. Abigail repeats the forecast, this time to David, in 1 Sam. 25:28: "For the LORD will certainly make a sure house for my lord." As I have suggested in an earlier volume, the succession of priestly houses in 1 Samuel 2 foreshadows not only the royal victories of David and his successors referred to by Abigail, but also the programmatic and historical defeat of kingship itself in the History. Throughout the rest of 2 Samuel and well into 1 Kings, this powerful theme of "building or making a house for God or human" will explore domestic issues of king and temple in order to form a complex picture of Israel's history.[2]

To understand the ideological importance of the narrator's seemingly incidental notice that Hiram's men built a house for David, we need to observe first of all how it fits into the overall progression of the chapter. Israel anoints David (vv. 1–5), he takes Jerusalem (vv. 6–9), Hiram's workers build David a house (v. 11), David takes more wives and concubines and has more children (vv. 13–16), and the LORD twice answers his inquiries, thus enabling him twice to defeat the Philistines (vv. 17–25). All these incidents exemplify the narrator's statements about the LORD being with David (v. 10) and explain David's growing awareness of this fact (v. 12). This rush of events, this march of history in David's favor, finds exultant expression in David's words, "The LORD has broken through (*pāras̩*) my enemies before me like a bursting flood" (v. 20) and in the LORD's words to David, "When you hear the sound of marching (*qôl s̩ecādāh*) in the tops of the balsam tree, then the LORD has gone before you to smite the army of the Philistines" (v. 24).

Thus everything in the chapter conspires to illustrate support for David, be it national acceptance by all Israel, the international assistance both of the king of Tyre, who supplied him with workers, and of the Jebusite women of Jerusalem, who supplied him with children, or, finally, the

divine inquiries that enabled him to predict victory over his archetypal
enemy. These successes signal that divine march whereby the LORD built
for David a sure house. Such sudden flashes light up the longer span of
history that began with the divine promise at the beginning of 1 Samuel "I
will build for him a sure house" (1 Sam. 2:35), that lead toward the History's disastrous climax in 2 Kings, "And [Nebuchadnezzar] burned the
house of the LORD, and the king's house and all the houses of Jerusalem;
every great house he burned down" (2 Kings 25:9), and that culminate
with the History's bittersweet notice that Evil Merodach freed the last
occupant of the house of David, "Jehoiachin king of Judah from (his)
house of imprisonment (*bêt kele'*)" (25:27). The LORD indeed had built a
sure house for David, but this house eventually turned into a house of
confinement, a prison.

However, verse 11 not only introduces into David's story this general
theme of building a house for someone, it also specifically refers to the
infusion of foreign elements that characterize the house of David from the
beginning. Notice how David's perception that the LORD had established
him king over Israel (v. 12) is immediately preceded by the reference to
Hiram's workers in verse 11 and followed by the statement about David's
wives and concubines from Jerusalem in verse 13. The international prestige and support that David receives through the king of Tyre having built
a house for him, on one hand, and the Jebusite wives having provided him
with "more sons and daughters," on the other, are what molds David's
perception of how the LORD was establishing his kingship over Israel. The
foreign builders of David's literal house, his palace, are workmen that
function as a model of the LORD's support of his kingship. The king also
acquires foreign workwomen, his Jebusite wives and concubines, who help
him build up his dynastic house.

This conjunction of foreign hands helping to construct both the literal
and dynastic house of David seems to receive approbation here through
the authoritative statements of the narrator in vv. 10 and 12. The LORD is
with David (v. 10) as foreigners build his house (v. 11); David knows that
the LORD has exalted his kingdom (v. 12), so the king engages foreigners
to fill his house with more sons and daughters (vv. 13–16).

Yet how can such a picture be maintained when 1 Kings 11:1–4 will contrast Solomon's love for foreign women with David's heart, which, these
verses assert, was true to the LORD his God? To suggest that the foreign
elements roundly condemned in Solomon's reign are present from the
beginning in David's reign—and this with the concurrent approval of the
LORD—is once again to declare the Deuteronomist's continuing view of
the paradoxical status of kingship within Israel: kingship came about
through both obedience and disobedience to the LORD, through Israel's

wanting to be like the other nations and the LORD's granting of this request, and, apparently, through a divinely approved infusion of foreign elements into the very building blocks of David's house, viewed as both physical abode and dynastic enterprise. As with all the other superficially apologetic narratives about David's rise to power, this account of how the LORD built a house for David with foreign hands and foreign material illustrates the pomp and prestige that traditionally surround David's glorious story, yet at the same time it quietly suggests that David's reign was little different from those that followed it.

A more fundamental problem that the History confronts is not why the LORD condemns Solomon, say, for practices already begun by David, even as he rejected Saul for actions far less obviously disloyal to the LORD than David would soon accomplish, but rather why and how the LORD at one and the same time appears to have approved and condemned kingship in Israel. If the Deuteronomist is busy describing for us the specific manner in which God built Israel a palace and Israel built God a temple, then an important dimension of the story seems to be whether it will be worthwhile to rebuild either.

With the introduction of *housebuilding* as a central image around which to construct this stage of the story, the Deuteronomist follows the same method that we have been describing throughout the History: nothing focuses issues better or outlines complexities more clearly than a concrete, almost visual, image that distills the author's message and the emotions animating it. We saw in our last chapter, for example, how the recurrence of homicidal and rapacious brothers and characters bent on fratricide helped to focus the story on larger issues of tribal or national murder and mayhem fostered by the pursuit of kings. Abner smites Asahel, and so Joab smites Abner; Amnon rapes Tamar, and so Absalom will have Amnon killed; Adonijah acts up and so Solomon has his brother and rival struck down—all these instances of brother pursuing brother use *blood brotherhood* to highlight the tribal and national fratricide that resulted from Israel's desire to be like the other nations.

In similar fashion, the Deuteronomist describes both the dynastic house of David and the national house of Israel—with all their attendant glories and final shame—through reciprocal images of Hiram helping to build physical houses for David and Solomon, their royal palaces, and of David's desire for, and Solomon's success in, the building of a material house for the immaterial LORD, his temple. Details surrounding both the building and the destruction of palace and temple may very well function as interpretive guideposts for our understanding of the LORD's promises concerning the dynastic house of David. To find out how much or how little the LORD promises when he says to David, "Your house and your kingdom shall be made sure before me forever" (7:16), one has only to attend to the manner in which palace and temple are conjoined in the narrative and their fates intertwined. A foreign king, Hiram, helps David with the building of his palace, as he will also help with the building of Solomon's palace and God's temple. Yet if the building of palace and temple go together in the story, so too does their destruction:

> And [Hiram's workmen] built a house for [David]. (2 Sam. 5:11)

> And [Nebuzaradan] burned the house of the LORD, and the king's house and all the houses of Jerusalem. (2 Kings 25:9)

As agents of a foreign king help to build these houses, so an agent of a foreign king will destroy them.

Finally, the conjoined fate of such *physical* houses in the narrative connotes the fate of the dynastic house of David:

> There was a long war between the house of Saul and the house of David; and David grew stronger and stronger, while the house of Saul grew weaker and weaker. (2 Sam. 3:1)

> And David became greater and greater (*hālôk wegādôl*). (2 Sam. 5:10)

> And [Nebuzaradan] burned down every great house (*kol bêt gādôl*). (2 Kings 25:9)

The house of David continued to exist beyond such domestic destruction, but it no longer could be called a great house.

Finding a Home for the Ark: Chapter 6

David and the people joyfully accompany the ark on its journey from Baale-judah to Jerusalem. At the threshing floor of Nacon, the LORD smites Uzzah, one of the two sons of Abinadab who are driving the cart carrying the ark. Angered by this, yet fearful of the LORD's outburst, David temporarily houses the ark with Obed-edom, the man from Gath. God blesses the house of Obed-edom, and this encourages David to resume the ark's joyful transfer to Jerusalem. The celebration ends when Michal scornfully confronts David, and the chapter ends with the narrator's notice of Michal's childlessness to the day of her death.

The thirty thousand men that David gathers together in verse 1, just before taking the ark to Jerusalem, constitute a mirror image of the thirty thousand Israelites slain in the account of the taking of the ark in 1 Samuel 4. This is the first of many details that demonstrate how the History's opening parable on kingship in 1 Samuel 1–7 foreshadows this chapter's triumphant events. I have already discussed some of these connections in a previous volume and will simply assume them in the present context. I want rather to concentrate on suggestions about how this chapter fits into its more immediate literary context, that is to say, how the events associated with the transfer of the ark from the house of Abinadab to the city of David continue to describe the spectacular rise of David, even as they intimate darker days ahead.

A number of details conspire to blur our vision of chapter 6. I can list some of them in order to give those who do not read Hebrew a feel for how difficult it is to understand what motivates the characters in this chapter. This is not to say that we cannot learn much from a careful compositional analysis of the story; it is, rather, to emphasize the limited nature of the insights that such an analysis can produce.

The chapter's frequent use of imperfective verb forms illustrates its hermeneutic challenges. A main function of such forms is to place the reader in the center of the action, often by presenting activity from the temporal perspective of characters: the narrator describes things as if the reader were observing what is happening in the story-world—even as the characters themselves do.

We read that the sons of Abinadab "were driving ($noh^a g\hat{\imath}m$) the new cart" (v. 3); that one of the brothers was walking ($hol\bar{e}k$) before the ark" (v. 4); that David and all the house of Israel were making merry ($m^e\acute{s}ah^a q\hat{\imath}m$) before the LORD" (v. 5); that David was dancing (?) ($m^ekark\bar{e}r$) and was girded ($h\bar{a}g\hat{u}r$) with a linen ephod" (v. 14); that David and all the house of Israel were bringing up ($ma^ca\hat{l}\hat{\imath}m$) the ark of the LORD" (v. 15); and that when the ark was "coming" ($b\bar{a}$') into the city of David, and Michal "looking down ($ni\acute{s}q^ep\bar{a}h$) from the window," she saw that David "was leaping (?) ($m^epazz\bar{e}z$) and dancing (?) ($m^ekark\bar{e}r$, as in v. 14) before the LORD" (v. 16).

There is a double dimension to these synchronic verb forms. In verses 3, 4, 5, 14, and 15, the narrator directly shows us someone leading, walking, playing, and so forth, but in verse 16 we not only see the ark coming and Michal looking out the window, we also see what Michal is seeing, that is "she saw David leaping(?) and dancing (?)." On one hand, the narrator tells us what is happening, on the other, what a character saw was happening. Given the convention of an omniscient narrator and the frequent appearance of unreliable or biased characters in biblical narrative, the distinction between an action that is directly presented by the narrator and one indirectly shown through the perception of a character can be significant. This is true whether the action is synchronic or, as is typically the case in narrative, retrospective. Thus, for example, what the narrator told us happened to the Levite's concubine in Judges 19 is one level closer to the reader than what the Levite in Judges 20 tells Israel has happened to his concubine. The differences between these two stories are important aids to interpreting the author's story.

What Michal saw in verse 16 is especially important because, upon seeing it, "she despised David in her heart" (v. 16). If it is fortunate that part of what she saw in verse 16 is already confirmed by the narrator as happening—David was *mekarkēr*-ing in verse 14—it is nevertheless unfortunate that, despite much scholarly speculation, what precisely Michal saw David doing (*mᵉkarkēr* and *mᵉpazzēz*) remains unclear. Given our ignorance about the particular meaning of these two verbs, we can hardly decide how these actions specifically or David's rejoicing generally or both in unison are intended to explain Michal's inner motivations at some level of character development within the story-world itself.

Another detail increases our puzzlement over Michal's strong reaction against David: she accuses David of "revealing himself as one of the *rēqîm* reveals himself" (v. 20). The meaning of *rēqîm* here may be related somehow to the "empty vessels" of Judg. 7:16 and 2 Kings 4:3 or to the "empty(?)" fellows of Judg. 9:4 and 11:3, but we still lack the kinds of contextual information that would make Michal's statement less opaque. Her accusatory comparison, therefore, remains semantically *empty*—at least with respect to relations between characters in the story-world.

Besides Michal's puzzling reactions in vv. 16 and 20–22, we have the LORD's sudden anger in verse 7. Amidst David's and Israel's apparently justified rejoicing, why does the LORD introduce this deadly note into the story? Uzzah seems to have acted to rescue a falling ark just as David was rejoicing before it, yet the one action displeases God, and the other provokes Michal's utter disdain.

What, finally, can David and Michal mean by their demeaning language in vv. 20–22? "You really have honored yourself!" Michal ironically asserts in verse 20; "I will make myself yet more contemptible than this, and I will be abased in my own eyes," David responds in verse 22.

If, having lost some of the vocabulary and contextual background against which the story sounds, we cannot be sure what David and Michal specifically are saying to one another within their own world, we still have sufficient contextual information to suggest what forms part of the dialogue between author and reader in this chapter. In terms of reporting and reported speech, chapter 6 contains mostly the reporting speech of the narrator. Yet paradoxically, the few reported statements of characters effectively condense the Deuteronomist's ideological and evaluative interests here, and help us clarify significant portions of the communication between author and audience, even though specific aspects of communication between characters continue to perplex us.

Seizing the Ark

The first character to speak is David, who in anger and fear over the LORD's sudden killing of Uzzah, the ark's transient caretaker, exclaims, "How (*'ēk*) can the ark of the LORD come to me?" (v. 9). I have elsewhere suggested that this question reverberates with the one previously uttered by the people of Beth-shemesh at the end of the ark account in 1 Samuel 6: "To whom shall [this holy God] go up away from us?" (v. 20).[3] Surely the city of David is where this holy God intends his ark to reside, yet the death of Uzzah causes a temporary failure of nerve on David's part.

The word *'ēk*, "how," is used in the History only rarely in exclamation (as in "How the mighty have fallen!" [1:19, 25, 27]) and usually indicates a questioning that is often, as here, tinged with fear. Earlier in 2 Samuel, David asked the Amalekite who claimed to have killed Saul, "How is it (*'ēk*) you were not afraid (*yārē'*) to put forth your hand to destroy the LORD's anointed?" (1:14). Samuel (1 Sam. 16:2), the servants of David (2 Sam. 12:18), and the elders of Samaria (2 Kings 10:4) all utter an anxious *'ēk*. These fearsome associations of "how" are epitomized by the priest who was returned to Samaria by the King of Assyria in order to teach its new immigrants "how (*'ēk*) they should fear (*yîrᵉ'û*) the LORD" (2 Kings 17:28).

David's question, therefore, initiates a fearful stutter that interrupts the ark's joyful journey toward Jerusalem. Like the ark's and David's temporary exile in Philistia in 1 Samuel, the ark's three-month stopover at the house of Obed-edom, the man of Gath, is yet another Philistine interlude in the story, reminding the reader that divine inevitability and the mysterious twists and turns of events are fellow travelers in the Deuteronomist's story. The LORD's unexpected outburst and David's temporary diversion of the ark once again exemplify the principle of false-start-as-providential-delay, a narrative pattern that we have seen operating at key junctures of the History. Amidst the triumphant frenzy of rejoicing that accompanies David's transfer of the ark to its royal abode, the murderous outburst of the LORD acts upon David and the reader as a check upon unbridled joy. If the LORD can break out (*pāraṣ*) upon David's enemies ("The LORD has broken through my enemies before me like a bursting flood" [5:20]), he is also capable of sudden outbursts against David's own servants, here the ark's caretaker Uzzah. As the presence of the ark was first harmful to

Philistines but then mysteriously noxious to Israelites themselves in 1 Samuel 4–6, so here in 2 Samuel 5–6 the LORD first bursts forth against the Philistines but then mysteriously erupts against an Israelite.

At least David's response to the LORD's outburst—fear, anger, and diversion of the ark—is understandable in terms of the story. Consider how Uzzah's act of touching or taking hold of the ark (*'āḥaz bᵉ*) is a graphic counterpart to David's more generalized and mediated action of bringing it up to "the city of David" (vv. 10, 12, 16). The meaning of *'āḥaz bᵉ* ranges from "touching or physically taking hold of" (Samson's doors in Judg. 16:13, the Levite's concubine in Judg. 20:6, the altar's horns in 1 Kings 1:51, walls in 1 Kings 6:6, and the ark here in 2 Sam. 6:6) to a less physical or personal "seizing or taking possession of" (judgment in Deut. 32:41, land in Josh. 22:9, 19, and the Amalekite in 2 Sam. 4:10). The meaning of *'aḥuzzāh* is "one's possession, that is, what one has taken hold of" so that Uzzah's apparently laudable action of taking hold of the ark in verse 6 is a graphic homology of David's apparently laudable action of taking possession of the ark in the chapter itself. Uzzah, in taking possession of the ark, is David's *agent*.

The story is intent upon making the reader aware of this parallelism first of all because David is aware of it. David's reaction—anger, then a fearful diversion of the ark to Obed-edom's house—wonderfully captures the motivation behind his words, "How can the ark of the LORD come to me?" If the LORD has broken out against Uzzah for taking hold of the ark, might he not also break out against David for also taking possession of it, whether selflessly or not? There is, then, an unpredictable danger, a risk, in seizing the ark. Both angered and terrified by the graphic revelation of Uzzah's death, David "was not willing to divert the ark of the LORD to himself (*lᵉhāsîr 'ēlāyw*), to the city of David" (v. 10), and so he removes the dangerous object to Obed-edom's house, as if to say, "Better him than me." Only after "the LORD blessed Obed-edom and all his household" (v. 11), does David apparently decide "better me than him." Yet even when the LORD's blessing encourages David to resume the ark's journey to Jerusalem, David is still sensitive to danger: instead of placing the ark in his own house, the one Hiram helped him build (5:11), he pitches a tent for it and offers sacrifices before it (v. 17).

Consider then how the LORD's smiting of Uzzah not only illuminates the understandable caution of David regarding possession of the ark of the LORD, it also interrupts David's and all the house of Israel's "making merry before the LORD" (v. 5). This initial complication parallels the sour note Michal will introduce into the celebrations toward the end of the chapter. By making Uzzah's grasping act homologous to David's, the

Deuteronomist indicates to readers that God's actions in the first half are somehow related to Michal's in the second half.

Housing the Blessed Ark

An important issue in the chapter is illustrated by the second instance of reported speech there, "And it was told king David, 'The LORD has blessed the house of Obed-edom and all that belongs to him, because of the ark of God.'" (v. 12).

We recognize that domestic matters involving physical, familial, dynastic, or national houses are taking control of the story, because the narrator increasingly uses *bayit*, "house," in chapters 6 and 7: we do not find such frequency again in the History until we get to 1 Kings 6–9, which speaks of Solomon's building operations.[4] Here in chapter 6, the ark is taken from the *literal* house of Abinadab (vv. 3, 4), is taken to, resides in, and is taken from the literal house of Obed-edom (vv. 10, 11, 12), and the people return each one to his literal house (v. 19); the LORD blesses the *familial* house or household of Obed-edom (vv. 11, 12) and is described by David as having chosen him over the familial house of Saul (v. 21), while David himself returns to bless his own household (v. 20); and the *national* house of Israel makes merry before the ark (v. 5) and noisily brings it up to Jerusalem (v. 15).

Amidst the wild rejoicing that characterizes much of the chapter, the account of the transfer of the ark to the city of David introduces the matter of how houses get blessed. The story here about how and where to house the ark is also about the kinds of houses within Israel that the LORD will bless. Notice all the blessing in this and the next chapter: the LORD is said to bless Obed-edom's house in vv. 11 and 12, David blesses the people and his own household in vv. 18 and 20, and David will even pray that God bless his house forever in 7:29. Nevertheless, given all this blessing, it is significant that the house of Obed-edom the Gittite is the only house, be it literal, familial, tribal, or national, that the LORD is said to bless in the entire History. Moreover, 2 Samuel 6 is the only place in the History where anyone actually blesses David's house—and it is David himself who does the blessing. Despite frequent references to various kinds of houses in the History, despite even the reciprocal themes of God providentially making or building a house for humans and humans building houses for both (the name of) God and their fellows,[5] and despite the abundant occurrences of God blessing (*bārak*) communities, individuals, and things—despite all this, Obed-edom's house, so far as the LORD is concerned, is the only blessed house in the entire History. Neither divine temple nor royal palace, neither familial or tribal house in Israel nor national house of Israel is ever said to be blessed by the LORD.[6]

When, therefore, the narrator tells the reader that the LORD blessed Obed-edom and all his house (v. 11) and when this information is relayed to David (v. 12), this *repetition* in the chapter on one hand, and its *uniqueness* in the History on the other, increase its significance in terms of both chapter and History. The LORD may first react against the idea of a royal house within Israel, yet after a significant interlude he ultimately promises to build one *forever.* Similarly, the LORD will first react against the idea of a house for the ark—a temple—yet again after a significant period he will allow one to be built. Such pregnant interludes are very much like the ark's stopover at the house of Obed-edom. God seems to be portrayed in the History as one who needs to be almost prodded toward kingship and all its trappings (palace, temple, and royal house of Israel) but then, after various false starts and providential delays, manages to cooperate with a vengeance. Throughout such vicissitudes, the LORD may assist in the building of various kinds of royal houses, he may allow David to request of him a blessing upon his house forever, yet nowhere in the History does the LORD bless any of them even for the moment.

Revealing David

The observation that Michal "despised [David] in her heart" (v. 16) prepares us for the contentious dialogue between them in verses 20–22. Their conversation begins and ends with reference to David's honor or glory: "How the king of Israel is honored today," Michal sarcastically begins in verse 20; "I *am* honored," David confidently states in verse 22. David's dishonor, Michal claims, consists in his having revealed himself before his servants' handmaids (*'āmāh*) like one of the *rēqîm* ("vulgar fellows" in the RSV). David counters that he was only making merry before the LORD, who, he taunts, chose him over her father's house. Moreover, he continues, he will become even more debased and contemptible in his own eyes, while the very handmaids of whom Michal spoke do (or will) honor him.

Details in the dialogue continue to puzzle readers. For one thing, many commentators see David's "revealing himself"[7] as a reference to his dancing almost naked, yet nothing in the text, so far as I can see, supports this view. In fact, David is wearing a linen ephod (v. 14), and efforts to describe him as "scantily clad" are difficult to justify. Michal's comparing David to *rēqîm* is another obstacle to understanding. Who are these *rēqîm* and how does a literal emptiness apply to them, if at all?

Michal's and David's double reference to "handmaids" (vv. 20, 22) is perhaps the clearest signal we have of authorial motivation in reporting their dialogue. The term "handmaid" ('*āmāh*) is central to the matter of David's honor or dishonor here because, throughout the Books of Samuel and Kings, women who are called handmaids work almost exclusively for the honor and glory of *David's* house. It is noteworthy that Michal here addresses David as "the king of Israel" and that '*āmāh* only appears in Samuel/Kings to designate a woman who by word or work furthers the cause of kingship in general and the glory of David's house in particular. Here is a review of the use of '*āmāh* in Samuel/Kings.

When Hannah prays to the LORD and requests a son or when she speaks to Eli about her prayers, she calls herself "your handmaid" (1 Sam. 1:11, 16). In terms of the opening parable about the birth of kingship in Israel, Hannah, the maidservant of the LORD and Eli, requests a son just as Israel later will request a king. And when Hannah receives her request, she praises the LORD for causing "the poor to inherit a throne of honor" (1 Sam. 2:6)

We next find the term on the lips of Abigail in 1 Samuel 25, who, after calling herself David's handmaid in verses 24 and 25, says to David, "Pray forgive the trespass of your handmaid; *for the LORD will certainly make my LORD a sure house* and evil shall not be found in you so long as you live" (v. 28). Abigail then requests, "When the LORD has dealt well with my Lord, *then remember your handmaid*" (v. 31). Abigail requests of David exactly what Hannah requested of the LORD in 1 Sam. 1:10: "remember your handmaid." Finally, if Michal ironically refers to David's glorification before the eyes of "the handmaids of David's servants" (2 Sam. 6:20), it is particularly suggestive that Abigail refers to herself as a handmaid of David's servants, "Behold your handmaid is a servant to wash the feet of the servants of my Lord" (v. 41).

After Michal's and David's references to '*āmāh* here in 2 Sam. 6:20 and 22, the next reference occurs in 2 Sam. 14:15 and 16, where the woman of Tekoa tells David, "And your handmaid thought, 'The word of my lord the king will set me at rest; for my lord the king is like the angel of the LORD to discern good and evil.' The LORD your God is with you" (v. 16). Further, in 2 Sam. 20:17, the wise woman of Maacah asks Joab to "listen to the words of your maidservant" and then counsels her townspeople to behead Sheba for opposing David's kingship.

In 1 Kings 1, Bathsheba twice calls herself David's maidservant (vv. 13, 17), and it is especially relevant how her association with David is the source of both honor and dishonor for David's house. David's murderous possession of *this* maidservant is the occasion for the LORD's curse on David's house: "Now therefore the sword shall never depart from your house, because you have despised me, and have taken the wife of Uriah the Hittite to be your wife" (2 Sam. 12:10). Even so, Bathsheba will become the maternal means whereby God builds David's house through the birth of Solomon.

Finally, *'āmāh* appears in the story of the two harlots in 1 Kings 3. After God has promised in a dream to give Solomon "both riches and *honor,* so that no other king shall compare with you all your days," it is Solomon's choice of the correct mother that proclaims his wisdom throughout Israel. While pleading her case before the king, only the innocent mother calls herself "your maidservant" (1 Kings 3:20). No other occurrence of "hand-maid" appears in Samuel/Kings.

It is particularly telling that, after the opening story of Hannah, the only women termed *handmaid* are those who speak to David, his commander Joab, or his son Solomon, and always in praise or defense of David or his son. None of the women, for example, who talk to Samuel, Saul, or any of their agents ever call themselves "your handmaid." The appearance of handmaidens in Samuel/Kings signals the glories of Israelite kingship in general and the Davidic throne in particular.

Whatever the embedded speech of Michal and David in verses 20–22 may mean in terms of personal characterization, this dialogue turns out to be another *mise-en-abyme* that encapsulates the Deuteronomist's story of David's rise as king of Israel in terms of the conflicting dimensions of his reign. The honor-bound maidens that surround David's *character-zone* throughout his life indeed voice their praise of him and further his inter-ests by their actions. Hannah, Abigail, the widow of Tekoa, and the wise woman of Maacah all personify the glory of David. David, then, is reported here as affirming Michal's statement: "by the maids of whom you have spoken, by them I *am* held in honor" (v. 22). Clearly, the dishonor invoked by Michal and the honor underlined by David are both affirmed by the Deuteronomist, who uses the larger story line to develop this dia-logue, and the dialogue to condense a significant dimension of the larger story line.

The King of Israel: Mixed Blessings

Michal looks down upon the joyful playing of David and Israel and calls it David's glorification—by which she means, of course, his dishonoring. A review of the language of chapter 6 indicates how David's bringing of the ark into a royal setting means both joy and sorrow, honor and dishonor.

David's playing before the LORD (*śāḥaq,* vv. 5, 21) was accompanied by joy (*śimḥāh,* v. 12) yet marred by death and derision. This conjunction of joyful play and painful result, signaled by *śāḥaq,* "to play, make merry," is normal in the History. When the lords of the Philistines gather "in joy," (*śimḥāh*) they call for Samson "to play for them." Such sport ends in the deaths of both player and spectators (Judg. 16:23, 25, 27). When David returns from slaying Goliath, the women come out with songs of joy (*śimḥāh*) and make merry (*śāḥaq*). Their song makes Saul so angry that he twice tries to kill David on the morrow (1 Sam. 18:6–11). And even in 2 Samuel 2, the one context in which *śimḥāh* is not explicitly attached to sport (*śḥq/ṣḥq*) in the History, the play again ends in tragedy: all twenty-four participants kill one another, and the spectators begin to battle each other (2 Sam. 2:12–17).

Perhaps, then, we ought to be less surprised by the outbreak of the LORD and the derision of Michal that spoil the sport in each half of the chapter. As far as the LORD is concerned, his smiting of Uzzah and the interruption of a joyful journey that it occasions may well represent the double bind that continues to unite the LORD to royal Israel. As for Michal, she is the daughter of her father, Saul, who took exception to the play that accompanied David as he returned "from smiting the Philistine" (1 Sam. 18:6): now, after David had "smote the Philistines from Geba to Gezer" (2 Sam. 5:25), David triumphantly returns to his own city only to be greeted with derision by Michal.

Both David and Michal agree that this merry making involves a glorification of David that is also in some sense dishonoring. Though we remain puzzled by this in terms of the personal motivations of characters within the story itself, we may nevertheless see how this dialogue voices the Deuteronomist's point of view on the past glories of David and his house.

Notice how David and Michal's confrontation brings together self-revelation (*niglāh*), honor (*nikbad*), despising (*bāzāh*), and being lightly esteemed (*qālal* in the *nifal*). Michal sees David somehow making merry before the LORD and despises him in her heart (v. 16); she talks ironically about how David "has honored himself by revealing himself today" (v. 20) and David responds that he "will appear even more lightly esteemed (*ûnqallotî*) than this" (v. 22). This conjunction of concepts surrounding the king of Israel—honor, self-revelation, despising, and being lightly esteemed—recalls most pointedly the words of the man of God in 1 Samuel 2 who quotes God as saying to Eli, "Did I not reveal myself to the house of your father? Far be it from me; for those who honor me I will honor, and those who despise me shall be lightly esteemed" (vv. 27, 30). Addressing itself immediately to the priestly house of Eli, this oracle does double duty as a prophecy of the rise and fall of royal houses in Israel, especially David's. In this oracle, God reveals himself, is honored, and makes those who despise him lightly esteemed. In the royal story of

2 Samuel 6, it is David, Israel's idolatrous replacement for God, who reveals himself, is honored, appears lightly esteemed, and is despised. Moreover, David, the one first despised by Goliath (1 Sam. 17:42) and now by Michal, will himself fulfill the oracle of God found in 1 Samuel 2. For God will repay David's sins with another oracle: "Now therefore I will not turn aside the sword from your house forever, because you despised me (*bāzāh*)" (2 Sam. 12:10).

Amidst all the triumphant honor surrounding the transfer of the ark to the royal city of David, and in spite of all the honor which the maidens will continue to heap upon him, David's own words forecast the fundamental message of his rule: to be honored is also to be heavy, *kābēd*, a burden. This burden of the house of David upon Israel will involve the paradox of being weighed down (*wᵉhāyîtî šāpāl*) and, at the same time, being a light-weight (*ûnqallotî*). Such mixtures of heavy/light, honor/dishonor, blessing/curse, and rejoicing/fear characterize David in chapter 6, even as they characterize the entire story of kingship in Samuel/Kings. The dialogue between David and Michal is a wonderful summary of the glory of David that was also his and Israel's burden. When Absalom later invites David and his servants to Baal-hazor, David refuses saying, "No my son, let us not all go lest we be burdensome (*nikbād*) to you" (2 Sam. 13:25). Such caution weighs upon the glory of David's house.

Barren Michal

If we are to understand the place of Michal, the spoilsport of David's glorious beginnings here in 2 Samuel 6, we need to review how the theme of women having sons has functioned in the narrative up to this point. In the opening chapters of 1 Samuel, kingship and the cause of the exile are tied together through two women's having sons. First, Hannah asks God for a son in chapter 1 as a figure of Israel asking God for a king in chapter 8: the birth of Samuel prefigures the birth of kingship. Then the loss of the ark, like the exile of Israel, is epitomized in the birth of Ichabod to the wife of Phinehas: "And she named the child Ichabod saying, 'the Glory has gone into exile from Israel for the ark of God has been captured'" (4:22). That the eventual victor, Samuel, prefigures the eventual victor, David, is nicely seen in the narrator's description of Samuel as a boy "girded with a linen ephod" (1 Sam. 2:18) and of David as a victorious king "girded with a linen ephod" (2 Sam. 6:14).

Here in 2 Samuel 6, as in 1–2 Samuel generally, a voice extolling the glories of Davidic kingship is counterbalanced by another voice intimating the connection between having children and building a royal house.

Whereas the Jebusite women *of* Jerusalem help David build his house (2 Sam. 5), Michal *in* Jerusalem does not. And whereas Hannah's asking for a son whom she would give to the LORD all the days of his life (1 Sam. 1:11) placed her in the role of a sinful Israel about to ask for a king, here in 2 Samuel 6 Michal's despising of David and her subsequent childlessness to the day of her death (v. 23) may represent an ideal Israel that never was. The royal glory (*kābôd*) about which Michal speaks and which David reaffirms in vv. 20–22 involves the abasement of Israel long ago signified by the birth of Ichabod, whose name means "No-Glory." The glory somehow departs from Israel when the ark of God is taken up in behalf of kingship. Michal's childlessness may represent the Deuteronomist's hope that the glory would one day return to Israel, and that Israel, like Michal, would remain kingless before the LORD to the day of her death.[8]

Voices: Chapter 7

In contrast to Chapter 6, where we find little reported speech, this chapter is mostly the reported speech of David (vv. 2b, 18b–29), Nathan (v. 3b), and the LORD (vv. 5–16). What the LORD says is especially important for understanding how and why this chapter has become such a popular staging ground for countless exegetical and literary-historical operations.[9]

The Voice of God: Nathan's Oracle

One way to focus upon that reported speech of the LORD we call Nathan's oracle is to appreciate the complex voice structure through which the oracle conveys meaning. Once we see the care with which authorial or editorial hands have fashioned God's words in verses 5–16, we may be less inclined to dissolve or deny its integrity in endless efforts to reconstruct its literary history.

In 2 Samuel 7, we find what is usual both in the History and in biblical narrative generally: most of the reported speech is direct quotation. Still, we do find Nathan quoting God in indirect discourse in verse 11: "And the LORD declares to you *that he will build for you a house.*" This brief shift to indirect discourse appears to have a functional importance which explains the oracle's obvious compositional features: its complexity, balance, and rigidity.

Look first at the complex nature of reporting and reported speech in verses 4 through 7. The narrator reports God's words in direct discourse in such a way that there are four levels of reported speech within them.

God's exact command to Nathan is the first level: "Go and tell my servant David" (v. 5a). God's words then descend to a second level by reporting exactly what Nathan is to say to David: "Thus says the LORD" (v. 5b). God's words reach a third level when Nathan directly reports the words of God he introduced through 5b: "Would you build me a house . . . ?" (vv. 5c–7). Finally, God's words in verses 5–7 conclude with a fourth level of reported speech in which God reports himself as never having said, "Why have you not built me a house of cedar?" (v. 7b). We see the complexity in verses 4–7 when we simply describe its voice structure: the narrator (v. 4) quotes God (v. 5a) quoting Nathan (v. 5b) quoting God (vv. 5c–7a) quoting himself (v. 7b).

A second feature of the oracle is the balance with which such complexities are found. The way verses 8–16 repeat the patterning of verses 5–7 is the most obvious illustration of such balance:

I. "Go and say to my servant David,	(5a)
'Thus says the LORD,	(5b)
"Would you build . . . ?" ' "	(5c–7)
II. "Now therefore thus you shall say to my servant David,	(8a)
'Thus says the LORD of hosts,	(8b)
"I took you from the pasture" ' "	(8c–16)

Despite the three levels of reported speech in verses 8–16, as opposed to four levels in verses 5–7, a similar pattern is found in both. The form of verses 8–16 further illustrates the balanced nature of God's words. For this second part of the oracle is itself divided into two parts:

A. 'Thus says the LORD of hosts,	(8b)
"I took you from the pasture" '	(8c–11a)
B. 'And now the LORD declares to you:	(11b)
1. that the LORD will make you a house (indirect discourse)	(11c)
2. "When your days are fulfilled" ' (direct discourse)	(12–16)

Notice that the second half (vv. 11b–16) of the second part (vv. 8b–16) of God's speech is again divided into two parts: Nathan quotes God first indirectly (11c) and then directly (12–16). These repetitions in patterning give God's words a balance that underscores the care with which they were composed.

A third characteristic of God's speech here is its rigidity from a compositional point of view. Nothing better illustrates the strong hold God has on the message Nathan is to convey to David than verse 11c's brief lapse into indirect discourse: "Moreover the LORD declares to you *that the LORD will*

make you a house." Ever since Bakhtin-Voloshinov emphasized the importance of reporting/reported speech in the study of language and literature, scholars and critics have been investigating the hermeneutic
potential exploited by the indirect ways one may report speech.[10] Once
one changes the wording of another's speech by reporting it either in indirect discourse or in the variety of other indirect ways a given language
allows, one moves from *representation* of speech toward *analysis and interpretation* of it. It is not difficult to see, therefore, that if the word being
reported is supremely authoritative, as God's words are here, then the
stature and authority of the reporter—here Nathan within the story-world
of the History—are enhanced whenever the reporter analyzes or interprets God's words by indirect means. In the Book of Deuteronomy, the
characterization of Moses as the greatest prophet of them all was established primarily by the supremely authoritative manner in which he indirectly reported the further words of God in chapters 12–26.[11]

When we look at the form and function of Nathan's reporting of God's
words in indirect discourse in verse 11, however, it is clear, first, that it
serves as a summary statement or headline of the directly quoted words of
God which end the utterance (vv. 12–16) and, second, that any prophetic
interpretation that this indirect quotation might suggest is neutralized by
its place within the larger utterance of God.[12]

Nathan's summary in verse 11c introduces the third section of God's
utterance in verses 12–16 and would seem to allow Nathan all the authoritative prerogatives belonging to such a practice.[13] Nevertheless, since the
indirect discourse is imbedded in the direct command of God, "Therefore
you shall say to my servant David, 'Thus says the LORD of Hosts'" (v. 8),
Nathan's choice of reporting God's words *indirectly* in verse 11c is only
superficially authoritative: God tells Nathan exactly what to say even in this
instance of indirect discourse, and allows him no room to interpret the
divine word. Since the narrator imbeds Nathan's indirect reporting of
God's word within the direct reporting of it commanded by God, all possibility of prophetic interpretation is removed. Far from enhancing
Nathan's prophetic authority, the move to indirect discourse within such a
compositional context reinforces Nathan's role in 2 Samuel 7 as mechanical mouthpiece of God.

If we wonder why Nathan is here so unlike the effective prophet-teacher
he turns out to be in 2 Samuel 12, we might look at what Nathan says on his
own account at the beginning of chapter 7. The chapter begins with David's
remark to Nathan that the king dwells in a house of cedars but the ark in a
tent. Nathan replies, "Go, do all that is in your heart, for the LORD is with
you" (v. 3). What is significant about Nathan's words to the "newly arked"
David is that they not only turn out to be contrary to the LORD's wishes but

also resemble Samuel's advice to the newly anointed Saul, "Now when these signs meet you, do whatever your hand finds to do, for God is with you" (1 Sam. 10:7).[14] On one hand, God cooperated with Saul's disastrous course of action ("Behold, a band of prophets met [Saul]; and the spirit of God came mightily upon him, and he prophesied among them" [1 Sam. 10:10]); on the other hand, here in 2 Samuel 7 God appears to protect David from a course of action that is unprecedented since Israel left Egypt. If it was wrong for a king to prophesy, it is also wrong for a king to "temple" the ark, "to build a house for [the name of] the LORD" (v. 13). Once again, house-building has profoundly negative connotations in the History. Nevertheless, the building of the temple, like the building of David's house, did occur, and the Deuteronomist's purpose is to situate both actions in a historiographic context that underlines their negative as well as positive aspects.

What is the significance of the chapter's depiction first of the king being misguided by his prophet and then of a prophet being corrected and constrained by his God? If we place these events next to 1 Samuel 10, where the king was also misguided by his prophet, but the prophet not constrained or corrected by his God, we have an important indication of the Deuteronomist's ideological point of view: even when directed by God's prophet through the interaction of "the custom of the prophet" and "the custom of the king,"[15] the king could still act against his and Israel's best interests.

There is something wrong, therefore, when a prophet counsels even one who has God with him to do either "whatever your hand finds to do" (1 Sam. 10:7) or "all that is in your heart" (2 Sam. 7:2). When the LORD did come to correct the prophet Samuel, it was to point out that human beings, even prophets and kings, look on outward appearances, but God looks on the heart (1 Sam. 16:7). Despite the presence of God's prophets around Israel's kings, and despite even the presence of God within their kings, Israel's social injustice and disruption are not only possible, they form the recurrent message of the Deuteronomist's historiographic account.

When, therefore, the Book of Judges ends its account of social chaos during the judicial period, it contrasts that period with the coming monarchic period in this way: "In those days there was no king in Israel; every man did what was right in his own eyes" (Judg. 21:25). As the royal history will go on to show, and despite commentators' perennial attempts to see in Judg. 21:25 a pro-monarchic point of view, social injustice will continue to dominate the Deuteronomist's account even in monarchic times. If a misguided prophet Samuel leads King Saul to do whatever his hand finds to do, and if a mistaken Nathan counsels King David to do all that is in his heart, then the narrator's statement about everyone doing what was right in their own eyes when there were no kings in Israel (Judg. 21:25) may invoke a contrast not between a kingless (or even judgeless) Israel, when every person did what was right in his or her own eyes, and a royal Israel, when people would begin to do what was right according to God's eyes, but rather between Israelites doing what was right in their own eyes and Israelites having to do what was right in their kings' eyes. The second situation will turn out to be as bad as the first.

Perhaps it was Nathan's mistake to assume that what was in David's heart to do—to build a temple for God—was seeing as God sees. Both to correct Nathan as he earlier had corrected Samuel and to protect David as he earlier had failed to protect Saul, the LORD issues a rigid prophetic statement in verses 5–16. So far in the History, it appears that the prophet may not speak of his own accord, nor should an Israelite take the initiative in seeking out a prophet for divine guidance; it is God who *sends* the prophet as his mouthpiece.

What, then, was God so careful to have Nathan say? When their content is emphasized, God's words to David easily divide up into three sections: vv. 5–7, 8–11a, and 11b–16. The first section deals with God's proper dwelling place in times past and present; the second discusses kingship under David (called here *nāgîd*); and the third concerns the building of the temple by one of David's offspring and the LORD's reciprocal promise to build David a dynastic house.

Building a Temple (7:5–11)

The LORD's initial reaction to David's suggestion in verses 5–7 is illuminated by a comparison with his words to Samuel in 1 Sam. 8:7–9. Not only does the LORD react negatively to David's proposal for a temple, just as he had reacted negatively to Israel's proposal for a king, he does so in both cases by using the same temporal formula to contrast previous practice to present reality. In 1 Samuel 8, God equates Israel's request for a king to rejection of the LORD and explains that Israel's actions have been consistent "from the day I brought them up out of Egypt even to this day" (1 Sam. 8:6). As Israel acted badly in the past, so they are continuing to do so by requesting a king. Here in 2 Samuel 7, the LORD uses the very same formula to make a similar point: the LORD has never dwelt in a house "from the day I brought up the people of Israel from Egypt even to this day" (v. 6). As it was wrong in the past for God to dwell in a house, so it is wrong for him to do so now.

Even in the other places in the History where this formula occurs, but where its wording is not as close to that of 2 Sam. 7:6 as 1 Sam. 8:6 is, its invocation is still confined to contexts that epitomize an especially disastrous turn of events. During the period of the judges, the Benjaminite outrage precipitating the civil war that concludes Judges sorrowfully exemplifies the social injustice that marked this epoch. When the Levite sent his dismembered concubine throughout all the territory of Israel, "all who saw it said, 'such a thing has never happened or been seen from the day that the people of Israel came up out of the land of Egypt until this day' " (Judg. 19:30). The rape of a Judahite woman by men of Gibeah provokes Israel's war against Benjamin, so the History's first invocation of this formula is in response to an especially heinous crime having widespread social, even national, consequences.

After its employment in 1 Sam. 8:6 and 2 Sam. 7:6, where the History reports God reacting in negative amazement first to Israel wanting a king and then to David wanting a temple, this formula is found in the History, for the last time, in the LORD's prophetic condemnation of Israel under Manasseh: "and I will cast off the remnant of my heritage, and give them into the hand of their enemies, and they shall become a prey and a spoil to all their enemies, because they have done what is evil in my sight and *have been provoking me* (*mak^{c}isîm*) to anger since the day their fathers came out of Egypt, even to this day" (2 Kings 21:15).

Not only does the reign of Manasseh constitute the worst reign in Israel's monarchic history, *it symbolizes the evil that Israel has been doing from the beginning.* Far from being an obviously slapdash attempt by some exilic editor to explain the fall of Jerusalem and the exile in the light of the LORD's promises to David here in 2 Samuel 7, the prophetic condemnation of Manasseh's reign in 2 Kings 21 uses language that depicts the History's clear vision of Israel's outrageous behavior from beginning to end. In the Book of Judges, when Israel continually sinned against the LORD, in 1 Samuel, when Israel requests a king, in 2 Samuel, when David wants a temple, and in 2 Kings, when Israel's worst king is condemned in language that makes his reign simply characteristic of Israel's behavior from the very beginning—in all these cases a repetition or variation of the same temporal formula signals an especially flagrant provocation of God by Israel.

We can see from this review that the Deuteronomist's parabolic and programmatic introduction to kingship in 1 Samuel 1–7 does *not* contrast judgeship to kingship as if comparing a golden period with the fool's gold that constituted Israel's monarchic era. Rather, the rejection of kingship and the return to some kind of judicial organization suggested by 1 Samuel 1–7 may simply be a recognition by the Deuteronomist that, although Israel was equally rebellious under both forms of government, at least God sent Israel judges through his own merciful initiative

(Judg. 2:18), whereas he sent them kings only at their own idolatrous insistence (1 Sam. 8:7–8).

The scope of the contrast between then and now, as introduced by the temporal formula in verse 6, narrows with God's question to Nathan in verse 7, "Did I ever say a word to any of the judges whom I commanded to shepherd my people Israel saying, 'Why have you not built me a house of cedar?'"[16] Instead of merely comparing Israel's anonymous past with David's present for the sake of emphasizing continuity, God's introduction of judges into the picture now makes explicit the virtual contrast in verse 6 between Israel's past judicial period on one hand and their present monarchy on the other. By this means we see a second connection between 1 Samuel 8 and 2 Samuel 7: both confront a crucial juncture in the story, a point where judicial and royal practices are contrasted. In 1 Samuel 8, Samuel the judge stands between Israel's premonarchic or judicial rejection of God and their coming rejection of God under King Saul; in 2 Samuel 7, Nathan stands between a LORD who rightfully dwells in a tent before the advent of kings and one whom David wants to put in a house. The more things change, the more they remain the same.

Verses 8–11 also cooperate in contrasting the period of the judges with that of kings; the LORD prophesies some kind of monarchic peace and stability in verses 8–10 and then distinguishes this from what was the case "formerly, that is, from the time that I appointed judges over my people" (vv. 10–11). The contrast between that judicial day and this royal day in verses 5–7 corresponds to the contrast between the judicial former times of verses 10b–11a and the royal present and future of verses 8–10.

A second aspect of the judicial/monarchic contrasts in verses 5–11 is spatial rather than temporal. Israel's situation under the judges is described mostly by verbs of *movement and instability*. God says, "I was moving about in a tent" and "In all the places where I moved about" (vv. 6, 7: *hithallēk*). God even commands Israel's judges "to shepherd the people" (v. 7) so that both leader and led participate in a mobile relationship. The spatial situation is much different in verses 8–11, where the LORD describes the present and future reality of Israel under Davidic rule. If judges were mobile shepherds in a metaphoric sense, David became king by ceasing to be a shepherd in a literal sense: "I took you from the shepherd's abode (*nāveh*), from following the sheep, to be prince (*nāgîd*) over my people" (v. 8). David's former *nāveh* in verse 8 corresponds to the LORD's *'ohel* in verse 6: both were portable.

The piling up of verbs of stability is especially obvious in this royal section. Though David is moved out of the *nāveh* (v. 8) and though God was with him "wherever he went" (v. 9), such movement is but preparation for present and future stability: "I will appoint a place (*wᵉśamtî*) for my people; I will plant them (*ûnta ͨtîw*); they will dwell (*weᵉšākan*) in their own place; they shall not tremble (or quake, be disturbed: *rāgaz*); I will set you down (or give you rest; *hēnî ͣḥ*)" (vv. 10–11).[17]

The LORD's reference, in verse 11a, to giving David rest (*hēnî ͣḥ*) from all his enemies ends this section not only because of the interruption of Nathan's words in verse 11b ("Moreover, the LORD declares to you"), but also because this use of *hēnî ͣḥ*, "to give rest or set down," forms an *inclusio* with the narrator's notice in verse 1, "and when the LORD had given [David] rest from all his enemies round about." David's rest turns out to be both the present peace noted by the narrator and the future peace prophesied by the LORD. The first is relatively transitory, the second will be firmly established; the one refers to David himself, the other to his throne. Only when David's son Solomon asserts, "But now the LORD my God has given me rest on every side" (1 Kings 5:18), will David's throne be said to be firmly established, his house set down or at rest. As 1 Kings 5ff. will indicate, these future events under Solomon are what 2 Sam. 7:11 is prophesying, thus providing the reader with a proper ideological context for the future building of the temple.

However inappropriate both royal house and divine temple are to be for Israel, it is important to see here that the building up of both will have a stabilizing effect upon the nation. The monarchies of David and Solomon were renowned in Israel's traditions, and the History will describe their successes in great detail; not the least of their glories was a permanence and continuity that could be compared to the dynasties of foreign nations: "I will make for you a great name, like the name of the great ones of the earth" (v. 9). Such considerations of continuity bring us to the third section of Nathan's oracle. For when the History speaks of family, dynasty, tribe, nation, or abode in terms of permanence and continuity, *bayit*, "house," comes naturally to mind.

The Permanence of Houses (7:11–16)

If the first two sections of God's speech related conditions of judgeship to those of kingship, the third section (vv. 11b–16) contrasts the kingship of David with that of Saul, "I will not take my steadfast love (*ḥesed*) from [your offspring] as I took it from Saul, whom I put away from before you" (v. 15). The permanence of David's house will succeed the aborted rule of Saul's.

Given the History's direct and indirect depictions of David's and Solomon's grievous failings, as well as of the repeated sins of those who later inhabited David's house, does not this rash and irrevocable promise demonstrate God's preferential treatment of David? When we see what the LORD has already done against the house of Saul and what he now promises to do for the house of David, it is difficult to recognize this God as the same one described by Moses: "For the LORD your God is God of Gods and Lord of Lords, the great, the mighty, the terrible God who is not partial and takes no bribes" (Deut. 10:17). God's apparent partiality toward David poses serious problems of interpretation for any reader who believes that the History makes sense. God's promise to David scarcely fits his past treatment of Saul, nor does it seem to be an apt introduction to the troubled life of David and the sinful lives of his descendants. Nevertheless, I want to suggest that the Deuteronomist carefully uses pro-Davidic traditions in order to depict David's house against the background of the mysterious justice of God. It may turn out that Saul's short reign and David's permanent rule are much more alike in the History than some of the statements exalting the house of David would lead us to believe.

We can understand how the third section of the oracle (verses 11b–16) fits into the immediate and general context by examining some formal features and narrative connections in 2 Samuel 7: frequent references to house (*bayit*), often in conjunction with perpetuity (*côlām*); the intimate connection of Nathan's oracle to the oracle in 1 Samuel 2; characterization of the LORD as the king's father; and God's formula for dealing with royal wrongdoing.

First, this chapter's emphasis on domestic perpetuity is easy to see: "house" occurs fifteen times and "forever" eight times.[18] Moreover, the frequent appearance in 2 Samuel of "house" and "forever" together is scarcely accidental, for this conjunction of words fits the pattern found throughout the rest of Samuel and Kings.[19] When we look at the distribution of "forever" throughout the rest of these books, the pattern we find there is remarkably similar: the word occurs twenty-three times elsewhere, and nine of these instances are in a context in which either a familial house or the divine temple is mentioned.[20] What these figures suggest is significant: whenever abode, family, tribe, or nation is referred to in Samuel/Kings as "house," something of the permanence which may from time to time be affirmed or denied of them is an important focus of this designation. To call an abode, family, tribe, or nation a "house" is *already* to call attention to the permanent aspects of such units with respect to the fortunes or misfortunes of time.

The Deuteronomist certainly concentrates on the special permanence of David's house in 2 Samuel 7. Yet one ought to remember two important facts concerning the perpetuity of David's dynasty. First, David's house is not the only familial house to which God promises perpetuity in the History: God said to Eli, "I promised that your house and the house of your father should go in and out before me *forever*" (1 Sam. 2:30). Second, such promised perpetuity, even when it is seen to be fulfilled in the History, does not preclude perpetual punishment as a distinguishing feature of, indeed a divine motive for, such permanence. In other words, God may choose to keep a house in existence *forever* in order that its punishment may be kept in force *forever*.

In fact, this second aspect of domestic perpetuity occurs in both of the cases in the History where God promises the permanence of a familial house. Thus, the "forever" in God's promise to the priestly house of Eli is not entirely revoked by the sins of Eli's sons or by Eli's complicity in such wrongdoing. Instead, God turns perpetual privilege into perpetual punishment. God decides that Eli's house shall endure in ignominy and without hope of future forgiveness: *"And every one who is left in your house* shall come to implore him for a piece of silver or a loaf of bread, and shall say, 'Put me, I pray you, in one of the priest's places, that I may eat a morsel of bread'"* (1 Sam. 2:36). "And I tell him that I am about to punish his house *forever*. Therefore I swear to the house of Eli that the iniquity of Eli's house shall not be expiated by sacrifice or offering *forever*'" (1 Sam. 3:13–14). With Eli's house, God turns perpetual election into an enduring existence that constitutes permanent rejection.

I have already suggested elsewhere how the priestly house of Eli and its fate in 1 Samuel 1–7 involve a narrative foreshadowing not only of all the royal houses of Israel throughout Samuel and Kings, but especially of David's royal house.[21] What happens now in 2 Samuel 7 is simply God's promise of perpetuity for David's house, as already foreshadowed in 1 Samuel 2. But it is especially important to realize that God's promise is preliminary to a series of reversals that will transform the supposed glories of the Davidic house into permanent shame.

One reason why God promises perpetuity to the house of David in this chapter is purely empirical: we may suppose that, at the time the History was composed, the house of David still stood. Indeed, the very last sentence of the History refers to that house's latest resident, Jehoiachin (2 Kings 25:29). Yet, another reason for the chapter's unusual emphasis on the enduring aspects of David's house may be far more important from the point of view of the History's predominant ideological message: Israel's punishment for wanting royal houses in the first place, as well as David's punishment for all the subsequent wrongdoing associated with his house, will both endure to the very moment when the History as we know it reached its final shape—whenever historians may surmise this to be. Woven into the History in complex ways that preclude the plausibility of last-minute editorial adjustments to an originally optimistic account of

Israel's monarchy is a brilliant step-by-step presentation of the fall of the house of Israel as it is linked to the fall of the house of David.

In 2 Samuel, therefore, it is not accidental that the very next "forever" to follow the eight forevers of 2 Samuel 7 is God's promise of perpetual punishment for the house of David: "Now therefore the sword shall not depart from your house forever (*ʿad ʿôlām*) because you despised me, and have taken the wife of Uriah the Hittite to be your wife" (2 Sam. 12:10). [22] This statement, like the statement of the LORD to Solomon in 1 Kings 11:11–13, is a Davidic analogue to God's words to Eli in 1 Sam. 3:13–14 and demonstrates that God's promise to keep a house in existence is not always benevolent. If God will not turn his "steadfast love" (*ḥesed*) away from David as he turned it away from Saul, neither will His sword be turned away from David. In the case of David's house, God's permanent love reveals itself as a two-edged sword.

A sword cannot remain over a house forever unless that house endure forever. Consider the perpetual penury of "every one who is left in [Eli's] house," who says, "Put me, I pray you, in one of the priest's places that I may eat a morsel of bread" (1 Sam. 2:36). This situation is but a foreshadowing of the History's last statement, those poignant words concerning David's latest descendant, Jehoiachin, "And every day of his life he dined regularly at the king's table; and for his allowance, a regular allowance was given him by the king, every day a portion, as long as he lived" (2 Kings 25:29–30).

I see little reason, then, for the elaborate literary–historical scenarios by which scholars have continually tried to remove the narrative incoherencies they suppose to exist within 2 Samuel 7 and between the chapter itself and other major sections of the History. Even here, where God is seen as irrevocably committing himself to keeping the house of David in existence, the aesthetic genius and ideological vision of the Deuteronomist insure that such explicit irrevocability is consistent not only with the past and future failings of both the house of Israel and the house of David, but also with the punishing disasters that will inexorably descend upon them in the History.

When, therefore, God refuses to give Saul precisely what he will later give David, he does so in these words: "Would that you had kept the commandment of the LORD your God, for then the LORD would have established your kingdom over Israel *forever*" (1 Sam. 13:13). That contrast between Saul's impermanence and David's permanence, like the contrast between God withdrawing "kindness" from Saul and allowing David to retain it (2 Sam. 7:15), is not between Saul's sins and David's faithfulness, nor between the punishment of a short reign and the blessing of a long one. Rather, the History is simply narrating the penalty of a short reign followed by the punishment of a long one.[23]

The permanence that normally belongs to literal houses and, by extension, to familial or dynastic units through the very designation of them as "houses" is accentuated the longer a house can endure through the vicissitudes of time. Consider a literal house like the temple: Solomon will tell God, "I have built thee an exalted house, a place for thee to dwell in forever" (1 Kings 8:13), and God will tell Solomon that he, God, has consecrated the house which Solomon had built in order to place God's name there forever (1 Kings 9:3). Consider even the house which God promises to build for David here in 2 Sam. 7:11: God promises that it will be established (*ne'eman*) forever (7:16), just as David prays for its everlasting establishment (*nākôn*: 7:26). Given the continued existence of houses—be they David's, Israel's, or God's—throughout the centuries surveyed by the History, how else can the Deuteronomist speak about such permanence except as a state of affairs established by the LORD for his own purposes? "Unless the LORD builds the house, those who build it labor in vain," sings the Psalmist (127:1). This historical foundation is precisely what the History builds into its story of the puzzling endurance of royal house and divine temple. The Deuteronomist's account is highly textured because of its elegant interweaving of the fates of the longstanding houses of David and of God; the account is bold because of the question its reading finally raises. *After* the destruction of the house of God, what do we do with the surviving house of David? This question, it seems to me, captures a fundamental aspect of the situation lying behind the composition of the Deuteronomic History.

The King's Crimes

We can now understand God's words in verses 14–15 about his treatment of the king who will build a temple for the name of the LORD. Why does God invoke divine paternity here: "I will be his father and he shall be my son" (v. 14a)? And how will God punish this royal culprit: "I will chastise him with a human rod and with human scourges" (v. 14b)?

References to the fatherhood of God are extremely rare in the History, being found only here and in Deut. 32:6. Instead of grounding my discussion upon ancient Near Eastern language of royal grants to faithful vassals, as many biblicists have done, I want rather to describe how God's language in vv. 14–15 has a legislative context in Deuteronomy 17 and a predictive force in the narrative following 2 Samuel 7.

Deuteronomy 17 is a legal counterpart to Nathan's oracle in terms of both structure and content. We have seen how the oracle in vv. 6–11 consistently relates conditions during the judicial period to those during the coming monarchy. In similar fashion, the legal matter discussed in Deuteronomy 17 involves a distinction between central legal administrations, first, under "the judge who is in office in those days" (v. 9), and then under the one whom "you shall set as king over you" (v. 15). Concerning the supreme tribunal needed to decide difficult cases, when Israel becomes a monarchy, the king must "learn to fear the LORD his God by keeping all the words of this law and these statutes and doing them, that he may not turn aside from the commandment" (vv. 19–20).

But what if the king does not faithfully carry out his rights and duties? How can an Israelite, in cases too difficult for local courts, expect justice at the highest governmental level if the king himself "turns aside from the commandment" (v. 20)? What recourse does Israel have in such circumstances where decisions must be made "between one kind of assault (*negaᶜ*) and another or between one kind of legal right (*mišpāṭ*) and another" (v. 8)? If the king is exploitative, then we have the very circumstance that demands a supreme tribunal in the first place. Who settles the case between the legal rights of the king and those of his subjects?

Deuteronomy 17 offers no answer to this problem, but 2 Samuel 7 does: God says, "When [your descendant] commits iniquity, I will judge (or chastise: *hôkîᵃḥ*) him with a human rod and human assaults (*negaᶜ*)" (2 Sam. 7:14). When the king's crimes make impossible, at the highest human level, a fair judgment between one assault and another, the LORD will punish the king with correspondingly human assaults. Let the punishment fit the crime.

Nathan's oracle also illuminates the legislation of Deuteronomy 17 by defining the precise relationship between royal faithfulness and the continued existence of royal houses. Deuteronomy 17 promotes royal obedience to the law in order that the king "may continue long in his kingdom, he and his children in Israel" (v. 20). It would appear from this that the continued existence of a royal house depends upon continued obedience to the law of God. However, the explicit language of 2 Samuel 7, as of the History taken as a whole, provides a formula that is as historiographically responsible as it is ideologically profound: even when a Davidic king sins, "my steadfast love shall not depart from him, as I took it from Saul. Your house and your kingdom shall be made sure forever before me" (2 Sam. 7:15–16).

From a historiographic perspective, David's house did remain in existence even to the end of the History as we now have it. Nevertheless, from an ideological point of view, the History uses a permanence-of-punishment formula to question the traditional exaltation of David's house as having endured "because David did what was right in the eyes of the LORD and did not turn aside from anything that he commanded him all the days of his life, except the matter of Uriah the Hittite" (1 Kings 15:5). The nature of this endurance is clarified through "the matter of Uriah the Hittite" when 2 Sam. 12:7–14 implies that God's perpetual love (*ḥesed*) includes a perpetual sword (*ḥereb*): "Now therefore, the sword shall never depart from your house, because you have despised me, and have taken the wife of Uriah the Hittite to be your wife" (v. 10).

David's solitary "faithfulness" no more kept his house in existence than Manasseh's disobedience alone brought down the temple of God. God can be seen continually punishing David's house for as long as that house continues to exist as a recognizable social entity. The History's ultimate conceptual authority continually saturates Israel's pro-Davidic traditions with such negative connotations. By the end of the History, then, recurring phrases such as "for the sake of David my servant" no longer single out David in an unambiguous way. At the end also, there remains a mystery: among the great houses built up in the History—the house of Israel, the house of David, and the house of God—the one house actually destroyed was the only one that was *incapable* of punishment or repentance, that is, the temple.

David's Response (7:18–29)

The tone of David's response to the amazing promises of God concerning the permanence of the king's house aptly characterizes David, while the content of his response displays the contours of the Davidic history in an especially profound way.

Concerning David, it is almost as if he cannot believe his ears. That he was God's favorite he already knew, but God's promise that his own house would endure forever is good fortune he could scarcely have hoped for. David sets the tone of his prayer by centering its preamble (vv. 18–24) and its petitions (vv. 25–29) around the theme of greatness (*gādôl*): God is great (v. 22) because he has wrought great things in behalf of David (v. 21) and Israel (v. 23). Therefore, God's name will be great so long as David's house remains established (v. 26). David knows that the enduring greatness of his house depends upon God fulfilling his promise, and so he centers his petitions around this relationship.

Here as elsewhere, "now therefore" (*wᵉᶜattāh*) signals the transition from antecedent to consequent in speech. In David's case, the preamble to his prayer (vv. 18–24) provides background for his requests in verses 25–29, where his triple "now therefore" (vv. 25, 28, 29) increases in breathlessness as the requests that follow decrease in length. The first "therefore" requests fulfillment of God's word, the second assumes it, and the third specifies its nature: "Now therefore, confirm forever the word concerning your servant's house" (v. 25); "now therefore, your words are true and you have promised this good thing" (v. 28); "now therefore, bless the house of your servant that it may continue forever before thee" (v. 29). In other words, fulfill your promise; your word is true; bless my house forever. In his prayer, David makes no mention of the very matter that occasioned Nathan's oracle in the first place; the temple is forgotten as David seizes upon God's unexpected promise with a fierce tenacity that reveals his character as effectively as anything else that has concerned him so far in the story.

God's words appear to contain a divinatory aspect that is scarcely lost upon David or the reader. God's promise of a permanent house despite explicit recognition that David's seed would sin (v. 15) leads David to believe that the one thing standing in the way of the continuance of his house is not the future disobedience of its occupants but a present lack of effective truthfulness on the part of its builder, who has just promised to establish the house forever. And so we see David concentrating the force of his first two *now therefores* on a *certainty* about God's words being fulfilled. We have seen in 1 Samuel how Saul's downfall centered around his increasing desire to know for sure what would befall him. The vision provided him by the woman of Endor in 1 Samuel 28 underlined Saul's tragic quest for certainty. Now, it seems, the LORD once more offers David what he continually denied Saul: providential intelligence that insures one's future.

We can almost hear David exultantly saying of his own house what Agag said of his own person, "Surely the bitterness of death is past" (1 Sam. 15:32). Yet in the very next verse the narrator showed how mistaken Agag was; it will take the rest of the History that follows 2 Samuel 7, however, for the Deuteronomist to demonstrate how David could be right in accepting God's promise of a permanent dynastic house yet unaware of the punitive reasons the LORD might have for granting such permanence.

In spite of David's limited vision here, the Deuteronomist still uses the beginning and end of David's prayer in a multivoiced way to foreshadow the contours of the coming narrative. Look first at the opening statement in David's prayer: "Who am I and what is my house, that thou hast brought me thus far?" (v. 18). Not only does this utterance indicate David's humble response to God's amazing promise, it also nicely summarizes the central question which the entire Davidic history seeks to answer. The Deuteronomist surrounded the *character zone* of David in 1 Samuel with a series of questions that follow him throughout his career.[24] In

2 Samuel 7:18 we have the final and most specific formulation of the central question motivating the entire monarchic history. If we hear the humble words of David in this question, we also sense in it the narrative program of the Deuteronomist.

Consider also the distinction that David makes in verse 21: "You have done all these great things on account of your word and according to your heart" (v. 21). It is possible that David makes the same mistake about God's promise of a permanent house that Samuel made about which of Jesse's sons was to be anointed king. God said to Samuel, "man looks on the outward appearance; but the LORD looks on the heart" (1 Sam. 16:7). Samuel thought that tall would follow tall, so that when tall Eliab appeared, the prophet, like Agag in the previous chapter, uttered a "surely" (*'ākēn* in 15:32; *'ak* in 16:6). However, it was according to God's heart that small should follow tall, so that David was the one to be anointed king. Here in 2 Samuel 7, David hears the word of God but may not understand how it will be fulfilled according to God's heart. Attending to the LORD's contrast between his treatment of Saul and his promised treatment of David (v. 15), the king understands that his permanent house will succeed Saul's temporary one. But his prayer also indicates that he fails to understand the heart of the matter: that long does not have to follow short as blessing follows curse.

Consider, then, the final request of David, one which reveals the precise manner in which David mistakes Nathan's oracle and the Deuteronomist interprets it. David ends his prayer by surrounding God's promise of domestic longevity with a double request for God's blessing on his house: "Please *bless* the house of thy servant, that it may continue forever before thee; and with *thy blessing* shall the house of thy servant *be blessed* forever" (v. 29). David equates the permanence of his house with the fact of God's blessing; such an understanding is at the heart of his prayer.

My discussion of 2 Samuel 6 above suggests why David's request for God's blessing upon his house here in 2 Samuel 7 is so significant for our understanding of the Deuteronomist's account of monarchic Israel: the house of Obed-edom the Gittite is the only house of any kind that the LORD is said to bless in the entire History. David, of course, has no way of knowing what the reader has been made aware of since 1 Samuel 2–3: a house may last forever so that its iniquity may not be expiated forever (1 Sam. 3:14).

Does David understand that his behavior and the behavior of those who will occupy his house will determine whether that house will endure as a sign of God's blessing or of God's punishment? Surely, many of the traditions that the Deuteronomist used in composing this History were as complacent about the enduring house of David as David is overtly humble about it here in 2 Samuel 7. The brilliant way in which the Deuteronomist explains how God will fulfill his promise to David in spite of David's and his house's dismal record of flouting God's law throughout the coming History is perhaps the best sign of the narrative's historiographic honesty and ideological complexity. At any rate, coming events will fashion a fascinating answer to David's initial question, "Who am I, O LORD God, and what is my house, that thou hast brought me thus far?" (2 Sam. 7:18).

·4·

SERVANTS
(8:1–10:19)

Every good servant does not all commands. (Shakespeare, *Cymbeline*)

'Tis mad idolatry to make the service greater than the god. (Shakespeare, *Troilus and Cressida*)

Who Is David?

The question of David's with which I ended the last chapter—"Who am I, O LORD God, and what is my house, that thou hast brought me thus far?" (2 Sam. 7:18)—expresses the formidable challenge which readers face when they try to understand this David who speaks. If one addresses the History's overall characterization of David, complications to a coherent picture abound. In terms of the larger story line, after predominantly overt glorification of David from the moment he enters the narrative in 1 Samuel 16 until now, the story just ahead beginning in chapter 11 characterizes David and his house in the bleakest of terms: David's adulterous murder of Uriah, Amnon's incestuous rape of Tamar, Absalom's execution of Amnon and revolt against David. The short view in David's story is from rags to riches, the longer view from rags to rogues.

When we add to this apparent unevenness of plot what authoritative voices in the History have to say about David, we perceive a dissonance that threatens to destroy whatever integrity we recognize in the story. On one hand, voices in the story, whether omniscient or fallible, evaluate the life and career of David in the most positive of terms. For example, when the voice of the narrator introduces us to sinful Abijam of Judah, it explains the LORD's actions in this way: "Nevertheless for David's sake the LORD his God gave [Abijam] a lamp (*nîr*) in Jerusalem, setting up his son after him, and establishing Jerusalem; because David did what was right in the eyes of the LORD and did not turn aside from anything that he commanded him

88

all the days of his life, except in the matter of Uriah, the Hittite" (1 Kings 15:4–5). The narrator's high estimation of David here was already foreshadowed by God's previous words to Jeroboam, which managed to ignore even the matter of Uriah: "Yet you have not been like my servant David, who kept my commandments and followed me with all his heart, doing only that which was right in my eyes" (1 Kings 14:8). Amongst characters of lesser authority, Solomon echoes these views as he prays to the LORD with filial devotion: "Thou hast shown great and steadfast love to thy servant David my father, because he walked before thee in faithfulness, in righteousness, and in uprightness of heart toward thee" (1 Kings 3:6).

On the other hand, this matter of Uriah the Hittite, so quickly disposed of in 1 Kings 15, has a far more significant influence on David's life and house in 2 Samuel 12, where God tells David, "Now therefore, the sword shall never depart from your house because you have despised me, and have taken the wife of Uriah the Hittite to be your wife" (v. 10). The single exception to David's righteousness in 1 Kings 15 burdens David's house with perpetual punishment in 2 Samuel 12. Moreover, not only will David's sin continue to hover over his house like a dark cloud, the vaunted righteousness of two other kings of Judah almost overshadows David's. The narrator extols Hezekiah in terms that excel even those used to describe David: "[Hezekiah] trusted in the LORD the God of Israel; so that there was none like him among all the kings of Judah after him, nor among those who were before him. For he held fast to the LORD" (2 Kings 18:5–6). And as David is lost in Hezekiah's glory, so Hezekiah in Josiah's: "Before him there was no king like him, who turned to the LORD with all his heart and with all his soul and with all his might, according to all the law of Moses; nor did any like him arise after him" (2 Kings 23:25). In terms of righteousness and obedience to God's law, Hezekiah surpasses David just as Josiah does Hezekiah.

So we find ourselves puzzling over the preeminence of David in Samuel/ Kings very much as we puzzled over the uniqueness of Moses in Deuteronomy, where one authoritative voice asserted, "there has not arisen a prophet like Moses" (Deut. 34:10), after God had prophesied through Moses, "I will raise up for them a prophet like you" (Deut. 18:18). Let us see how competing claims over the primacy of David fare through a careful examination of the tribute paid to David in 2 Samuel 8.[1]

God's Greatest Servant (8:1–18)

The reader's unavoidable realization that David is the preeminent servant (*ᶜebed*) of God in the History goes to the heart of the problem of David's characterization. From Deuteronomy through 2 Kings, God and the narrator call only prophet or king servants of the LORD. The narrator calls the prophets Moses, Ahijah, and Jonah, as well as King David, servants of the LORD.[2] Similarly, the LORD regards as his servants only the prophets and King David.[3] These two voices of authority in the History call David the LORD's servant more often than they so designate all the prophets combined, Moses included (thirteen out of twenty times).[4] More to the point, David is the only king of Israel in the entire History whom the story's conventionally omniscient voices designate as servant of the LORD.

Nevertheless, as I have indicated here concerning David—and have suggested in a previous book concerning Moses—the authoritative and reliable voices of narrator and LORD are often multivoiced vehicles for the Deuteronomist's voice, which recognizes David as the preeminent servant of the LORD even as it succeeds in putting such traditions of Davidic glorification into historiographic and ideological perspective. The manner in which the Deuteronomist consistently positions David in the story is an aesthetic marvel. The History's abiding practice of putting in their place David and all those who glorify him now continues in 2 Samuel 8.

Saving the Servant of God

The first time that the LORD—or anyone else for that matter—is reported calling David God's servant is when Abner quotes God as attaching Israel's coming deliverance to David's loyal service: "For the LORD has promised David, saying, 'By the hand of my servant David I will deliver ($h\hat{o}\check{s}\hat{i}^{ac}$) my people Israel'" (2 Sam. 3:18). God subsequently calls David "my servant" twice in 2 Samuel 7, verses 5 and 8, and David echoes God's language fully nine times: 7:20, 21, 25, 26, 27 (twice), 28, 29 (twice).

God promised in 2 Samuel 7 to build David a house and to magnify his name (v. 9) and 2 Samuel 8 now sets about fulfilling these promises. David's stunning series of victories over Edom, Moab, Ammon, Philistia, Amalek and other nations illustrates how "David won a name for himself" (8:13) and how "the LORD delivered ($h\hat{o}\check{s}\hat{i}^{ac}$) David wherever he went" (8:6, 14). David's success and his service of God go hand in hand in the story; how can readers make sense of this connection, and how does the History's multivoiced presentation of God's deliverance of his servant parallel David's service of the LORD?

Nothing is more frequent in the History than an authoritative voice (God, prophet, or narrator) promising deliverance to those who obey God's law and disaster to those who do not. Nevertheless, the story itself and the authorial voice that shapes it contradict this retributive ideology constantly. In spite of God's frequent threats and blandishments over the law, the reader cannot finish the History without being convinced that there is little connection between the salvation or deliverance ($y\bar{a}\check{s}a^c$) that actually comes to an individual or a group in the story and the merits of those so favored. The merits or demerits of someone delivered by God are, more often than not, irrelevant to the deliverance itself.

At one end of the History, the entire Book of Judges shows God persistently delivering a continually sinful Israel.[5] At the other end, 2 Kings illustrates just how irrelevant to God's deliverance is the obedience of the one delivered. God delivers even a foreign nation, Syria, through its leprous commander Naaman (2 Kings 5:1). Then, under the sinful reigns of Jehoahaz and Jeroboam II, God delivers Israel, even though the narrator explicitly states that neither of these kings turned aside from their sins (2 Kings 13:5–6; 14:24, 27). Finally, to underline the mysteriousness of God's salvation, the History has God announce, through Isaiah, that he will deliver Jerusalem "for my sake and because of my servant David" (2 Kings 19:34). This divine rationale is especially surprising, given the more immediate lifelong loyalty of the reigning king, Hezekiah, of whom the narrator has just affirmed, "There was none like him among all the kings of Judah after him, nor among those who were before him" (2 Kings 18:5). If God often *does* punish people for their disobedience, the History surely shows him more typically delivering those who do not deserve it. The impact on the reader of the History's climactic destruction of Judah at the end of 2 Kings, therefore, comes not just from the retributive force this divine act obviously displays, but especially from the divine indulgence of Israel that it finally displaces.

We see, then, that here in 2 Samuel 8, as earlier in the life and career of David, the LORD's actual deliverance of the man after his own heart has no necessary connection with any loyalty to the LORD that we may suppose on David's part. From the moment David enters the picture, he comes across as someone who is as much self-serving as God-fearing. The very first words we hear from him immediately establish this feature of his character: "And David said to the men who stood by him, 'What shall be done for the man who kills this Philistine?'" (1 Sam. 17:26).[6] Even in the most propagandistic stretches of David's story, as in 1 Samuel 24–26, where, for example, Abigail praises the LORD, and David praises Abigail, for stopping David "from delivering oneself with one's own hand and thus from incurring bloodguilt" (1 Sam. 25:26, 31, 33), and where David preaches how wrong it would have been to kill Saul because Saul, like David himself, was the LORD's anointed (1 Sam. 24:7, 11; 26:9, 11, 16, 23), the Deuteronomist keeps underlining David's self-serving motives for action.

David's Servant—and God's

What makes 2 Samuel 8 so significant from an ideological point of view is its depiction of the basis for David's traditional reputation as servant of the LORD. That subservient voice that we so often hear in the History, and have described by the term *authoritarian dogmatism,* typically offers one simplistic explanation for David's reputation as preeminent servant of the LORD and for God's permanent deliverance of him and his house. For example, David "did only what was right in God's eyes" (1 Kings 14:8). On the other hand, that authorial voice I associate with *critical traditionalism* constantly overrides such blatant propaganda not only by overtly detailing the darker sides to David's life, as in 2 Samuel 11 and the chapters following, but especially by subverting even the glorious accounts of David's career in all the various ways I have been describing since 1 Samuel 16. In the previous chapter, I suggested that David's house endured for God's own punitive purposes; here I want to suggest that the Deuteronomist promotes David's special service to God as historiographically accurate at the same time it emphasizes David's self-serving character.

The victories of David over Israel's enemies in 2 Samuel 8 describe God's deliverance of David wherever he went. The immediate result of this deliverance is the same in both of the verses in which it is mentioned: the defeated nations "became servants to David" (vv. 6, 14). And what do servants or vassals do? They bring tribute or gifts (*noś'ê minḥāh* in verses 2, 6) to the one they serve. We often see this particular act of servitude elsewhere in the History: the nations over whom Solomon ruled "brought tribute and served [him] (*ᶜābad*) all the days of his life" (1 Kings 4:21); "at the time of the offering of the gift (*minḥāh*), Elijah said, 'O LORD, I am thy servant (*ᶜebed*)'" (1 Kings 18:36); and when Shalmanesar came up against him, "Hoshea became his vassal (*ᶜebed*) and paid him tribute (*minḥāh*)" (2 Kings 17:3). In the History, to bring tribute to someone goes hand in hand with serving that person.

As the defeated nations show their servitude to David in 1 Samuel 8 by paying him tribute, David is shown expressing his own servitude toward the LORD by turning over to him the silver, gold, or bronze that he had received from his newly acquired servants. "And Joram brought with him articles of silver, of gold, and of bronze; these also King David dedicated (*hiqdîš*) to the LORD, together with the silver and gold which he dedicated from all the nations he subdued" (vv. 10–11). God delivers David so that subservient nations bring him tribute; David then expresses his own servitude by dedicating this tribute to the LORD.

By showing David immediately consecrating to the LORD these valuable signs of servitude, the Deuteronomist relates an early practice of David's that qualifies him, in one important sense at least, as the LORD's servant par excellence. David was the first king in Israel, this story suggests, to enrich the treasury of the LORD that one day would be housed in the temple. Indeed, the long account of Solomon's building of the temple in 1 Kings 6–7 ends with a statement which singles out this founding act of David's divine servitude: "Thus all the work that King Solomon did on the house of the LORD was finished. And Solomon brought in the things which David his father had dedicated, the silver, the gold and the vessels, and stored them in the treasuries of the house of the LORD" (1 Kings 7:51). Far from using all the wealth from the nations simply to enrich his own house, David shares this wealth with the house of the LORD. And so, it turns out, David helps to build up the LORD's treasury long before his son Solomon will house it in the temple.

Within Israel's traditions as represented in the History, then, we see David becoming the LORD's special servant not because "he did only what was right in the LORD's eyes"—his life and career as depicted in the History emphatically correct such overblown statements—but because, the Deuteronomist seems to be saying, David helped to establish the power and wealth of the Jerusalemite priesthood in fundamental ways that lasted to the very destruction of the temple. Chapter 8 offers us a glimpse into an important practical reason for David's reputation as God's servant: David served the LORD more through his fiscal policy toward the Jerusalemite priesthood than by his obedience to the law. Powerful priestly voices within Israel's establishment may have repaid David's initial beneficence by continuing to polish his reputation even up to the time when blame had to be meted out for the fall of Jerusalem. In this way, the Deuteronomist seeks to explain how and why Israel continued to regard David as the LORD's servant long after the king's behavior should have weakened, if not destroyed, the moral basis for the epithet.

Everything in 2 Samuel 8 appears in David's favor, yet one final feature of the chapter illustrates once again the History's penchant for using pro-Davidic traditions against themselves. Having been delivered by the LORD and victorious over the nations surrounding Israel, David shows himself to be both magnanimous toward God by sharing tribute with him and responsible toward the people by fulfilling royal obligations: "So David reigned over all Israel; and David administered justice and equity to all his people" (v. 15). David also assigns military, administrative, and priestly positions in verses 16–18; there is little hint here of the royal abuses that were prophesied by Samuel in 1 Samuel 8 and would be fulfilled during Solomon's reign.

Yet even while David's glories fill the chapter, it ends with a statement which suggests how David's service of God could operate in a self-serving way. No matter how much tribute the king assigned to the LORD's treasury—presumably under the control of the LORD's priesthood—it is still the king himself who appoints the high priests, here Zadok and Ahimelek (v. 17). Not content, however, with controlling the LORD's treasury through royal appointment of the priests who oversaw it, David also makes his own sons priests (v. 18). Such a move will have far-reaching effects once the temple is built. How better to insure the interests of the House of David within the treasury of the house of God than for the king not only to appoint his own priests but even to appoint his own sons as priests?

If, theologically speaking, part of the reason for Saul's abortive rule was his disastrous mixing up of kingship and prophecy, perhaps part of the reason for David's traditional success, seen here primarily from a political point of view, was his efficient conjoining of kingship and priesthood. In any case, 2 Samuel 8 allows the reader to glimpse something of the complex relationships established in the History between God's deliverance of David and David's abiding service of God. Politically speaking, David's tribute to God here may be seen as earning him the title of servant of the LORD; ethically speaking, that is, from the point of view of the personal justice and equity administered by the king to all his people (v. 15), David's reputation as God's special servant is off to a credible start. Nevertheless, as the coming chapters will demonstrate, that reputation—like God's deliverance of David—will be shown to be not wholly merited.

Chapter 9: Problems of Coherence

"Is there anyone left of the house of Saul, that I may show him kindness for Jonathan's sake?" This question of David's begins 2 Samuel 9. Given the events that have already transpired in the story, here is a compassionate query that could easily strike terror in the heart of anyone belonging to Saul's house who might hear of it. After all, David has been as singularly unsuccessful in his efforts on behalf of Jonathan as he has been eminently successful on his own behalf. After David had concluded the covenant with Jonathan to which his question in 2 Samuel 9 refers ("Do not cut off your loyalty from my house forever," Jonathan had implored in 1 Sam. 20:15), forces external to David conspired to kill off the inhabitants of Saul's house one by one, even as these same forces appeared to shield David from any complicity in such deaths. Thus David had no part in the deaths of Saul and his three sons in 1 Samuel 31, but only because the lords of the Philistines had stopped him from going down into battle against Saul and Jonathan (1 Samuel 29). When Joab's men detained Abner in order that their master could murder him, we read that "David did not know about it" (2 Sam. 3:26). Nor did David know of Ishbosheth's murder until Rechab and Baanah brought his head to the king (2 Sam. 4:8). By the time David comes to question whether there is anyone left (*nôtar*) in Saul's house, the reader cannot help but wonder whether David's loyalty (*ḥesed*) for the sake of Jonathan counts for anything. To interpret David's belated success in protecting Mephibosheth, the remnant of Saul's house, therefore, demands that we explain it within the context of David's singular inability to translate his covenantal loyalty to Jonathan's house into practical protection of its inhabitants. We must look backwards and forwards in the story if we are to understand the form and function of David's *ḥesed*, his lovingkindness, to Mephibosheth here in chapter 9.

Biblicists usually point to narratives about Mephibosheth as literary historical indicators of the present jumble within the text. We first encountered reference to Mephibosheth in 4:4;[7] this verse, we are told, is out of place and probably belongs here at the beginning of chapter 9. How and why the displacement is supposed to have taken place is difficult to say, despite the ease of speculation about it. When Ziba questions Mephibosheth's loyalty to David in 2 Samuel 16, the king will give back to Ziba the land which he had earlier restored to Mephibosheth in 2 Samuel 9. Finally, in 2 Samuel 19 Mephibosheth will successfully defend himself against Ziba's accusations of disloyalty and prompt David's offer to return to him half of Saul's land.

In addition to 4:4, the case for a meaningful progression of events concerning David's actions for the sake of Jonathan is further weakened by the events in 2 Samuel 21, where David hands over the descendants of Saul to the Gibeonites. Once again we are counseled by those who know about such things that the events in chapter 21 are out of order: from an editorial point of view, the chapter probably belongs before chapter 9, since the events within it can best be understood as having occurred before the events of chapter 9. This jumbled picture in the text is another indication of ancient editorial misadventure.

Although 2 Samuel 21–24 may give the appearance of material that has been hastily appended to the much more discursively coherent story preceding it, we shall see that this characterization is misleading. There are some hints of architectonic order within and among these apparently haphazard and scattered references to Mephibosheth's affairs, and I will indicate in a moment how 2 Samuel 9 functions as the hub of a well-connected story that has a number of definable levels to it. These levels extend successively backwards and forwards in the text, thus widening the story's focus of interest to the point where we can say something about the Deuteronomist's ideological perspective here in 2 Samuel 9. The placement and sequencing of the passages that are most directly connected with the Mephibosheth affair suggest the high degree of care—or at least habitual patterns of thought—according to which these passages have been shaped into the final form of the History. But before discussing this aspect of 2 Samuel 9, I need to say something about the language we find within it.

Obeisance or Worship (9:1–13)

Chapter 9 is filled with the language of servitude: some form of $^c\bar{a}bad$, "to serve," occurs ten times within it.[8] Ziba's servants become Mephibosheth's and must work ($^c\bar{a}bad$) the land for the lame prince, yet both lord and master remain David's servants; David designates Saul as Ziba's (erstwhile) lord, and Ziba himself calls David his lord. Moreover, just as language of "bringing tribute" (*nos'ê minḥāh*) represents the servitude of nations toward David (8:2, 6), so also language of bowing down, of doing obeisance (*hištaḥwāh*), indicates Mephibosheth's acknowledged servitude to David (9:6, 8).[9]

Nothing could be more suitable to the situation than that Ziba, "a servant of the house of Saul," now says to King David, "Your servant is he" (v. 2). Mephibosheth also appropriately says to David, "Behold, your servant" (v. 6). Is not, then, Mephibosheth's double action of obeisance (*hištaḥwāh*) in David's presence (vv. 6 and 8) simply what one who calls himself David's servant should do in such circumstances: "He fell on his face and did obeisance" (v. 6)? It may be entirely appropriate for the defeated nations of chapter 8 to express their servitude toward David by bringing him tribute, and for Mephibosheth to express his by bowing before the king, yet there is indication that such acts of obeisance as Mephibosheth performs in chapter 9 are especially significant in terms of the History's major ideological emphases. A survey of the use of this verb *hištaḥwāh* in the History reveals a narrative and ideological consistency that places enormous ideological weight upon the Israelite who does obeisance and the lord who receives it.

The manner in which English versions of the Bible translate this verb immediately isolates the ideological importance and complexity of the action to which it refers. The agent is often called servant (*^cebed*) and the recipient lord or master (*'ādôn*). Abigail well expresses each participant's role in this transaction: "She rose and bowed down (*wattištaḥû*) and said, 'Behold your handmaid is a *servant* to wash the feet of the servants of *my lord*'" (1 Sam. 25:41). When the lord so acknowledged is human, the RSV, for example, will translate the Hebrew verb as "bow down" or "do obeisance." When, however, the lord is divine, or thought to be so, the RSV will typically use the verb "to worship," as throughout the Book of Deuteronomy, where "to serve other gods" and "to worship them" are almost always used in tandem: "Take heed lest your heart be deceived and you turn aside and serve other gods and worship them" (Deut. 11:16).[10] This variable practice of the RSV is meant to indicate that when the "lord" to whom one bows down is divine, submission amounts to an act of worship, but when the lord is human, an act of mere deference. A simple matter, then, with little consequence for our understanding of the History's characterization of David as exemplified here in 2 Samuel 9. Mephibosheth knows his place in David's presence; it is at the king's feet, bowed down in homage to his royal lordship.

Yet matters are not so simple after all. In the History, mere human beings are said to receive the homage to which *hištaḥwāh* refers only after Israel has entered its royal phase, when this particular act of submission or deference toward fellow human beings becomes so common that, from 1 Samuel 8 onwards, humans—mostly kings or their retinue—receive reverence in this manner more often even than gods do: twenty-four to eighteen occurrences respectively.[11] The History is significantly consistent on this point. Despite the numerous prophets, judges, priests, and other "lords" to whom this verb might be thought appropriately to have applied in Deuteronomy, Joshua, and Judges, only deities and no humans (apart from the uncanny and unearthly commander of the LORD's army in Josh. 5:14) receive such homage throughout these books. And in eleven of these fifteen instances, "to worship" (*hištaḥwāh*) these gods is explicitly "to serve" (*ʿābad*) them also.[12]

Such a pattern suggests that this particular act of homage, which Israelites typically performed in the presence of their royal lords, as Mephibosheth does here in 2 Samuel 9, is not as ideologically innocent as it might at first appear to be. Only *after* Israel rejected the LORD by asking him for a king and the LORD responded by equating kingship with "forsaking me and *serving other gods*" (1 Sam. 8:8) do we find in the History Israelites who bow down to human beings with this special act of homage. The History makes it crystal clear that this submissive practice—referred to by *hištaḥwāh*—of bowing down before one's fellow human being is one of those unseemly actions belonging to the royal baggage that weighed Israel down during the monarchic period.

If to "bow down or worship" (*hištaḥwāh*) is explicitly synonymous with "to serve" (*ʿābad*) almost always in the Book of Deuteronomy, and often throughout the rest of the History, then the History's solution to Israel's royal problems, as 1 Samuel 7 has described it, once more takes on added

meaning: when Samuel tells Israel to serve the LORD *only* (1 Sam. 7:3; see
v. 4 also), the Deuteronomist means us to understand this to command
Israel not only not to serve other gods, but also not to serve *kings*.[13] Intimately connected with serving kings, I am suggesting, is the very act of
"bowing down before them," as Mephibosheth does before David; to bow
down before the LORD *only*, the Deuteronomist teaches throughout the
History, means one ought not to bow down before kings.

We can obtain considerable insight into the implications of this Deuteronomic connection between royal service and royal submission by comparing the History's practice of singling David out as God's preeminent
servant—as I described it above in discussing 2 Samuel 8—with its corresponding practice of presenting David and his retinue as the predominant
lords whom Israelites "worship" or before whom they do obeisance. As we
have seen, despite all the kings in Israel's history, only David is God's "servant" according to the authoritative voices of God and the narrator; conversely, of all those fellow human beings before whom Israelites bow down,
King David and his retinue turn out to be Israel's preeminent lords. Moreover, even though it is another king or prince who is first given obeisance
in this manner in the History, it is David himself who bows down, indeed
initiates the practice of doing so: he bows down before Jonathan in 1 Sam.
20:41 and before Saul in 24:9. If there is a forward-looking element of self-
protection in the future king continually speaking with abhorrence about
raising one's hand against the LORD's anointed in 1 Samuel 24 and 26,
then there may literally be an aspect of *self-service* in David's initial obeisance to King Saul and to his heir Jonathan: David himself begins the practice that will typify Israel's almost unswerving respect for *his* lordship in
the coming story.

Is There *Still* Anyone Left?

David begins 2 Samuel 9 with four successive questions: "Is there still
anyone left of the house of Saul?" "Are you Ziba?" "Is there not still
someone of the house of Saul?" "Where is he?" (vv. 1–4). David's queries
engender an immediate question on the part of the reader: what does
David mean by his double use of "still" (*ʿôd*) in verses 1 and 3? The
adverb seems to refer to some happening that has brought the house of
Saul into imminent extinction. Biblicists, wise in the ways of ancient tam-
pering with the text, can make a strong case for the events of 2 Samuel 21,
where David hands over to the Gibeonites seven descendants of Saul for
execution, being chronologically precedent to the events here in 2 Samuel
9. Nevertheless, whether or not 2 Samuel 21 is displaced, readers ought to

ask whether it makes any sense where it is; this is a question that literary historians almost never ask, because they typically, perhaps unavoidably, need to concentrate on textual and interpretive disruption in order to construct their genetic theories about how the text got into its present shape.

When, therefore, we ponder the significance of David's "still anyone left," (*côd 'ăšer nôtar*), we must first look at matters from our own vantage point as readers. What have we previously encountered, and what will we encounter later in the story, that may shed light on David's repetitious "Is there *still* anyone (left)?" After all, we have just seen how this chapter's unusually definite emphasis on the language of servitude ("servant," "lord," "work [*cābad*] the land," "bow down") finds its focus in the patterns of such language-use that precede and follow the chapter. What does it mean in 2 Samuel 9, therefore, that David does not know whether, nor the reader why, there might *still* be someone left of the house of Saul?

Compositional Patterns of Meaning

The further we read backwards and forwards, the greater we develop our depth of vision. Three successive steps will place 2 Samuel 9 in proper context.

The first step concentrates on Mephibosheth himself—his introduction, fate, and significance in the story. It is immediately obvious that the introduction to Mephibosheth (4:4) appears as unexpected and "out of place" as the story about the Gibeonite revenge in chapter 21, which contains the History's final reference to him (v. 7).[14] In addition, 2 Samuel 9 stands at some distance from the story's introduction of Mephibosheth in 4:4 and from two subsequent accounts, in 2 Samuel 16 and 19, involving him. How do these distanced references to Mephibosheth before and after 2 Samuel 9 affect our understanding of the story at its most superficial level?

Our being introduced to Mephibosheth early on in 2 Sam. 4 does make some sense, since we may then read about the murder of Ishbosheth in this chapter with the knowledge that, despite the prior deaths of Saul's three sons in 1 Samuel 31 and Ishbosheth's death here in 2 Samuel 4, there still remains someone else of Saul's house. When they come to 2 Samuel 9, then, attentive readers already know the answer to two of David's questions as he utters them. What follows in 2 Samuel 16 and 19 concerning Mephibosheth is a pair of reversals that show David backtracking on his prior decisions. After having restored all of Saul's lands to Mephibosheth in 2 Samuel 9, David gives them all back to Ziba in chapter 16, only to reverse himself once more by restoring half again to Mephibosheth in chapter 19. The primary effect of all this on the reader, it seems to me, is to characterize David as a person easily given to expedient decisions that can conflict with his own prior commitments. We wonder whether David is really the appropriate person to "show the kindness of God" (2 Sam. 9:3) to anyone, least of all to remnants of a rival house.

We take a second step in our understanding of what is at stake in chapter 9 by extending its context even further backwards and forwards in the story. When David tells Ziba and Mephibosheth of his intention to show *ḥesed* (kindness) to Mephibosheth "for Jonathan's sake" (vv. 1, 7), this language necessarily returns us to 1 Samuel 20, where David entered into a covenant, binding himself to respect Jonathan's request not "to cut off your loyalty (*ḥesed*) from my house forever" (v. 15). David's "kindness' in 2 Samuel 9 also moves us forward to 2 Samuel 21, where our wonder about the appropriateness of David's *ḥesed* will turn first to surprise and then to certainty, as we finally learn why David had asked, earlier in the story, "Is there *still* anyone left?": the account in 2 Samuel 21 appears to be of a *previous* decision of David's, that is, before the events in 2 Samuel 9, not to keep faith with Jonathan. Mephibosheth, the one still left in Jonathan's house, is a living reminder of David's complicity—whether justified or not—in transforming Saul's house into a barren establishment, and his own pact with Jonathan into a broken covenant. However 2 Samuel 21 got to be where it is, the effect of its location is not to render incoherent what precedes it, but rather to enlighten readers, in a wonderfully surprising way, about what they thought they already knew. There is some pleasure in this delayed revelation; something deliberate is going on in terms of narrative architecture.

One reason why these first two contexts of 2 Samuel 9 suggest a compositional plan is their similar placement and function: these successive contextualizations work at a distance and with an effect that finally pleases by enlightenment and surprise. In these two contexts, 2 Samuel 9 is at the center of a narrative movement that becomes increasingly clear: 2 Sam. 16:1–4 and 19:25–31 both show us David reversing an earlier decision narrated in 2 Samuel 9, so that we wonder at his tendency to backtrack on prior decisions; 2 Samuel 21 then reveals important expository information that sheds light not only on David's benevolence toward Mephibosheth in 2 Samuel 9 but also on his inconstancy toward him in 2 Samuel 16 and 19. David showed *ḥesed* to Saul's house only after he allowed the Gibeonites' sword to descend upon most of its occupants. The History gradually enlightens the reader about David's motivation—works toward closure, as some theorists would say—first by showing this character backtracking on past decisions, and then by having the narrator present a surprising flashback that sheds light upon that character's previous decisions in the story.

David as Mephibosheth

A third look backwards and forwards reveals the final and most comprehensive context for our understanding of 2 Samuel 9 and the language we find in it. At this level of contextualization, we encounter, as directly as we ever will, the compositional plan of the royal history itself. The story of David has its ultimate significance only within a history of monarchic Israel that is fundamentally *social* rather than personal. Paradoxically, what David does for Mephibosheth in 2 Samuel 9 receives its widest significance when we read it in the context of what precedes and follows it at the furthest remove. Such specific textual connections mirror and confirm the similar constructions of the two narrower contexts we have already discussed; they also bring us closest to the ideological point of view of the entire History.

Elsewhere I have described how 1 Samuel 1–7 offers the reader a wonderful overture to the entire monarchic history to follow.[15] By looking back at this opening narrative, we will find our most important context for interpreting David's actions toward Mephibosheth in 2 Samuel 9, for in the oracle of the man of God in 1 Sam. 2:27–35 we have a multivoiced foreshadowing of what is to take place in the coming monarchic history. At the level of its glorification of royalty, it rehearses in a particularly graphic way the victory of the house of David over the house of Saul.

Look again at the characteristic language and background of the story in 2 Samuel 9. David inquires whether there is still anyone left (*nôtar*) of the house of Saul. There is, and this remnant is Mephibosheth, the lame son of Jonathan. Now although David acts in this chapter to restore Saul's lands to Mephibosheth, the emphasis concerning his showing *hesed*, lovingkindness, to Mephibosheth is clearly on allowing him "always to eat at the king's table." "You shall *eat at my table always;* your master's son *shall always eat at my table;* so Mephibosheth *was eating at David's table,* like one of the king's sons; for he *was eating always at the king's table*" (vv. 7, 10, 11, 13). Moreover, even when David commands Ziba to work the land for Mephibosheth, it is "so that your master's son may have bread to eat" (v. 10). David is the one to whom God promised in 2 Samuel 7: "I will build you a house. Your house and your kingdom shall be made sure for ever before me" (vv. 11, 16). Because God took his steadfast love (*hesed*) from Saul (v. 15) and chose David, David is now in a position to give bread to the one who is left (*nôtar*) of Saul's house, to the one who "came to David and did obeisance" (*wayyištaḥû:* vv. 6, 8).

In a previous volume, I discussed how many details within 1 Sam. 2:27–36 find a glorious fulfillment in the establishment of David's kingdom here in 2 Samuel. I want here to describe how the closing verse of this oracle, 1 Sam. 2:36, finds its fulfillment in the demeaning situation of Mephibosheth as 2 Samuel 9 describes it. What first leads us to identify Mephibosheth as a royal embodiment of this fallen priestly house is his designation as "someone left of Saul's house" (*'ăšer nôtar lᵉbêt šā'ûl*)" (2 Sam. 9:1). Such language echoes the language of the oracle in 1 Samuel 2, which ends, "And everyone who is left (*hannôtar*) in your house" (v. 36). Although we find the construction, *nôtār*, "someone or something left (over)" elsewhere in the History, 1 Sam. 2:36 and 2 Sam. 9:1 are the only texts that speak of the "remnant of a house," the first ostensibly referring to a priestly house and the second to a royal one.[16]

Moreover, in 1 Sam. 2:36 this remnant "shall come to bow down (*lᵉhištaḥwôt*) before [the faithful priest]"; the narrator also says of the lame son of Jonathan, "Mephibosheth came to David and did obeisance" (*wayyištaḥû:* vv. 6, 8). I discussed above how consistently the History employs this verb of servitude, *hištaḥwāh*. It is noteworthy, therefore, that the use of this verb in 1 Sam. 2:36 is the only instance in the History before the onset of kingship in Israel where a human being is so reverenced. I am suggesting that its usage here reinforces the numerous royal dimensions that are everywhere present within the oracle.

A final indication that 1 Samuel 2 finds a narrative fulfillment in 2 Samuel 9 is the prior text's emphasis on the fallen's remnant's servile position in relation to the eating of bread. 1 Sam. 2:36 continues, "he shall come to do obeisance for a piece of silver or a loaf of bread, and shall say, 'Put me, I pray you, in one of the priest's places, that I may eat a morsel of bread.'" Admittedly, there is a difference of emphasis between the fallen Elide and the lame Mephibosheth: the oracle has the Elide coming to the faithful priest and requesting food to eat at one of the priest's places, whereas in 2 Samuel 9 it is David who takes the initiative. Nevertheless, the condition of subservience symbolized by the remnant's dependence upon his successor even for the basic necessities of food unites both situations in a remarkable way.

If we have any doubt that our look backwards to 1 Samuel 2 provides an appropriate context for what takes place in 2 Samuel 9, we need only look forward to the end of 2 Kings 25, which provides a proper conclusion to 2 Samuel 9—a climax that surprises us in very much the same way as both 2 Samuel 16 and 19 and 2 Samuel 21 do through their successive revelations about the background and aftermath of 2 Samuel 9. The passage in

2 Kings allows us to put 2 Samuel 9 in proper ideological perspective and to hear the voice of the Deuteronomist shaping Mephibosheth's situation in order to comment upon David's. The reader is surprised, first, by David's reversal of previous decisions affecting Mephibosheth (2 Samuel 16 and 19), then by the narrator's late revelation of David's decision that brought about this remnant of Saul's house in the first place (2 Samuel 21), and, finally, by the Deuteronomist's climactic depiction, in 2 Kings 25:27–30, of the remnant of David's house, Jehoiachin, as little different from the remnant of Saul's house, Mephibosheth.

Is There Anyone Left of the House of David?

A hint that what happens to Mephibosheth, the remnant of the house of Saul in 2 Samuel 9, is compositionally connected to what happens to Jehoiachin, the remnant of the house of David in 2 Kings 25, lies in the immediate linguistic and thematic similarities between the two passages, as intermediate and final fulfillments respectively, of God's prophetic—and the Deuteronomist's programmatic—oracle in 1 Samuel 2. As 2 Samuel 9's emphasis on Mephibosheth's eating bread continually (*tāmîd*) at the king's table looks backward to the servile remnant of Eli's house requesting to be given "one of the priest's places that I may eat a morsel of bread" (1 Sam. 2:36), it also looks forward to the last words in the History, whereby the Deuteronomist provides the reader with one final graphic image of the conquered remnant of David's house, Jehoiachin: "And every day of his life he ate bread regularly (*tāmîd*) at the king's table, and for his allowance, a regular (*tāmîd*) allowance was given him by the king, every day a portion as long as he lived" (2 Kings 25:29–30). Once we realize that the History employs the phrase, "to eat continually," (*'ākal tāmîd*) only in 2 Sam. 9:7, 10, and 13 and 2 Kings 25:29, and combine this fact with the thematic similarities between the situations surrounding both passages, there is little reason, I believe, to doubt deliberate intentions—be they called editorial, authorial, or whatever—to fashion the details of the larger history in such a way as to have the affairs of Mephibosheth comment on the affairs of Jehoiachin, and vice versa. The details of what happens to the house of Saul and the details of what happens to the house of David are ideological carriers and reciprocal models for each other.

Look at the thematic similarities that tie together these beginning, intermediate, and final instances of the History's meditation on the rise and fall of houses. At the start, the LORD's building of a sure priestly house results in a kind of perpetual remnant ("every one who is left in your house") continually subservient to the "faithful priest" whom the LORD has raised up (1 Sam. 2:36). We then see this priestly situation as an uncanny precursor not only of the situation involving Samuel and Saul but more especially of that between the house of Saul and the house of David: Mephibosheth stands in relation to David very much as the remnant of the house of Eli stood in relation to the faithful priest of the LORD's sure house. But the story does not end simply with the glorification of David's house, because, in perhaps the History's most perceptive move, the fate of Saul's house—and of Mephibosheth as remnant and permanent emblem of that fate—turns out to be a narrative model of what will befall David's house as well, with Jehoiachin as remnant and final emblem of *its* fate. In my beginning is my end, T. S. Eliot might have David say.

Yet there is more to this homology of houses than the linguistic and thematic ties that bind their occupants, even after the structures themselves have collapsed. What really clarifies the matter of authorial or compositional intentions to compare these houses—especially despite the almost overwhelming differences between them—is the History's attention to detail whereby the continuing vicissitudes of one house will mirror and model those of the other. To see what David's initial act of beneficence to Mephibosheth means in terms of larger ideological issues, we need to see how David's changing position toward Mephibosheth foreshadows God's toward the house of David. What David simply calls "kindness" (*ḥesed*) in 2 Sam. 9:1 and 7, he calls "the kindness of God" in 9:3. David, after the fall of the house of Saul, will be shown "graciously" dealing with Mephibosheth very much as God will be shown "graciously" dealing with David before the collapse of his house.

For the Sake of David My Servant

A review of David's changing relations toward Mephibosheth first shows the king restoring Saul's lands to him and giving him a place at the royal table: what had apparently gone to Saul's *servant* Ziba, David now returns to Jonathan's son; David becomes Mephibosheth's provider and protector (2 Samuel 9). But then, on Ziba's accusations of Mephibosheth's disloyalty to him, David gives Saul's lands back to Mephibosheth's *servant* Ziba, who immediately does obeisance (*hištaḥwāh*) before his lord, David (2 Sam. 16:1–4). The narrator next recounts how and why David offers to restore half of Saul's land to Mephibosheth, who surprisingly refuses the offer (2 Sam. 19:25–31). The final entry in the story of David's variable relations with Mephibosheth relates the circumstances of the Gibeonite revenge that began this association between lord and servant (2 Samuel 21). The present overall arrangement of events concerning Mephibosheth is a narrative expression of the idea that one's end is one's beginning.

Now if there is anything that helps the reader understand the constancy of David toward Mephibosheth in the midst of all this variability, it is David's explanations at the beginning of the story, "that I may show him kindness for Jonathan's sake" and "do not fear, for I will show you kindness for the sake of your father Jonathan" (2 Sam. 9:1, 7) and the narrator's corroborating statement at the end, "But the king spared Mephibosheth, the son of Saul's son Jonathan, because of the oath of the LORD (*ᶜal šᵉbuᶜat YHWH*) between them, between David and Jonathan the son of Saul" (2 Sam. 21:7). Mephibosheth's continued existence, however reduced and subservient it may be, testifies to David's and the LORD's continuing *ḥesed* or kindness toward him. A permanent reminder of the LORD's rejection, Mephibosheth is a continual sign of his kindness also.

Consider, then, the changing fortunes of the house of David as the History will narrate them: the vicissitudes of David's house, as different from Saul's as master is from slave, seem mysteriously to blend into those of Saul. They share a trajectory in which lord becomes servant, and, throughout it all, the motivation behind the LORD's treatment of David's descendants sounds like that behind David's treatment of Jonathan's son. David's "for the sake of (*baᶜabûr*) Jonathan" turns into God's "for the sake of (*lᵉmaᶜan*) David."

The sins of David's son Solomon provoke God to declare, "I will surely tear the kingdom from you and give it to *your servant*. Yet for the sake of (*lᵉmaᶜan*) David *your father* I will not do it in your days" (1 Kings 11:11–12). We recall that all the land of Saul was twice in the hands of his servant Ziba, and twice restored (either all or in part) to Mephibosheth (2 Sam. 9:7, 9; 16:4; 19:30). We also recall that the explanation for these acts of kindness toward Mephibosheth was "for the sake of (*baᶜabûr*) *your father Jonathan*" (2 Sam. 9:7) and "because of the oath of the LORD (*ᶜal šᵉbuᶜat YHWH*) between David and Jonathan" (2 Sam. 21:7). In both cases, kindness toward a son which acts against a servant's interests— David's restorative action in behalf of Jonathan's son Mephibosheth against his servant Ziba, and God's delaying tactics in behalf of David's son Solomon and against the interests of Solomon's servant, Jeroboam—is authoritatively explained to be "on account of your father." Moreover, in 1 Kings 11 the tribe of Judah will remain under the control of David's house in spite of Solomon's sins; once again, the LORD promises this "for the sake of (*lᵉmaᶜan*) David my servant" (1 Kings 11:32, 34). Thereafter, when the LORD refuses to destroy Davidic rule or even Judah itself, the motive given, despite Abijam's and Jehoram's sins or Hezekiah's righteousness, is always "for the sake of (*lᵉmaᶜan*) David [my servant]" (1 Kings 15:5; 2 Kings 8:19; 19:34; 20:6).

By the time we get to Jehoiachin, who "did what was evil in the sight of the LORD" (2 Kings 24:9), the LORD's rescue of Judah and preservation of the house of David, divine actions that the reader (and Israel) have grown accustomed to expect "for the sake of David my servant," do not occur, and we are left with an exiled Jehoiachin, who becomes a Mephibosheth writ large in the last sentence of the History. Even though the house of David lasted for centuries and the house of Saul only for decades, and despite the enduring glories of one and the permanent shame of the other, the perspective of the History is that these royal houses are remarkably similar over the long view, that is to say, as determined by the two-edged "kindness of the LORD."

One result of this transformation of Mephibosheth into Jehoiachin is that David is now replaced by the king of Babylon. Hovering over both great kings is the omnipotence of God, who, in spite of the free will of his more powerful creatures, uses their actions to achieve his own purposes. Whatever we may suppose David's motivations to have been, whether generally throughout his career or specifically in his decisions concerning Saul's house, and however our suppositions might color perceptions of David's character, Sternberg's apt dictum about the LORD as creator of plot in biblical narrative is pertinent: the Deuteronomist seems to be telling the reader that Mephibosheth will live not only because this suits David's purposes, but especially because it suits God's, who wants the beginning of the house of David to foreshadow its end.

Finally, the History credits Moses with the first use of the narrative formula in which the LORD deals graciously with sons for the sake of their fathers. Moses explained that Israel would possess the land for this reason: "Not because of your righteousness or the uprightness of your heart are you going in to possess the land, but that [the LORD] may confirm the word which he swore to your fathers" (Deut. 9:5). What was true for Israel's occupying and remaining in the land will hold true in plans for regaining it. The king of Babylon and Jehoiachin may have succeeded David and Mephibosheth, yet in the last analysis, the players are God and Judah, who replace both sets within the social dimensions of the History. At the end, Judah in Babylon embodies the "lovingkindness of the LORD" and his long awaited justice at one and the same time; this exiled nation is *hannôtar,* the living remnant that now suffers "the pangs of dispriz'd love" as it once enjoyed "the law's delay."

From David's Kindness to Syria's Servitude (10:1–19)

After the provocative and multivoiced presentation of Mephibosheth in chapter 9, chapter 10 comes as something of an anticlimax. Relating the circumstances leading up to David's defeat of Ammon and Syria, this chapter not only looks backwards to the summary account in chapter 8, it also prepares for the coming account in chapters 11 and 12 that deal with David's murder of Uriah during battle with Ammon and with that crime's effect upon David's house. The bridge between what precedes and what follows is formed by the loving kindness with which David begins the chapter ("And David said, 'I will show kindness [*'e^{ce}śeh ḥesed*] with Hanun, the son of Nahash, as his father showed kindness to me'" [v. 2]) and the servitude of Hadadezer and his royal vassals by which the narrator ends it ("And when all the kings who were servants of Hadadezer saw that they had been defeated by Israel, they made peace with Israel, and became subject to them" [v. 19a]).

After This

Chronology is the most obvious problem that confronts the reader of chapter 10. The chapter begins with the temporal marker, "after this (*wayhî 'aḥ^{a}rê kēn*)," which locates specific acts or events in some sort of chronological sequence.[17]

The occurrence of this phrase at the beginning of 10:1 indicates that what follows in the chapter itself follows upon David's gracious acts toward Mephibosheth in chapter 9. At the same time, the content of chapter 10 clearly indicates that what occurs within it is to be understood as resulting in the state of affairs described much earlier in chapter 8, namely, how "the Syrians became servants to David and brought tribute" (8:6). How does one make sense of these opposing directions in the text?

One way to understand the book's overall chronological orientation is to build upon the idea, suggested above, that events in the account of the Gibeonite revenge in chapter 21 are to be understood as having occurred *before* David's reinstatement of Mephibosheth in chapter 9. Using the occurrences of *wayhî 'aḥ^{a}rê kēn* as guidelines in this regard, I want to suggest further that 2 Samuel's plot is best distinguished from its story by seeing 2 Samuel 8 as a summary account of David's entire career as servant of the LORD and lord of those nations that were to become his servants or vassals. It follows, then, that not just chapter 10 but everything that follows the summary in chapter 8 belongs before it chronologically as the filling in of narrative detail. Thus we should not be surprised that the events of chapter 10 culminate in chapter 8; all the events that follow chapter 8 in the book precede it in a similar way. If chapter 10 contains details about how certain nations became David's vassals, the chapters to follow will provide a more comprehensive—and corrective—account of an even more important issue, how David, in addition to paying him tribute, otherwise served the LORD.

The "after this" in 2:1 separates the events in 2 Samuel 1 from those that follow in chapters 2–7: how David gets settled in Jerusalem and gets promised a permanent house. Then, "after this" in 8:1 is a global introduction to a summary account of David's career in matters of tribute, as international lord and loyal servant of the LORD. After chapter 9 narrates the Mephibosheth affair, the formula in 10:1 introduces David's affair with Bathsheba, and its aftermath, followed by the same phrase in 13:1, introducing the history of Absalom in chapters 13–20. The story of Absalom is neatly divided into two parts: concerning his conflict with Amnon in chapters 13–14 and concerning his revolt in chapters 15–20. We notice that "after this" in 15:1 nicely separates these two phases of Absalom's career. Introductory "after this" occurs finally in 21:18; we notice here that there is still (or once again) war with the Philistines, and also that, so far along in the book, we are still (or once again) at a specific point in the story that precedes the narrator's summary account in 2 Samuel 8.

Apart from these chronological considerations, it is not an easy matter to situate 2 Samuel 10 within its literary context. It is true that David shows *ḥesed* to Hanun because of his father Nahash, just as in 2 Samuel 9 David showed *ḥesed* to Mephibosheth for the sake of his father Jonathan. It is also true that David consoles (*nāḥēm*) Hanun after the death of his father (10:2, 3) just as he will console Bathsheba after the death of their son (12:24). Nevertheless, there is not much to say about the obviously unfair, but perhaps understandable, interpretation that the Ammonite princes give to the consoling servants which David sends (10:3), nor do I know why so much that follows in the chapter happens by halves.

In the initial rebuff of David, his servants are humiliated when Hanun "shaved off half the beard of each and cut their garments in half" (v. 4). Also, the battle accounts in the chapter proceed by divisions of two. The Ammonites at the city gate and the Syrians in the open country (v. 8) cause Joab to divide his army in two, under his and his brother's direction (vv. 9–12). After the Ammonites and Syrians flee, and Joab returns to Jerusalem (vv. 13), a second battle ensues between the Syrians, now divided into eastern and western troops (v. 16), and Israel, now led by David himself. A clear narrative purpose for all these halvings—if there is one—is not obvious.

What is clear, however, is that by the end of chapter 10, just before the narrator, at long last, gives readers their first unambiguous glimpse into the heart and soul of David, everything has gone David's way: Syria and its vassals are cowed (10:19), and David is set to demolish Ammon (11:1). The Deuteronomist is now set to dismantle from within what the story has so far mostly exposed from without: the glorious house of David, lord of nations and servant of the LORD.

·5·

MESSENGERS
(11:1–12:31)

Fame, if not double-faced is double-mouthed,
And with contrary blast proclaims most deeds;
On both his wings, one black, the other white,
Bears greatest names in his wild airy flight.
(John Milton, *Samson Agonistes*)

Kings or Messengers

It may be that there is no more deliciously ambiguous verse in all the History than 2 Sam. 11:1: do "kings" (*mᵉlākîm*) or "messengers" (*mal'ākîm*) go forth in the spring of the year? The question is an ancient one, for early textual witnesses already testify both to the widespread presence of "messengers," indicated by an aleph in the disputed word, and also to "kings," indicated by the absence of the aleph.[1] It is commonly assumed that one must make a choice here, whether on textual, literary-historical, or other grounds, and it is not difficult to mount a defense of either alternative.

Look first at some suggestive reasons why many ancient Hebrew manuscripts should have "kings" (*mlkym*) rather than "messengers" (*ml'kym*) in this verse. In terms of the immediate story, the reference to kings going forth (to battle) sets up an ironic contrast between the beginning and end of the verse, that is, between what normally takes place at this time of the year on one hand, and this particular instance on the other, when "David was remaining at Jerusalem" (v. 1). This verse signifies that David, who has been a hands-on king, now becomes a stay-at-home, one who conducts military affairs at a distance. Had he been where the military action was, David would never have seen Bathsheba when he did, and the history of the house of David might have been different. In a word, when we construe "kings" at the beginning, the verse progresses toward an abruptly forceful climax that clearly introduces what follows.

The story in chapter 11 goes on to reinforce this narrative raising-of-eyebrows over David's domesticity when it reports Uriah's pointed response to David, "The ark and Israel and Judah dwell in booths [or "at Succoth"]; and my lord Joab and the servants of my lord are camping in the open field; shall I then go to my house, to eat and to drink, and to lie with my wife?" (v. 11). Uriah's subsequent willingness to eat and drink to excess in *David's* house (v. 13) surely signifies that sleeping with Bathsheba is the crucial issue, yet just as significant in Uriah's words is the contrast between his stated devotion to God and country and David's position, who, while all Israel is encamped in battle, is content not only to eat and drink in his own house, but also to have slept with the wife of one of the men he had sent into battle—so Bathsheba remains the crucial issue in respect to David also.

It is not just the David-Bathsheba affair that argues for the customary going forth of "kings" in verse 1: the larger story line later on makes a point of justifying David's decisions not to go forth to battle, as kings normally do. During Absalom's rebellion, "David sent forth (*šālah*) the army. The king had said to the people, 'I also will definitely go forth (*yāṣo' 'ēṣē'*) with you.' But the men said, 'You shall not go forth (*lo' tēṣē'*). For if we flee, they will not care about us, for now there are ten thousand such as we; therefore it is better than you send (*šālah*) us help from the city.' The king said to them, 'Whatever seems best to you I will do.'" (18:2–4). Here David is shown remaining at home in the city because of the counsel of his men. And further in the story, David's narrow escape from death at the hands of Ishbibenob even causes David's men to swear, "You shall not go forth any more (*lo' tēṣē' ᶜôd*) with us into battle, lest you quench the lamp of Israel" (21:17). Despite Israel, in the beginning, wanting their kings to go forth like those of other nations, there seems to have arisen a tradition about David that foolish kings went forth where even angels (*mal'ākîm*) feared to tread. At any rate, David's behavior in chapter 11 is in contrast with that of other kings: they normally go forth, but he remains at home.[2]

Another reason why "kings" ought to go forth in 11:1 centers around the overall distribution of "kings" and "messengers" throughout the rest of the History: kings are often said to go forth (*yāṣā'*), but apart from the instance of *mal'āk* here in 11:1, messengers never do. Indeed, the story of Israel's romance with kingship begins with Israel's insistence that they have a king who *does* go forth: when Samuel counsels them against the having of kings, they insist, "No! but we will have a king over us, that we may be like all the nations, and that our king may govern us and go forth (*yāṣā'*) before us and fight our battles" (1 Sam. 8:19–20). The subsequent history shows many instances when kings, whether Israelite or not, either go forth or, for various reasons, are counseled not to.[3] The manifold activities of messengers throughout the History seem to make their going forth in 11:1 possible—but hardly as probable as the going forth of kings.

Nevertheless, there is much to be said for the going forth of messengers in 11:1. For one thing, a contrast in this verse between adventuresome kings and a domestic David clearly sets up the statement about what David *did* do: he sent (*šālaḥ*) Joab, his servants, and all Israel to ravage (*šāḥat*) the Ammonites and besiege Rabbah. Precisely because "David was remaining in Jerusalem" (v. 1), he is constrained often to act at a distance throughout the chapter by sending messengers, who act or perform as his mouthpiece and his agent. David's messengers seize Bathsheba in verse 4, and his messenger is to return to Joab and encourage him in verse 25. This is the messenger whom Joab has just used to convey information to the king that the murder of Uriah had been accomplished. All in all, there are five references to messenger(s) in 2 Samuel 11 (in addition to the disputed occurrence in verse 1), an unusually high frequency when one looks at the distribution of *mal'āk* in the History.[4] Thus, the chapter's subsequent emphasis on messengers as the means by which things get done is a plausible argument for the going forth of messengers in its opening verse.

When we also realize that the most typical action involving messengers—within the History and in the very nature of the case—is *to send them* (*šālaḥ*), even the progression of verbs in 11:1 favors the presence of "messengers" in this verse: "In the spring of the year, when [the] messengers go forth, David *sent* . . . "[5] Just as David's initial decision to communicate and act at a distance sets up the special frequency of *mal'āk* in this chapter, that decision also explains why *šālaḥ* occurs more often in 2 Samuel 11 (twelve times) than anywhere else in the History.[6] Because David remained in the city and within his own house, his emissaries roam the chapter to accomplish his purposes; the story is about how David continually sends—or is sent—commands, information, and people. The period covered by chapter 11, therefore, is precisely a time when *messengers* go forth.

What are we to do in the face of such textual and compositional ambivalence? This verse, I would suggest, is too intricately ambiguous to be the result simply of textual or editorial misadventure, and, consequently, one does not have to choose between kings and messengers, because both meanings hover over the verse from the start—whatever one may decide about original orthography. The verse clearly doubles back on itself in a marvelous display of narrative virtuosity: at a time when kings go forth, David did not, making it a time, therefore, when messengers must go forth; at a time when messengers go forth, David, remaining in Jerusalem, sent Joab, his servants and all Israel to ravage Ammon. I suppose this circular progression of meanings may have happened by chance, but almost everything we know about this chapter and the History conspires against a merely happy accident.

One is certainly justified in raising questions about orthography: is the aleph of *mal'āk* original to the text, as the predominant Masoretic testimony has it (therefore, "messengers") or ought it to be absent, as many Hebrew manuscripts and most ancient versions testify (therefore, "kings")? If there is conscious wordplay here, as I am suggesting, then which word was written down to suggest the other? As outlined above, the distribution of verbs attached to the two nouns throughout the History indicates that the paronomasia is probably based upon a more familiar construction of kings going forth being turned on its head, as it were, through this story about how messengers went forth when one king decided not to. Nevertheless, we cannot rule out an alternative, that the wordplay itself (kings/messengers going forth) was well known, even traditional, at the time of its usage in this narrative. Whatever may be the case, the fact that kings often go forth in the History, but messengers only here in 11:1, suggests that the *lectio difficilior* (*mal'ākîm*) ought to be orthographically retained, even as its dual reference is to be emphasized. Indeed, the story in chapters 11–12 is very much a meditation on messengers and their messages, as well as a reflection of the Deuteronomist's larger message about King David and his house. And of all the messages in this story about David, Nathan's will turn out to be very much like the Deuteronomist's in miniature. But for now, it may be helpful to spend a moment on the role that specific context plays in the reader's production of their meaning.

Artful Story or Artificial Context

Modern readings of chapters 11–12 tend to praise the quality of the story, even as some treatments of 2 Samuel struggle with the placement of that larger unity (2 Samuel 9–20: called, variously, the Court History or the Succession Narrative) whose critical stance toward David the Bathsheba affair most obviously and mysteriously initiates. Thus, while discourse-oriented scholars, often inspired by the groundbreaking article of Perry and Sternberg in 1968, as well as by Sternberg's revision of it in 1985, emphasize the story's artfulness by highlighting the many gaps by which it provokes the reader to reflective constructions of meaning, many source-oriented readers still wrestle with the apparently artless and incoherent manner in which it has been contextualized within the larger story line of the History.[7] Given the abundant and valuable analyses of Sternberg and others of the inner workings of chapter 11, I will simply mention some of their many insights before concentrating rather on the central question of the story's supposed contextual incoherence. Along the way, I hope to provide a proper context for the story's celebrated gaps. How do these particular gaps function within the Deuteronomist's larger speech plan?

Here then are some useful details about chapter 11 that modern readers emphasize and that illustrate how an artful story requires its readers' participation—and increases their pleasure as well. To begin with, attentive readers have come to realize that since Bathsheba is in the process of purifying herself from uncleanness, probably menstruation, when David lies with her (v. 4), what he earlier saw from his roof—a woman bathing (v. 2)—is simply being specified now by the narrator as ritual ablutions. This readerly inference conveniently establishes David's paternity and removes any possibility of Uriah's role in the pregnancy that Bathsheba announces to David in verse 5. Another insight proceeds from interpreting David's command for Uriah to go home and "wash your feet" (v. 8) as a probable euphemism for "go sleep with Bathsheba," an obvious attempt of David's to shift the public and private perception of the child's paternity from his own to Uriah's. Finally, as Perry and Sternberg—and others following them—have so provocatively shown, the story is filled with multiple gaps that force the wary reader to reflect upon what is supposed to be going on in the story.

Of these and many other matters by which readers, both modern and ancient, have illustrated the literary quality and subtlety of the David and Bathsheba account, the central issue of the story's multiple gaps—and readers' struggles with closing them—promises to give us the best access into what Bakhtin would call the *speech plan* of the history of David and of the royal history that forms its illuminating context.

Source-oriented readers who see chapters 11–12 as part of the so-called Court History (9–20) are fairly unanimous in recognizing this account of the second half of David's career as the prose masterpiece of biblical narrative. In this view, they are in agreement with discourse-oriented scholars like Sternberg, who have demonstrated, with superb literary detail, what genetic biblicists have tended only to assert, through sweeping statements about the sober objectivity of a supposedly eyewitness account. Where scholars differ is over the contextual coherence of the larger story of David's downfall that chapters 11–12 initiate.

On one hand, genetic scholars tend to struggle with the abrupt change of fortune that separates 2 Samuel 11–1 Kings 2 from what precedes it in 1 Samuel 16–2 Samuel 10. If the Court History is subtle and superb in its literary crafting, its black-on-white placement is scarcely credible to some biblicists. So Van Seters will remove the entire Court History from the Deuteronomist's masterful narrative because, however brilliant both gem and setting are individually, they clash in tandem and mar the historiographic and ideological unity of the entire narrative.[8] On the other hand, a discourse-oriented reader like Sternberg will view the location of chapter 11 within the composition of the book as artfully pinpointing "the where and why of David's change of fortune" seen "within the structure and progress of the text as a whole."[9] Is, then, the *placement* of this pivotal story of David and Bathsheba a question of art or artifice?

So the burden of my treatment of chapters 11–12 will be on the function of the, by now, well-known gaps that are filled or unfillable in these chapters; I need not repeat in detail what Perry and Sternberg have already demonstrated in brilliant fashion, namely, that 2 Samuel 11 is an ancient instance that illustrates the general structure of literary texts: such artful constructions normally demand multiple systems of gap-filling. Rather, I want to discuss the *specific* function of the filling or not of *specific* gaps in this particular story within its own particular context. Why are chapters 11–12 so pivotal in the writing of the history of David specifically, and of the royal history of Israel more generally? We shall see how a main function of 11–12 is to close, in a particularly effective way, gaps that have plagued the reader all along: who *is* David and why did God promise him an everlasting house?

Of course, such questions are simply responses to a message that comes to us through the words of a narrator and characters, both of them messengers who, as Nabal said about David's messengers, "come from I do not know where" (1 Sam. 25:11) and who speak in behalf of an authorial voice or voices. Fortunately, chapters 11–12 pivot around the play and place of messengers who themselves act as models for the Deuteronomist's own messengers, and who provide clues that help us fill out some wider gaps in the History: what is its overall speech plan, and what might be the historical situation to which it is but a response? We need to see how and why the sending of messengers and their messages in chapters 11–12 helps to illuminate these chapters as the absolute core of the story of David and the house that God built for him.

Messengers in Chapters 11–12

The obvious thing about messengers in the History is how they typically act and are acted upon: messengers tend to be sent (*šālaḥ*) by someone in order to speak or declare a message.[10] Nevertheless, a messenger is also an agent who works or acts in behalf of a sender; this basic function of a *mal'āk* is graphically seen in the cognate word, *mᵉlā'kāh*, which is a common word in Hebrew for "work or occupation." So messengers, besides being distant communicators, are also agents who act or work at a distance for their dispatchers. Throughout the History, then, we read about messengers—whether from God or from humans—who sit, reach out, touch, watch, prophesy, salute, take, bring back, spy out, besiege, smite, destroy, encourage, discern, invite, inquire, and so forth.

When we examine the activities of the particular messengers in chapters 11–12, we also find this general pattern: messengers function both as communicators and as agents of those who send them. Joab commands his messenger to speak to David (v. 19); this messenger comes and declares all that Joab sent him to declare (v. 22); his words are directly quoted by the narrator (v. 23); David in turn commands him to return with a message for Joab (v. 25); and Joab sends messengers requesting David to leave Jerusalem for the front (12:27). In addition, messengers act at a distance as David's agents: David sends messengers—Joab, his servants, and all Israel—to ravage the Ammonites and to besiege Rabbah (11:1); David sends messengers to take and bring Bathsheba to him that he might sleep with her (v. 4); and David commands his messenger to return to Joab to encourage or strengthen him (*wᵉḥazzᵉqēhû*: v. 25).

David's decision to remain in Jerusalem (11:1–12:29) results, then, in a veritable profusion of messengers that are even more numerous than those who are explicitly referred to as "messengers" within these chapters. I have already emphasized the general picture: people and messages are dispatched (*šālaḥ*) more often in 2 Samuel 11 than in any other chapter in the History.[11] There are four distinct groups or individuals who are explicitly called messengers in 11–12: first, Joab, his servants, and all Israel (v. 1); then those who take Bathsheba to David (v. 4); then the one who brings news of Uriah's death to David and who returns with David's response to Joab (vv. 18, 19, 22, 23, 25); and finally, the one Joab sends to David in 12:27. Beyond these, chapters 11–12 are heavily populated with virtual emissaries who are sent by various characters to communicate or act in their behalf. In addition to the explicitly designated messengers in these chapters, there are six additional groups or individuals who function as messengers: the person(s) David sends to inquire about the identity of the woman he has seen bathing (v. 3); the one(s) Bathsheba sends to David to declare her pregnancy (v. 5); the individual(s) David sends to Joab in order to recall Uriah (v. 6); most poignantly, Uriah himself, whom David proposes to send (v. 12) and actually does send, carrying his own death sentence (v. 14); those whom David sends to fetch Bathsheba after Uriah's death (v. 27); and the prophet Nathan, whom God sends to announce punishment of David and his house (12:1) and to proclaim Solomon's new name, Jedidiah (12:25). It is fair to say that there are more messengers, explicit and implicit, in chapters 11–12 than anywhere else in the History.

Moreover, when we look at how these implicit messengers act in chapters 11–12, we find them doing just what explicit messengers do throughout the History. As Ahaziah will send messengers to *inquire* (*drš*) of Baalzebub about his own sickness (2 Kings 1:2, 3, 16), so David sends (messengers) to inquire (*drš*) about the woman (11:3). As the messenger sent by Joab to David will *declare* (*higgîd*) and *say* (*'āmar*) (11:22–23) and as countless messengers do throughout the History, so Bathsheba sends (messengers) to declare (*higgîd*) to David and say (*'āmar*) (11:5). As Saul sent the pieces of his oxen throughout all the territory of Israel "by the hand of messengers," (1 Sam.11:7), so David sends his letter to Joab "by the hand of Uriah [his messenger]" (11:14). As Joab will send messengers to David to gather together (*'āsap*) the rest of the people for battle (12:27–28), so David sends (messengers) to bring (*'āsap*) Bathsheba to his house (11:27). And as the LORD sends his messenger to speak or say God's words elsewhere in the History, so the LORD here sends the prophet Nathan (his messenger) to speak (*'āmar*) his words (12:1).[12]

Messages and Their Variety

The profusion of messengers that we have been discussing leads us to explore the various ways in which characters convey their messages in chapters 11–12. We find that reported speech is either written or oral; whispered or clearly spoken; highly coded to say more than the obvious or else obviously straightforward; innocent or manipulative; conveyed directly or, most of the time, through a messenger; emphasizing explanation or lacking it; and forming informational gaps or filling them.

The most obvious feature of the reported speech in these chapters flows from the story's emphasis on messengers. Roughly three-fourths of all the reported speech in 11–12 concerns communication at a distance: the sending of messengers, the messages that are conveyed by them, and the direct responses to such messages.[13]

When we look at the many distanced messages that pervade chapter 11 and that appear to lead up to the pivotal message of Nathan in chapter 12, we are reminded of the analogous compositional situation in 1 Samuel 9–10. As the many merely human "prophecies" of 1 Samuel 9 led up to the crucial prophecies of God's prophet Samuel in 1 Samuel 10,[14] so here the many varied messages that scatter themselves throughout 2 Samuel 11 lead up to the critical message that the LORD sends David through his prophet Nathan in 2 Samuel 12. If 1 Samuel 9–10 was a meditation on the rights and duties of the prophet as they pertain to the rights and duties of the king (*mišpaṭ hannābî'* related to *mišpaṭ hammelek*), 2 Samuel 11–12 is a meditation on the modes and functions of messengers as they pertain to the rights and duties of kings (*mišpaṭ hammal'āk* related to *mišpaṭ ham-*

melek). It will turn out that *mišpaṭ hammal'āk* /*hammelek* and *mišpaṭ hannābî'* are both united in Nathan's confrontation with David.

What kinds of messages do messengers convey in chapter 11? We find straightforward or clear messages given in the form of statement (Bathsheba's "I am with child" [v. 5]), rhetorical question (David's messenger returning with "Is not this Bathsheba, the daughter of Eliam, the wife of Uriah the Hittite?" [v. 3]), and command (David's "Send me Uriah the Hittite" [v. 6] and his written command to Joab to murder Uriah [v. 15]). We find messages that are secret or highly coded in order either to exclude the *messenger* from the message's content or intent (as David's written message to Joab in verse 15 keeps Uriah in the dark, and the messages between David and Joab in verses 19–21 and 25 keep their messenger relatively ignorant of the crucial information conveyed within them) or else in order to keep the *receiver* of the message from initially discovering the message's true intent (as Nathan's parable in 12:1–4 draws David into a wrong conclusion about it). We find messages that differ in delivery from their formulation when dispatched (as, for example, the messenger's statement in 11:23–24 diverges in a number of ways from the message Joab gives him in verses 19–20). We find an explicitly written message like David's in verse 15, in contrast to those that are either obviously oral (like Nathan's messages in 12:1–4, 7–12 and the message about Bathsheba in 11:3) or else possibly written or oral (like most of the other messages in these chapters). We find messages that either wrongly anticipate the response of the receiver, as Joab's message in verses 15–20 does, or else successfully manipulate the receiver's response, as Nathan's parable does in 12:1–7. And most importantly, we find in these chapters messages that either help to form gaps in the receiver's mind, as Nathan's parable is intended to do, or fill up gaps in knowledge, as do Nathan's further message in 12:7–12 and the messages generally in chapters 11–12. This last contrast of messages—their ability to form or to fill a gap—helps greatly to put chapters 11–12 in proper context. In chapter 12, Nathan will form a gap in David's mind and then fill it, in a manner that mirrors the way in which the Deuteronomist, in chapter 11, will fill in a gap in readers' minds about David that previous chapters worked very hard to form.

Closing the Gap in Chapter 11

There are not many places in the Bible where a character's reputation is so suddenly and effectively demolished as in 2 Samuel 11, where the phrase, "character assassination" rather accurately expresses the double focus of the story: both David's character and the character Uriah are dispatched.

What makes so effective this sudden bursting of "the bubble reputation," which the author has allowed David to enjoy from the beginning, is its accomplishment amidst all the gaps in the story that commentators since the publication of Perry and Sternberg's famous article have been wont to emphasize. What does Uriah know of his wife's affairs? What does David believe about Uriah's knowledge of the adultery? Why does Joab carry out David's command to murder, but change the plan David had set out for accomplishing the act? Why does Joab's messenger fail to relate his message exactly as Joab had stipulated? And what do Joab's reference to Abimelech's being killed by a woman, and the chapter's emphasis on "approaching too close to the wall," have to do with the chapter's main concerns?[15]

Whether one believes that any of these gaps are capable of closure or not, the marvel of the story is that none of them detracts from the absolute clarity with which this chapter, like the next, answers for the reader the question David earlier asked of God, "Who am I, O LORD God, and what is my house, that thou hast brought me thus far?" (2 Sam. 7:18). It is *this gap* in the characterization of David, amidst David's ongoing successes and growing reputation, that has plagued the reader since 1 Samuel 16: why is David the man after God's own heart, and why is he portrayed from the start as a quintessential winner in the face of gigantic odds that, at the beginning, are personified in Goliath himself?

For Sternberg, the multiple systems of gap-filling which he finds in the David and Bathsheba story are a general feature of many literary texts, and have various functions that illustrate for him the constructive force of ambiguity in the reading process. Yet we can apply this useful insight into the inner workings of chapter 11 even to the *context* of the story line itself. This larger picture also involves a process of the forming and filling of gaps, but these gaps are much wider than and paradoxically remain unaffected by the local ones—resolved or irresolvable—that here in chapters 11–12 tend to slip by the lazy reader and challenge the attentive one. Gaps in messages have a way of tricking the unwary, as David will find out in chapter 12.

In chapter 11 there is nothing ambiguous about the fact of David's adultery, his unsuccessful attempt to render paternity ambiguous by bringing Uriah home to sleep with Bathsheba, and his murderous command, so cruelly placed in the hand of his messenger-victim. The story establishes David's guilt not by a privileged view into his thoughts or motivations but by a sober recitation of reported actions and reported speech (mostly messages) that either directly or indirectly indict David with unexcelled force. So when the chapter ends with the narrator's statement that "the thing that David had done was evil in the eyes of the LORD," readers already know this, even as they come to understand that the narrator's sober recitation of the affair has been far from disinterested.

Sternberg is certainly correct when he points out, in an important footnote, that "within the composition of the book, therefore, [chapter 11] is a central chapter in that it pinpoints the where and why of David's change of fortune."[16] This observation, however, helps to raise a further question that goes to the heart of the Deuteronomist's speech plan concerning the history of David's house specifically and Israel's generally: having pinpointed the why and wherefore of David's sudden change of fortune, what is the why and wherefore of the suddenness itself within the overall plan of the Deuteronomist? After all, at the center of the story of David we find something much more akin to the bursting of a bubble than to the relaxed deflation of a balloon. The tragic turn of events that follows chapters 11–12 is but a consequent reverberation of the explosive events of these earlier chapters. The success and adulation that have constantly accompanied David up to now were only questioned by the Deuteronomist's subtle hints, which, here or there, helped us to wonder whether there was more—or less— to David than met the eye. In previous chapters and a previous book, I have suggested some of these indirect challenges to the narrator's surface adulation of David.

But now the voice of the Deuteronomist is as extreme in its description of the fall of the house of David as it was in its building up. The following disintegration is, as it were, implosive, and flows from the sudden collapse of the narrator's overtly positive characterization of David. Whether David originally served God but now seriously fails him, or whether readers only now find out the kind of calculating and self-serving person David has always been, is perhaps one of those gaps in the story that must remain unresolved—in Sternberg's terms, a constructive ambiguity about the characterization of David. What *is* clear, however, is that chapter 11 offers readers a sudden flash of recognition about David that constitutes a turning point in his life: this sudden illumination *of* David is followed in chapter 12 by a moment of recognition *by* David that reflects the very turning point or pivot of the entire History. The core of the message of chapter 12 revolves around the revealing strategy of the prophet Nathan, the messenger God has sent to David. As the Uriah incident, in all its stark openness, is the moment of recognition for readers concerning the History's characterization of David, so Nathan's parable triggers that moment of recognition when David discovers that he has been found out and what his fate will be. In addition, God's message to David in the first part of chapter 12 (vv. 1–15), and its denouement in the death of David's son in the second part (vv. 16–25), will constitute that *anagnoresis* or *peripeteia* (technical terms normally used for the kinds of sudden illumination and cognitive turning point that *characters* experience in literature) by which readers, too, may suddenly perceive the overall vision and specific speech plan of the History. It is perhaps fitting to say that 2 Samuel 12 is the hermeneutic center of the entire royal history, as 1 Samuel 1–7 was its interpretive introduction.

The Scope of Nathan's Parable

At first glance, the story in chapter 12 is relatively clear: God is displeased with David and *sends* (*šālaḥ*) Nathan to him to deal with the situation. Given chapter 11's emissary emphases as I have described them, Nathan is God's *messenger*, and there are two possibilities about the message itself: (1) Nathan's parable in verses 1–4 and God's explanation of it in verses 7–12 are both part of God's message to David, the first intended by God to trick David into a self-condemning statement, and the second, God's detailed explanation of how this parable applies to David; or (2) God's words in verses 7–12 are supposed to represent the complete message God sent David, and the parable is simply Nathan's ploy to trick David into condemning himself and to soften him up for the impact of God's words in verses 7–12. Nothing in the story inclines us one way or the other in this regard. Still, either choice preserves the force of the story, and readers are carried along in the same direction, whichever possibility they choose. Nathan speaks his parable, and David takes it too literally, thus passing judgment on himself just before God does, by word (v. 7–12) and by action (vv. 15b–25).

Beneath the deceptive simplicity of this summary lies an account that is comprehensive enough to embrace the entire history of Israel. As Nathan tricks David into jumping to conclusions too precipitously, so a Deuteronomic voice tricks its audience into hastily condemning David—and paradoxically condemning themselves in the process. Here are some details about chapter 12 that contribute to its being as deceptive for readers as Nathan's parable is for David.

The parable is both spare and strange at the same time. Its plot line is simplicity itself: in a certain city there lives a rich man and a poor man. The rich man, who is unwilling to part with his own possessions, takes a ewe lamb from the poor man in order to act in behalf of a wayfarer. (It is unclear what the rich man does for the stranger.) The uncanny power of the parable lies in its dependence on words that are either rarely used in the History, or else so vaguely general in meaning that they can easily be applied to a variety of similar situations. Unusual words in the parable act as efficient checks upon any unrestrained application that might be based solely upon the vague generality both of its plot and of its more common words.

For example, *all* the players in the parable, rich man, poor man, wayfarer, and lamb, are designated by words that are rarely used in the History: ewe lamb (*kibesāh*) occurs only here in chapter 12, and its masculine form, *kebeś*, is never found in the History; two of the words used to designate the wayfarer (*hēlek* and *'ōreah*) are rare in form;[17] even a relatively common reference to "rich" and "poor" is conveyed by roots used but rarely in the History (*ro'š*, "poor" and *cāśîr*, "rich").[18] At the same time as all the principals are so uncommonly designated, the crucial action performed by the rich man in behalf of the wayfarer is only vaguely specified—not once but twice. What the rich man is unwilling to do for (*cāśāh le*) the wayfarer out of his own flocks, he does for him (*cāśāh le*) with the ewe lamb that he has taken from the poor man (v. 4). But what is it that he *does* with the ewe lamb? The taking itself is specified as to motivation (the rich man spared taking from his own flocks, and so had to take from the poor man) but not as to purpose (to do *what* for the wayfarer?). Why is Nathan's choice of words vivid in its designation of characters but vague in its description of actions? It matters not that Israelite readers might have immediately known what the rich man does for the wayfarer. The important thing is that the specific action is twice referred to only generally.

David's response (in verses 5–6), both wrong in reference and partially right in condemnation, continues the parable's vagueness even as it initiates an appropriate note of explanation. We know that David roundly condemns the rich man for taking the ewe lamb, yet the rich man's actions are no more specified in David's words than they were in the parable, even though David gives a reason for his condemnation of the man: "the man who had done this" (v. 5); "*because* he did this thing; *because* he did not spare [the poor man's ewe lamb]" (v. 6). Is David incorrect not only for mis-referencing the story itself, but perhaps also for directing his condemnation solely to the rich man and to his action of *not sparing*? Just how deeply does David's misunderstanding run?

The words of God in verses 7–12 and Nathan in verses 13–14 are authoritative interpretations of the parable and its consequences, and are characterized by their *largesse* in specifying action as well as offering explanation for the LORD's wrath. God indicates his own motivation through the use of "because," just as David did through his use of "because."[19] In a moment, I shall discuss the actions God specifies in applying the parable, but for now I want simply to indicate how David's assessment of the parable may be even more mistaken, and God's explanation of it much less transparent, than we commonly believe.

The words that Nathan uses to spring his trap on David illustrate the deceptive ambiguity that is tightly coiled within the parable. After David's indignant response in verses 5–6, Nathan accuses him: "You are the man (*hā'îš*)" (v. 7). But which man in the parable is Nathan talking about? David has roundly condemned "the man (*hā'îš*) who has done this thing" (v. 5), obviously referring to the rich man of Nathan's story. But does Nathan's accusation refer only to the man in the story to whom David is referring, or could Nathan be saying something more?

The question is important, because each of the human players in the parable is finally called *hā'îš* by Nathan: "the rich man (*lā'îš hecāšîr*)," "the poor man (*hā'îš hārō'š*)" and "the man who comes to him (*lā'îš habbā' 'ēlāyw*)" (v. 4).[20] We can reasonably suppose that these final formulations in verse 4 are important, since "the rich man" is earlier called "the rich [man] (*hecāšîr*)" and "the poor man" is earlier called "the poor [man] (*hārō'š*)" (vv. 2–3), that is, these adjectives are also used alone, that is, as substantives without the accompanying noun, "man." Similarly, the way-farer in verse 4 is first designated as "the one coming to him (*habbā' lô*)" and finally as "the *man* coming to him (*lā'îš habbā' 'ēlāyw*)." We see, then, how *hā'îš* can refer to any one of the three persons in the parable, the benefactor, recipient, or victim, but in David's misguided but partially accurate interpretation only to one person, the rich benefactor. The question, therefore, is this. Which of the men in the parable is Nathan identifying with David when the prophet says, "You are *the man*"? And when God gives *his* explanation of the parable, does he restrict his application simply to the rich man, as David did, or does he widen the scope of the parable to include not just the immediate context of chapter 11 but even the entire career of David?

Who Is the Rich Man?

We find out in verse 7 what we probably already suspected: Nathan's story is parabolic or allegorical, while David's mistake in verses 5–6 is to take it to be historiographic or literal. Wrong though David obviously is about the genre of Nathan's little tale, is David correct at least in seeing the rich man as its villain, just as we feel certain in seeing David as the villain of the parable's immediate context? There is much in the authoritative interpretations of God (vv. 7–12) and Nathan (vv. 13–14), and in the stark story of chapter 11, to support both condemnatory positions. What contextual features, formal or otherwise, confirm most readers' tendency to identify the rich man in the parable with David in the larger narrative?

If we look first at God's explanation of the parable in verses 7–12, it is obvious that the many wives of David (vv. 8, 11) and the one wife of Uriah

(vv. 9, 10) correspond to the (very many) flocks and herds of the rich man (vv. 2, 4) and the one ewe lamb of the poor man (vv. 3, 4). Also, the one animal owned by the poor man is feminine, *kibᵉśāh* (as we have said, the only lamb designated by this root in the History), and obviously corresponds to the wife of Uriah. Moreover, God specifies David's sin as one of *taking* (*lāqaḥ*) Uriah's wife as his own (vv. 9, 10) just as the rich man spared *taking* from his own flock and *took* the ewe lamb from the poor man (v. 4).

Comparing the parable in chapter 12 with the account in chapter 11 leads us to similar conclusions: the ewe lamb was "like a daughter (*kᵉbat*)" to the poor man (12:3), an obvious play on the very name and genealogy of Uriah's wife given in 11:3, "Bathsheba, the daughter of Eliam (*bat šebaᶜ bat 'elîᶜām*)"; the rich man's sin was to *take* (*lāqaḥ*) the ewe lamb (12:4), just as David "sent messengers and *took* (*lāqaḥ*) [Bathsheba]" (11:4); and *eating, drinking, and sleeping* all join the poor man and his ewe lamb in the parable (12:3), just as David's problem in chapter 11 involved Uriah's refusal to do the expected, that is, to *eat, drink, and sleep* with Bathsheba (11:11). Surely there can be little doubt that the context of Nathan's parable forces us to identify David with the rich man, Uriah with the poor man, and Bathsheba with the ewe lamb, and that the parable itself, like David's interpretation of it, necessarily portrays the rich man as a villain. A brief discussion of God's explanation in verses 7–12, however, ought to make it clear that when Nathan accuses David with the words, "You are the man (*hā'îš*)" in verse 7, he means much more than, "You are the rich man of my story."

Look first at God's opening words to David in 12:7–8: "I anointed you king over Israel, I delivered you out of the hand of Saul; and I gave you your master's house, and your master's wives *into your bosom*, and gave you the house of Israel, and of Judah; and if this were too little, I would add to you as much more." This recitation of God's beneficence to David is, of course, background for the indignation God expresses over David's betrayal of him through the murder of Uriah and the taking of Bathsheba. The basis for God's present displeasure with David is *what he has done for the man*: he took from Saul and gave to David.

We see immediately that the parable's deliberately vague emphasis on the rich man *acting for* the wayfarer (twice in verse 4) allows us at this point to see God in 12:7–8 initially explaining the parable in this way: "As the rich man took the poor man's possession and acted in behalf of the way-farer, so I took Saul's possessions and gave them to you, O David." Before the *present* of David's betrayal lies the *past* of God's benevolence. In verses 7–8 God applies the parable to an antecedent situation before he applies it to what is at hand. The parable remains the same, but the names must first be changed to protect the innocent: at this phase of God's application of the parable, the rich man, God himself, is no villain, but simply the one who takes the ewe lamb from the poor man (that is, the kingship from Saul) and acts for, *ᶜāśāh le*, the wayfarer (*hēlek, 'orēᵃḥ*) or the man who comes (that is, hands over to David all that poor Saul possessed).

At this stage in God's speech, the hierarchy of players is remarkably similar to that of the parable. The rich man possesses many flocks and herds; below him is the poor man who owns but one animal; below even the poor man, who has a family and presumably a home, is the wayfarer, someone like a sojourner, one who comes for a time into the city of the parable;[21] and below even this wanderer is the ewe lamb, transferred by the rich man from the poor man to one who is below him on the social scale. The story from 1 Samuel 13 to 2 Samuel 10 is one that fulfills Samuel's word to Saul, "But now your kingdom (*mamlᵉkāh*) shall not continue; the LORD has sought out a man after his own heart" (1 Sam. 13:14), even as it is background for God's word to David in 2 Sam. 12:7–8. Because Saul *spared* (*ḥāmal*) Agag and the choicest of his flocks (1 Sam. 15:9), the LORD *spared* (*ḥāmal*) taking from his own flocks and took rather from Saul's, that is, took Saul's kingship and transferred it to Saul's servant, David. The LORD was right in not sparing Saul, and David will be wrong both in not sparing Uriah and in focusing on the man's action in Nathan's story as necessarily evil for "not sparing (*ḥāmal*)" (12:6).

What best conjoins the ewe lamb in the parable and David's kingship in the larger story is precisely God's reference in 12:8 to what he did for David: he transferred Saul's royal wives to David, "I gave you your Lord's wives into your bosom (*ḥēq*)." We recall that the poor man's lamb used to lie in his bosom (*ḥēq*: 12:3) before it was taken away. Before ever the ewe lamb represents the one wife David took from Uriah, it represents the many wives God took from Saul and gave to David.

This reversal of fortune whereby David succeeded Saul as king over all Israel had already been foreshadowed in the Deuteronomist's introduction to kingship in 1 Samuel 1–7, and it is in this introductory parable that we find an important passage that sheds light upon the parable here in 2 Samuel 12. In 1 Samuel 2, Hannah rejoices over the son she had requested from the LORD and sings about the glories of kingship soon to be recounted in the History:

> The LORD makes poor[22] and makes rich (*ᶜāšar*);
>   he brings low, he also exalts.
> He raises up the poor from the dust;
>   he lifts the needy from the ash heap
> to make them sit with princes
>   and inherit a throne of honor. (1 Sam. 2:7–8)

We see, once again, how the use of relatively rare terms in Nathan's parable (here "rich/poor") helps to limit the appropriate applications that its more general language might otherwise allow. Although David hears that Saul will make rich the man who kills Goliath (1 Sam. 17:25), and despite David's humble insistence to Saul's servants that he is but a poor man ('*iš roš*: 1 Sam. 18:23), it is really *God* who makes poor and makes rich (1 Sam. 2:7). The LORD's words in 2 Sam. 12:7–8 are simply another way of saying that he had impoverished Saul to enrich David. Later in the story it will be Solomon whom the LORD makes rich (1 Kings 3:11, 13; 10:23). We begin to understand, then, how the heart of Nathan's parable is a multifaceted meditation on kingship that transcends the narrow boundaries of David's present sins.

I have already described how the language of the parable and its context supports the usual explanation of the parable in which David is the rich man, Uriah the poor man, and Bathsheba his ewe lamb. This understanding is not wrong—simply incomplete. For only when God turns to David's *present* sins in 12:9–10, does he, God, twice use the language of *taking* (*lāqaḥ*): as the rich man took the poor man's lamb, so David took Uriah's wife. The parable meant one thing according to the past perspective of 12:7–8, yet means quite another according to the present perspective of 12:9–10. The key players shift roles accordingly: in relation to the LORD, who makes rich, his beneficiaries, Israel's kings, are still poor; yet in relation to other humans, their subjects, these kings are rich and can exploit the poor beneath them.

Finally, when God's interpretive words in vv. 11–12, and Nathan's in vv. 14–15, shift to the future, the players within the parable once again change in application. Since the ewe lamb of the parable points especially to the women of Saul in the LORD's past application (12:7–8) and to Bathsheba in his present application (12:9–10), it is obvious that it now comes to refer most pointedly to the women of David in the LORD's reference to the future in 12:11–12: "I will take *your women* before your eyes and give them to your neighbor and he shall lie with *your women* in the sight of the sun." As God took Saul's women and gave them to David, so he will give David's women to his sons, first Ammon and then Absalom. Moreover, as God took Saul's kingdom from Saul to give to David, so God will *take* (*lāqaḥ*) the kingdom out of the hands of David's son Solomon and give ten tribes to Jeroboam (1 Kings 11:35) and to the king of Assyria (2 Kings 17), finally delivering the remaining tribe of Judah to the king of Babylon (2 Kings 24–25).

In this third phase of the LORD's multiple explanation of the parable (12:11–12), God is once again the rich man, but David is now the poor king whose beloved lamb is to be taken from him and given to "the one who comes," first to Absalom for a time, then to Jeroboam, Assyria, and finally Babylon. Here the formal connections between the parable and its context are especially clear: the rich man took the ewe lamb; David took Uriah's woman; and God will take David's women. David's sins centered around sleeping with Bathsheba, who should have slept with Uriah; David's punishment will soon involve his son sleeping with David's own daughter (2 Samuel 13) and another son sleeping with David's concubines (2 Sam. 16:21–22). Both instances are graphic images of the internal disintegration of David's enduring house, and both form the two-edged sword that will never depart from that house.

The scope of Nathan's parable embraces the entire career of David and the history of his house, not just the immediate situation. When Nathan says to David, "You are *the man* (of my story)," he means many things at once: David *was* the wayfarer, "the one who comes," insofar as his past dealings with God are concerned (12:7–8); he *is* the rich man when his present crimes are brought into the picture (12:9–10); and he *will be* the poor man when God's punishing future for him and his house arrives (12:11–12). When applied to the story as God and Nathan apply it (12:7–15), and as the larger story line suggests that it be interpreted, the parable shifts in meaning as it structures the various phases of the royal history. Yet here as elsewhere in the History, there is a social dimension to the story: the fate of the house of David and that of the house of Israel are so intertwined that Nathan's parable, as interpreted by God and Nathan, may very well explain not only the complex history of David, but even that of Israel itself.

Nathan and the Deuteronomist: A Coincidence of Plans

In verse 12 God tells David, "For you did it secretly (*bassāter*); but I will do this thing before all Israel, and before the sun." This contrast between doing something secretly and doing it openly is at the heart of the History, and the parable of Nathan, with its accompanying explanation, forms a key image of how the History conveys its messages. For David is not the only character in chapters 11–12 who has acted secretly: God's own messenger, Nathan, himself conveys a disguised message in the story of verses 1–4, and then declares it "openly before Israel and before the sun," by pointing to David and rehearsing its successive meanings in verses 7–15. The secret strategy is successful: in his reaction to the story, David fails to realize that he is both judge and defendant in this case. As the reported speech of Nathan within 12:1–12 mirrors the critical situation of David in chapters 11–12 (David—secret sin: exposure; Nathan—secret message:

explanation), so also is the authorial perspective concerning the larger story of David reflected in the words of its messengers—the narrator and the character, Nathan—which judge David first secretly then openly.

The obvious point of view dominating 1 Samuel 16–2 Samuel 10 created a safe and traditional picture of David, a characterization marked by flattering brush strokes that evoked superficial adulation. It was relatively easy to condemn Saul and praise David, given God's rejection of the first and obvious choice of the second. Aspects of the story that did cast David in a less attractive light were indeed present, but rarely in an obtrusive way—as if there was danger involved in the tale being too directly critical of the man after God's own heart. After the debacle of Saul's reign, David's glorious successes seemed to allow Israel to glory in a king who could gladden every heart. It was, again, almost as if readers were being lulled into believing that Israel's request for a king in 1 Samuel 8 was not such a bad idea after all. Saul, not the institution of kingship, had gone wrong, so that David became kingship's best advertisement. Poor Saul may have deserved to die, yet kingship, as David practiced it, ought to be restored fourfold.

With 2 Samuel 11–12 as introduction to 2 Samuel 13–1 Kings 2, the Deuteronomist now presents David as openly as Saul was once presented: David, also, "is the man." The primary difference between David's story and Saul's is this: the sign of Saul's punishment was the impermanence of his house, whereas the permanence of David's house will be the sign of his: God promises David, "The sword shall never depart from your house" (2 Samuel 12:10).

The pedagogical impact—or moment of recognition—provided David and the story's readers by Nathan's oracle is scarcely a novel move in the History. Very much the same tactic lies behind the account of the fall of Eli and the rise of Samuel in 1 Samuel 1–7: ostensibly about the fall and rise of *priestly* houses, these chapters are also an extended introduction to the rise and fall of *royal* houses. Bedecked in soiled priestly garb, old Eli appropriately falls to his death in 1 Samuel 4, a fate that David will later proclaim the rich man to deserve in 2 Samuel 12:5. However, the royal history that follows Eli's story, like that which follows Nathan's parable, avoids such easy proclamations. As Nathan accuses David, so a Deuteronomic voice accuses its Israelite audience. If it is clear, finally, that David is a royal *taker* who deserves the punishment to come, then the Deuteronomist's audience ought now to realize that it too has been tricked into forgetting that the fate of the house of David and that of the house of Israel have always been inextricably intertwined. The sword that will never depart from David's house hangs over Israel's house as well. This social and ideological dimension of Nathan's parable prepares us for understanding its aftermath in the death of David's son in 12:15–25.

There is a clear and present danger in conveying an unpalatable message too directly. Very often in such cases, immediate danger awaits the messenger. We know that the Amalekite lad who brought news to David about the death of Saul and his sons lost his life for his efforts (2 Samuel 1 and 4), and we can easily understand why "the servants of David feared to tell him that the child was dead" (2 Sam. 12:18). Yet the servants convey their message by chance, in much the same way as Nathan conveyed his by design; Nathan spoke in parable, while "[David's] servants were whispering together (*mitlaḥªśîm*), and David perceived that the child was dead." That is, only *after* David got the point of their whispering, did they declare outright to him, "[The child] is dead" (12:19). This patterned mode of communication exercised both by David's prophet and by his servants in chapter 12 might appear to be happenstance were it not for the larger similarity between the communicative stance of Nathan in chapter 12 and that of the Deuteronomist—with respect to the basic speech plan of the entire History as well as to the many local instances I have been emphasizing as examples of *mise-en-abyme* within it.

We cannot often tell whether this or that dialogue or narrative event which appears similar to the History's overall speech plan is authorially deliberate (as, within the story, Nathan's strategy is from his point of view) or unwitting (as the servants' whispering is in 2 Samuel 12). After all, such homologies can result either unconsciously or from a deliberate speech plan. Which of the striking images found within the History—whether they are brief like the fall of Eli from this throne (1 Sam. 4:18) or extended like the priestly parable of 1 Samuel 1–7—is employed by design and which through unconscious needs of ideology may be impossible to decide. Nevertheless, when the image extends over a relatively long stretch of narrative, and is colored by repeated literary allusions to the larger picture (as in 1 Samuel 1–7), then something deliberate like a plan probably lies behind such reflective structures.

To illustrate, then, just how central Nathan's parable is to that larger story we call the History, I want now to apply that parable to the plot-line of the History in much the same way as I have explained God's words as doing with respect to the history of David's house. There may be nothing more here than the whispers of common ideology or comparable thought patterns. In a previous chapter, I suggested that the words of the man of God to the house of Eli in 1 Sam. 2:27–36 clearly foreshadow the permanent punishment that will plague the house of David to the end.[23] Similarly, Nathan's parable, seen as appropriate to David's entire history, is probably appropriate to Israel's as well. Whether the result of speech plan or mind-set, the following similarities in plot, tone, and language are worth considering.

Look at Nathan's parable as a summary of the history of Israel from Deuteronomy through 2 Kings, and let the ewe lamb represent the land of Canaan and its cultural heritage. The plot would go something like this. The LORD, he who "makes poor [*hifil* of *yāraš* "to dispossess"] and makes rich [*hifil* of *ᶜāšar*]" (1 Sam. 2:7), dispossesses the nations and gives the land of Canaan to Israel, the traveler or sojourner. Still living in the same city, that is, the land of Canaan, Israel becomes rich, and the nations it dispossessed poor (Deuteronomy–Judges).

The time comes, however, when Israel is no longer willing to take its form of government from its own religious and cultural heritage (a Yahwistic theocracy), and so takes it from the very nations it dispossessed: kingship is established in Israel (1 Samuel 8). The move at first appears politically successful, but in reality God decides to take the land away from Israel: the LORD successively gives the land to "the one who comes," first the North to Assyria, and then the South to Babylon (1 Samuel–2 Kings).

I earlier summarized the formal reasons why Bathsheba and the ewe lamb of Nathan's parable must merge in the account of 2 Samuel 11–12. If we now look at the language and tone of God's application of the parable to David's situation with respect to kingship, we can see how that application also fits the language and tone of authoritative statements, elsewhere in the History, about Israel's situation with respect to the land.

First, in 12:7–8 God summarizes the story of David up to that point by emphasizing his *giving* of kingship to David and his *delivering* of David from the hand of Saul. In similar fashion, God's words to Israel in Judg. 6:9 neatly summarize the story from Deuteronomy until then: "I delivered you from the hand of the Egyptians, and from the hand of all who oppressed you, and drove them out before you and gave you the land." "The land which the LORD gives Israel" is a constant refrain in the larger story line, very much as the giving of kingship to David is a refrain of God in 12:7–8 ("I anointed you; I gave you Saul's wives, his house, the house of Israel, and so much more").

Second, in 12:9–10 God characterizes David's murder of Uriah and taking of Bathsheba as despising (*bāzah*) him and his word, and in 12:14 Nathan calls David's actions "utterly scorning (*nā'aṣ*) the LORD." Not content with what the LORD had given him, David took for himself what belonged to Uriah, a *foreigner*. It is significant that the only cases of despising (*bāzah*) the LORD in the entire History occur here and in 1 Sam. 2:30, in the midst of a programmatic prophecy about the history of royal Israel ("The LORD declares, 'Those who despise me shall be lightly esteemed'"). As for Nathan's reference in 12:14 to David's "scorning (*nā'aṣ*) the enemies of the LORD" (a euphemism for scorning the LORD himself), the only other occurrence of such language in the History concerns Israel's attitude, once God has given it the land: "For when I have brought [the people of Israel] into the land flowing with milk and honey, which I swore to give to their fathers, and they have eaten and are full and grown fat, they will turn to other gods and serve them, and scorn (*nā'aṣ*) me and break my covenant" (Deut. 31:20).

Although the history of Israel in the land is one of almost constant disobedience, there nevertheless is an obvious turning point in the story in 1 Samuel 8, where the language and tone of God's words to Samuel sound very much like God's words to David in 2 Sam. 12:9–10: God said to Samuel, "They have not rejected you (*mā'as*), they have rejected me from being king over them" (1 Sam. 8:7). As David turns to a foreigner, Uriah the Hittite, and takes what was his, so Israel turned to the nations surrounding it to take what was theirs: "No, but we will have a king over us, that we also may be *like all the nations*" (1 Sam. 8:19–20).

Third, as David's fate in 2 Sam. 12:11–12 will correspond to his own sins (since you took Uriah's wife, "I will take your women and give them to your neighbor" [v. 11]), so Moses foretold the corresponding fate of Israel, who will want kings in order to be like the other nations: "Like the nations that the LORD makes to perish before you, so shall you perish" (Deut. 8:20). The LORD's double punishment of David by first handing over the kingship of ten tribes to Jeroboam (1 Kings 11) and then kingship over Judah to the king of Babylon (2 Kings 24–25) actually reflects the LORD's two-stage punishment of his people, Israel, first by giving the North to Assyria, and then by giving the South to Babylon: "And the LORD said, 'I will remove Judah out of my sight, as I have removed Israel' " (2 Kings 23:27).

In short, Nathan's parable about a rich man and a poor man—and about those who live in the city and one who comes to it—fits the larger story of the house of Israel in much the same way as it is interpreted by God to fit the particular story of the house of David.

·6·

WOMEN
(13:1–14:33)

King's daughters are among thy women of honor. (Psalm 45)

Thro' all the drama—whether damned or not—
Love gilds the scene, and women guide the plot.
(Richard Sheridan, *The Rivals*)

The Immediate Context of the Rape of Tamar

A review of Nathan's parable and God's interpretation of it in 2 Samuel 12 will set the stage for an understanding of the events narrated in 2 Samuel 13.[1] In the previous chapter I suggested that the power of the parable to pinpoint David as "the man" derives from its threefold perspective on David's past, present, and future. This triple view is itself facilitated by the parable's underdetermined references to what the rich man does with the ewe lamb that he takes from the poor man, that is to say, what he does for the wayfarer. I also suggested that the interpretive words of God in verses 7–12 are characterized by their largesse in specifying those actions of David that explain the LORD's wrath. Nevertheless, as the words of Nathan and God are able to *interpret* the parable in a threefold manner largely because the language of the parable was underspecified at central points, so now the narrator immediately begins a brilliantly conceived sequence of events which the reader can view as fulfillments of God's words precisely because the divine interpretation itself in chapter 12, despite being specific in reference to David's past sins, was also sufficiently general with respect to David's future punishment.

First, take the LORD's careful references to the *women* in David's past, present, and future: "I gave into your bosom the women of your lord (v. 8); you took the woman of Uriah the Hittite to be your woman (v. 10); I shall take your women from before your eyes and give them to your neighbor ($r\bar{e}^{ac}$) (v. 11)." In the past, David was the wayfarer to whom God,

131

the rich man, gave the women of Saul. Now, in the narrative's present, David becomes the rich man who steals the woman belonging to Uriah, the poor man. Therefore, God prophesies, David shall become the poor man whose women God will take and give to those royal pretenders who are to come upon the narrative scene.[2]

What allows God's prophecy about David's fate to have a surplus of meaning is the divine use, first, of "women," a word that here refers not only to wives and concubines but also to *daughters* and, second, of $r\bar{e}^{ac}$, a general term used in various contexts for national, tribal, and familial kinsmen on one hand, or simply for companions and friends on the other.

Notice how God's reference to the "women" of David's past (12:8) looks back to Saul's daughters rather than to his wives or concubines. The narrative has nowhere mentioned David's acquisition of Saul's wives or concubines, but rather has concentrated upon David's dealings with Saul's daughters, Merab and (especially) Michal. And in order to make it clear that "the women of your master" (v. 8) is a divine reference to Saul's daughters rather than wives, the narrator puts these women in David's bosom in verse 8 just as the parable, in verse 3, placed the ewe lamb in the poor man's bosom, and adds, "it was like a daughter to him." It is obvious, therefore, that the first way in which the divine punishment of David prophesied in verse 8 takes place in the narrative is not through Absalom's taking of the king's concubines in 2 Samuel 16, but rather through Amnon's rape of his father's daughter here in 2 Samuel 13.

Second, it is scarcely accidental that David's multifaceted punishment is to be carried out by David's $r\bar{e}^{ac}$ or $r\bar{e}^{c}\hat{\imath}m$, his fellow or fellows (12:11). "Fellow," like "brother," can mean fellow citizen, fellow tribesman, or fellow kinsman. For example, we have Solomon's reference to an Israelite's sin against a fellow (citizen) in 1 Kings 8:31, David's sharing of spoil with his fellow tribesmen in 1 Sam. 30:26 and, in our present story, Amnon's conspiring with his fellow kinsman, Jonadab, who, we are told, is the son of Shimeah, David's brother (2 Sam. 13:3). As we think about the generic appropriateness of "fellow" in God's words of punishment to David in 2 Sam. 12:11, we can see once again why the immediate focus of the story in 1–2 Samuel is not so much on brothers or fellows in a tribal or national sense but on brothers or fellows in a familial sense. As David was both son and fellow citizen of Saul—Saul's "neighbor" to whom God has given the kingdom (1 Sam. 15:28; 28:17)—so now Amnon and Absalom, as both sons and fellow kinsmen of David, are, both of them, David's neighbors, to whom God promises to give the women in David's life (2 Sam. 12:11), first his daughter to Amnon in 2 Samuel 13 and then his concubines to Absalom in 2 Samuel 16. As God's words to David in 2 Sam. 12:10–12 enlarge the scope of Nathan's parable, so also the subsequent narrative in 2 Samuel 13–1 Kings 2 enlarges the scope of God's words in 2 Samuel 12.

2 Samuel 13: Shadows and Light

Key aspects about the story of the rape of Tamar appear irresolvably ambiguous at this point in the narrative. Most uncertainties revolve around the inner disposition of David in the affair. After the rape of Tamar and her subsequent desolation, the narrator informs us, "When King David heard of all these things, he was very angry" (v. 2). Yet what precisely was David angry about? The rape only, or also Absalom's counsel to Tamar to hold her peace "for Amnon was her brother and she should not take the rape to heart" (v. 20)? We know that Amnon hated Tamar with a very great hatred (v. 15) and that Absalom hated Amnon because of the rape (v. 22); did all this fraternal hatred anger David also? Then, when David, his sons, and all his servants weep very bitterly (v. 36), are these tears of relief that the sons whom David thought Absalom had killed were alive, or only tears of sadness that Amnon himself was dead? Again, when Absalom flees, the narrator states "David mourned for his son day after day" (v. 37). This statement, appearing right after the king' weeping and Absalom's fleeing, seems deliberately ambiguous: which son does David mourn, the one alive or dead, the exile or the corpse? And finally, the last verse of the chapter, verse 39, remains opaque both because, as S. R. Driver pointed out long ago, *watt^{e}kal dāwid hammelek* is "untranslatable," and because we cannot be sure about the meaning of *niham* in this verse: whether David "was comforted" or "changed his mind" about Amnon, that he was dead. In short, while Tamar's, Amnon's, and Absalom's inner dispositions of hatred and desolation are clear in the chapter, David's position "about all these things" remains opaque.[3]

Such questions surround the events of this chapter and fill it with ambiguity that may or may not be dissolved in the story to come. Nevertheless, there is much else in the chapter that the narrator presents with utmost clarity.

If 2 Samuel has an unusually large number of references to sons, daughters, brothers, and sisters, one chapter within it, chapter 13, refers to children and siblings more often than any other chapter in the book does: seventeen times and ten times respectively. The chapter begins to examine the family of David through a narrative microscope.

At the same time, this immediate emphasis on family also involves deeper associations of tribe and nation. From now on, the fate of David's house will parallel the individual fates of the northern and southern

houses, as well as of the entire house of Israel, and statements about
relations between fellows ($r\bar{e}^{ac}$) and brothers ('$\bar{a}h$) in the story will often
have familial, tribal, or national dimensions that are marvelously intertwined—whether by conscious artistry or by implicit ideology we may not
always be able to determine. Nevertheless, we can learn much about the
variable perspectives within 2 Samuel 13 by seeing the chapter both from
within and from without, that is to say, by looking first at its internal structure and then at one of its most revealing literary contexts.

A favorite means of the Deuteronomist for incorporating authorial
intentions into the narrative is to construct certain narratives in two parts,
one of which reaffirms a similar theme, message, or perspective of the
other. As we saw, for example, in 1 Samuel 16, God's provision of David as
his king in the first part of the chapter parallels Saul's provision of David
as his musician in the second part, by means of a number of linguistic and
narrative interconnections.[4] Similarly in 2 Samuel 3, the story of David's
apparent ignorance of Joab's role in the murder of Abner is immediately
followed by an account of Israel's certain knowledge of David's lack of a
role in that murder. So too, here in 2 Samuel 13 the rape of Tamar
(vv. 1–20) is immediately followed by the revenge of Absalom (vv. 21–39)
and each half of the story contains words, phrases, and perspectives that
reverberate with those in the other half.

Consider first that the combination of a request and a refusal culmi-
nates in a violent fraternal crime in each half of the story: Amnon entreats
Tamar, "Come and sleep with me, my sister" (v. 11) and Absalom pres-
sures David, "Let the king and his servants [that is, his sons] go with your
servant [that is, your son]" (v. 25). Tamar's refusal results in Amnon
raping her, and David's refusal is followed by Absalom having Amnon
killed. Consider also the curiously dual role that Jonadab plays in the
chapter: he counsels Amnon in the first half and David in the second. In
each case, what he advises comes to pass: Jonadab's words to Amnon in v. 5
("Lie down on your bed and pretend to be ill; and when your father
comes to see you, say to him, 'Let my sister Tamar come and give me bread
to eat, and prepare the food in my sight, that I may see it, and eat it from
her hand'") are confirmed by the narrator's words in the following verses.
Similarly, Jonadab's words to David in v. 32 ("Let not my lord suppose that
they have killed all the young men the king's sons, for Amnon alone is
dead, for by the command of Absalom this has been determined from the
day he forced his sister Tamar") are verified by the narrator's previous and
subsequent accounts. Amnon indeed gets Tamar alone in the first part,
and Absalom indeed murders Amnon alone in the second part. Consider
again how, in the first section, what Tamar says, hears, and does closely

parallels what David says, hears, and does in the second. First, David refuses Absalom in words that clearly are patterned after Tamar's refusal of Amnon: "No (*'al*) my brother, do not (*'al*) rape me" (v. 12) is followed by David's double refusal to Absalom, "No (*'al*) my son, we all shall not (*'al*) go" (v. 25). Second, the words that David and Tamar hear are also similar: "Do not take this to heart," Absalom tells Tamar in verse 20; "Let not my lord the king so take it to heart," Jonadab tells David in verse 33. And third, as Tamar sorrowfully tears the royal daughter's robe in verse 19, so David tears his royal clothes in verse 31. Then consider how David is not willing (*lo' 'ābāh*) to go at the request of Absalom (v. 25) just as Amnon earlier was not willing (*lo' 'ābāh*) to listen to the pleading of Tamar (vv. 14, 16). Consider, finally, what happens to David's children in the chapter: Absalom violates David's daughter and then hates her in the first half (v. 15); Absalom hates David's son (v. 22) and then murders him in the second.

When we also reflect upon the concurrent perspectives whereby both narrator and characters name various individuals in the story, we find that the events recounted here are clearly structured as an introduction to the larger story about David and his son Absalom that will concern the reader through chapter 19. Why does the narrator begin this account by stating, "Absalom, the son of David, had a sister" (v. 1) rather than "Amnon, the son of David, had a sister," if not to orient the reader to the main proponents and opponents in the coming seven chapters? And why does the narrator quote Amnon as admitting to Jonadab "Tamar is my brother Absalom's sister" (v. 4), instead of "Tamar is my sister," if not to indicate that Tamar's fate in the story is primarily a detail that motivates *Absalom's* actions?

It is true that the narrator's and Amnon's concurrent designation of Tamar as *Absalom's* sister may also function as implying that Tamar is only the *half-sister* of Amnon, a mitigating factor that Amnon may want to emphasize when he admits to Jonadab his incestuous feelings about Tamar. Nevertheless, Tamar is introduced not in her own right, and not so much as Amnon's half-sister, but precisely as the sister of Absalom: this story of the rape of Tamar and the murder of Amnon is primarily about David and Absalom, just as the stories about Sarah's and Rebecca's adulterous situations in Genesis 12, 20, and 26 are primarily about Abraham and Isaac.

Similarly, Amnon is introduced in verse 1 as David's son, so that he, like Tamar, appears in the story primarily for the sake of the larger story about David and Absalom which chapter 13 introduces. Tamar and Amnon are the two victims in the chapter that help to establish David and Absalom as the two antagonists of the coming chapters. And even between David and Absalom, the second is introduced in verse 1 as "the son of David" because the larger story is primarily about the house that is David's.

Sons of Israel and Sons of the King: A Narrative Background for 2 Samuel 13

We have seen how the word "brother" (*'āḥ*) in various contexts can refer either to national, tribal, or familial relationships, and how, in the Books of Samuel, there is a marked tendency for "brother" or "brethren" to denote a familial rather than a tribal or national connection—especially when these words appear in a context that involves or mentions "kings." Thus in 2 Samuel, "brother" denotes familial connections about two-thirds of the time, whereas in Deuteronomy, for example, it denotes such familial associations in only seven out of forty-two verses.[5] When we look at Judges, we find this pattern significantly confirmed in both its royal and non-royal contexts: where the text establishes a specific royal context, as in Judges 8–9, references to brothers are consistently familial rather than tribal or national.[6] Moreover, in Judges 19–21, a section that begins and ends with the same exclusionary statement, "In those days there was no king in Israel," "brother" almost always (five out of six verses) denotes a national relationship; only in 21:22 does "brethren" have an immediate familial sense. Of course, this suggestion about one facet of the History's worldview points to a tendency rather than an absolute rule, as Deut. 17:15 and 20 illustrate by their references to national rather than familial "brethren" in the explicit context of the Israelite monarchy to come.[7]

More immediately, however, in Judges 19–21, "when there was no king in Israel," (19:1; 21:25), we have a story which, in its remarkable similarity to, and significant contrasts with, 2 Samuel 13, helps us understand an important aspect of the rape of Tamar. On one hand, Judges 19–21 recounts the instigation and aftermath of a civil war between the sons of Israel, whom the text designates as (national) brethren.[8] The story is about the conflict between the tribe of Benjamin and its brethren, that is, between the sons of Israel. On the other hand, 2 Samuel 13 recounts the instigation and aftermath of a *familial* war amongst "the sons of the king," a conflict of familial "brothers" concerning their "sister."[9] Moreover, at the end of Judges, before there was a king in Israel, fraternal rape of a fellow citizen and the killing of national brethren plague the sons of Israel; in 2 Samuel, familial fraticide and fraternal rape within the royal family surround the sons (and daughter) of David.

A closer look at selected details within Judges 19–21 and 2 Samuel 13 suggests how each story echoes similar concerns, but with different reference points. Despite the many obvious differences between the outrages described in Judges 19–21 and those of 2 Samuel 13, specific language and related themes in these two pericopes indicate how their ideological concerns are remarkably similar—even though explicitly national and tribal conflicts are addressed in the earlier story and immediately familial ones in the later one.

The first significant aspect that ties together the language of the two stories is, as I have just suggested, their focus on a conflict arising between "sons" and "brothers": both of these words are national or tribal terms in Judges 19–21 but familial ones in 2 Samuel 13. If the Book of Judges states, "But the Benjaminites would not listen to the voice of their brethren, the sons of Israel" (Judg. 20:13), 2 Samuel 13 also uses the son/brother terminology, but what was a national conflict is now transformed into a familial one. Absalom entreats David, " 'Let my brother Amnon go with us.' And Absalom pressed him until he let Amnon and all the sons of the king go with him" (2 Sam. 13:26–7).

Second, the cause of the near fraticide of Benjamin in Judges and of the actual fraticide of Amnon in 2 Samuel is the sexual abuse of a woman who hears similarly callous language from her male companion immediately following both outrageous incidents: "Arise let us be going (*qûmî w^enēlēkāh*)," the Levite tells his concubine in Judg. 19:28; "Arise, be gone (*qûmî lēkî*)," Amnon tells Tamar in 2 Sam. 13:15.

Third, in both cases the crime is termed "foolishness or vile thing" (*n^ebālāh*), a relatively rare term in the History that, apart from Achan's stealing of the Lord's devoted things in Josh. 7:15, is confined to sexual misconduct.[10] "Do not do this vile thing," the old Ephraimite tells the men of Gibeah, exactly as Tamar pleads with Amnon. Indeed, given the limited usage of *n^ebālāh*, it may be significant that, out of six occurrences in the History and twenty-four occurrences in the entire Bible, only in these two stories do we find the term used in exactly the same expression.

Fourth, as one might expect from the similarity of the crimes involved, the abhorrence expressed over such deeds is similar in the two stories. After the crime in Judges, we hear, "Such a thing has never happened or been seen from the day that the people of Israel came up out of the land of Egypt until this day" (Judg. 19:30). And before the rape in 2 Samuel 13, we hear Tamar tell Amnon, "Such a thing is not done in Israel" (2 Sam. 13:12).

Fifth, the rape of a virgin is suggested in Judges 19 and accomplished in 2 Samuel 13. The Ephraimite suggests to the men of Gibeah, "Behold, here are my virgin daughter (*b^etûlāh*) and his concubine. Ravish them (*^cānāh*)" (Judg. 19:24). Tamar also is a virgin (*b^etûlāh*) who pleads with

Amnon not to rape ($^c\bar{a}n\bar{a}h$) her, but he does so nonetheless (2 Sam. 13:2, 12, 14).

Sixth, the language of pleading used by the Ephraimite and Tamar in the face of an impending rape is significantly similar in its vocabulary and syntax:

> Ephraimite: No (*'al*), my brothers, do not (*'al*) do this evil thing. (Judg. 19:23)

> Tamar: No (*'al*), my brother, do not (*'al*) rape me. (2 Sam. 13:12)

So far as I have been able to establish, such an expression (*'al* plus "brother[s]" plus *'al* plus verb) occurs nowhere else in biblical narrative.

Seventh, there is a double expression of familial unwillingness (*lo' 'ābāh*) in each story. The son is not willing to stay with his father-in-law in Judges 19:10, just as the father is not willing to go with his son in 2 Samuel 13. Again, just as the rapists were not willing (*lo' 'ābû*) to listen to their national brother, the Ephraimite, so Amnon is not willing (*lo' 'ābāh*) to listen to his familial sister, Tamar (Judg. 19:25; 2 Sam. 13:14, 16).

Finally, we see not only linguistic connections between the two stories but even similarities in plot structure, of both a general and specific character. Most obviously, the Levite and Israelites in Judges 19–21 resort to killing on a tribal or national scale as revenge for the crime committed by the men of Gibeah, just as Absalom resorts to murder within his own family as revenge for the crime of Amnon. More specifically, however, in each story the narrative offers some indication that those who should have protected the abused women actually fail in their responsibility: not just the rapists are guilty, the women's supposed protectors are also. Thus, the conduct of the Levite and of Israel in Judges 19–21 may be as reprehensible as that of the men of Gibeah and Benjamin.[11] Similarly Absalom counsels Tamar to hold her peace about the rape, thus confining her to his house as a desolate woman (2 Sam. 13:20), and David, although angry at his son's rape of his daughter (2 Sam. 13:21) does nothing about it. We saw how tribal brothers treated tribal brothers when there *was* no king in Israel; the story in 2 Samuel 13 is about how familial brothers treat familial brothers when there *is* king in place. Matters have not improved with the advent of kingship.

We see from all this that what happens to brothers within the house of David is another, more concrete, way of telling the reader what is happening to brothers within the house of Israel. The "neighbors" in Judges 19–21 are immediately national or tribal, while those in 2 Samuel are immediately familial. Nevertheless, the story of David's family continues to reflect the story of the family of Israel.

Ambiguity in 2 Samuel 14

There are many more references to speaking (*dābar*) and saying (*'āmar*) in 2 Samuel 14 than in any other chapter of the book.[12] This chapter is very much about the words that one speaks or says, and what they mean. More specifically, it is about words that one has *someone else* speak: "So Joab put the words in her mouth" (v. 3); and "it was [Joab] who put all these words in the mouth of your handmaid" (v. 19). Coupled with the complications of reported speech is the presence of a number of verbal and narrative ambiguities: convoluted or awkward language combines with narrative opacity to make interpretation difficult.[13] Here are two crucial features of the chapter that combine to challenge our understanding.

First, the simple preposition *ᶜal* is equivocal at three important moments in the chapter. The word appears eleven times here, and in eight instances the meaning is straightforward. It is clear what is happening when people fall on (*ᶜal*) their face in obeisance (vv. 4, 33), or when reference is made to a remnant "upon (*ᶜal*) the face of the earth" (v. 7). The woman from Tekoa clearly acknowledges guilt on or upon (*ᶜal*) herself and upon (*ᶜal*) her father's house (v. 9), and we easily understand how Absalom's abundant hair "lay heavy upon (*ᶜal*) him" (v. 26). We also find this preposition in its clearly oppositional sense of "against": "And now the whole family has risen up against (*ᶜal*) your handmaid" (v. 7). Finally, the word's common meaning of "about or concerning" fits Joab's command to the Tekoite to be like a woman who "mourns for (*ᶜal*) the dead" (v. 2).

Nevertheless, in three central instances in the chapter, we cannot be sure whether this preposition avoids a sense of opposition. Our initial perspective in the chapter depends upon knowing what Joab thinks about David's attitude toward Absalom: does Joab perceive that David's heart grieved *for* Absalom or inclined *against* him (v. 1)? After he hears the woman's initial statements, does David promise to give orders *concerning* her or *against* her (v. 8)? And finally, does the woman accuse David of having planned (*ḥāšab*) such a thing against (*ᶜal*) the people of God or for (*ᶜal*) them (v. 13)?[14]

Briefly put, does Joab use the woman from Tekoa to tell David that the king's attitude *against* Absalom needs to be changed, or simply that his feelings *on behalf of* Absalom need to be acted upon? Does David immediately side with the woman or against her? And does she accuse David of acting for or against the people of God?

We ought not to be surprised about questions concerning what Joab's perception of David's attitude might be in 14:1, since the narrative's ambiguity here seems part of the story. After all, as I mentioned above, the account of Amnon's rape of Tamar, and Absalom's retaliative murder of him, ends chapter 13 on a similarly ambiguous note: did David "change his mind about (*niham ʿal*) Amnon, seeing that he was dead" or was he "comforted about Amnon, seeing that he was dead" (v. 39)? If, in chapter 13, we are already unsure about whether David ends up for or against his dead son, whether David starts out in chapter 14 being for or against Amnon's murderer remains appropriately in doubt. Equally in doubt is the woman's statement about David's attitude toward the people of God in verse 13. In her story, the people are her opponents. Then ought she not to be accusing David of siding with the people, not against them? Only in verse 8 do we have a slightly clearer sense of the meaning of the preposition: it is likely that David gives orders in behalf of the woman, not against her.

A more important feature of chapter 14 reinforces the ambiguities surrounding *ʿal* in verses 1, 8, and 13. We know that in biblical narrative the message conveyed to a messenger by a sender is sometimes first verbalized by the narrator quoting the sender, before the message is then reported in the messenger's words to the receiver (as in 13:5–6), and sometimes not (as with Nathan's mission from God in chapter 12). In this respect, the narrator's account of Joab's sending of the woman in chapter 13 is like God's sending of Nathan at the beginning of chapter 12: at first, the narrator does not tell us precisely what the sender wants the messenger to convey to the receiver, so that when this messenger is reported—through direct discourse—delivering the message, we may wonder where the sender's words end and where the messenger's own words, if any, begin.[15] This second example of apparent ambiguity is so central to our understanding of chapter 14 that the chapter's thematic attention to questions about the messengers themselves works to reinforce our sense of uncertainty.

Ambiguous Messengers

Although no one explicitly refers to the woman of Tekoa as Joab's messenger (*mal'āk*), this is obviously her immediate function in the story. "You shall come to the king and speak to him these words," Joab commands her, "and Joab put the words in her mouth" (v. 3). If the woman clearly, but only implicitly, is Joab's messenger, she, for her part, actually affirms that David is "like God's messenger" (*mal'āk*: v. 17). In fact, the story sets up a number of similarities between David and the woman that involve their role as emissaries. The narrator introduces us to Joab's messenger by first calling her "a wise woman" (v. 2) and then reports her telling David that he is "wise like the wisdom of God's messenger" (*mal'āk*: v. 20). What will happen, the narrator wants us to ask, when the "wise" messenger of Joab meets David, who is "wise" like a messenger of God?[16]

Also, both messengers are ambiguous mourners, to say the least. When Joab tells the woman, "Pretend to be a mourner, and put on mourning garments, and behave like a woman who is mourning many days" (v. 2), this threefold use of the root *'bl* has accents of ambiguity that refer back to David, who "mourned for (*wayyit'abbēl ʿal*) his son day after day" (13:37). The ambiguity in 13:37 is whether David is mourning over the dead Amnon or the exiled Absalom. Although we will find out eventually that David mourned for Absalom when he died (19:1, 2), we are never sure whether he mourned for Amnon or not.

The woman's double comparison of David to a messenger of God in verses 17 and 20 recalls Achish's similar statement to David, "I know that you are as blameless in my sight as a messenger of God" (1 Sam. 29:9), even as her words look forward to Mephibosheth's similar attestation, "But my Lord the king is like the messenger of God; do therefore what seems good to you" (2 Sam. 19:27). What is obvious from the two affirmations of Achish and Mephibosheth that frame the Tekoite's words is that in all three assertions the reader has a much wider perspective on David than do those who praise him. How mistaken Achish was to trust David was clearly specified in 1 Sam. 27:8–12 and David's erratic decisions about Saul's property (giving it all to Mephibosheth in 2 Samuel 9, then returning all of it to Ziba in 2 Samuel 16, only to divide it between them in haste in 2 Samuel 19) makes the king a flighty angel of God indeed. Coming upon the heels of David's sin and God's punishing words and actions in 2 Samuel 11–13, the woman's praise of David sounds upon one's ears with unavoidably ironic tones. All three situations, therefore, underline in various ways how far off the mark are such servile statements about David, who is either a deceiver or a dupe at the point in the story when such comparisons are made. It may even turn out that David is both here in 2 Samuel 14.

If, then, the Tekoite woman only appears to be "like (*kᵉ*) a woman who is mourning" (v. 2), David only appears to be wise "like (*kᵉ*) a messenger of God" (vv. 17, 20). Certainly, David's decision to return Absalom to Jerusalem and to his presence will ultimately put David's wisdom to a severe test: far from being able "to distinguish between good and evil" (v. 17), far from "knowing all things that are on the earth" (v. 20), David is either duped—or at least pressured—by Joab into returning Absalom to the court. The woman prays in David's presence, "The LORD your God be with you" (v. 17), but she speaks at a point within the narrative when the LORD his God has already begun to punish David.

Joab's Ambiguous Message

Even though the narrative refers only in general to the words that Joab put in the woman's mouth (v. 2) before it reports the dialogue between her and David in direct discourse (vv. 4–20), it is still possible for the reader to infer what Joab's precise strategy might be. Even though the narrator from the beginning appears to inform the reader about Joab's strategy, the reader is still disposed to wonder where Joab's strategic words leave off and the woman's own words begin. It does not take angelic wisdom to suspect that Joab may indeed want David to see through his ploy.

The woman's eventual admission that she has been sent by Joab (vv. 19–20) may itself be part of Joab's indirect message to David—something like, "Bring Absalom back or I may side with him against you." In chapter 12, Nathan eventually told David that God was speaking to him through the parable of the rich man. In contrast, here in chapter 14 Joab may want David to discover by himself that he, Joab, is speaking through the Tekoite's story. When the woman tells David about "the man who would destroy me and my son together from the heritage of God" (v. 16), Joab may want David to suspect that this is precisely what he, Joab, is doing through the woman's words, namely, threatening David and his house.

For one thing, after Nathan's tricking of David in chapter 12, it is difficult to believe that David would not immediately see the woman's story as an obvious reflection of his own situation, and a ploy in behalf of Joab's advocacy of Absalom. Joab's strategy, therefore, may simply be a thinly veiled attempt to urge David to return Absalom to the court. After all, when David turns to Joab and commands him to bring back the young man, Joab responds, "the king has granted the request of his servant" (v. 22).

Moreover, whereas it is possible that some readers might have been as surprised as David when Nathan transformed his account into a parable with the words, "You are the man!" (12:7), it is much less likely that David is taken in by the Tekoite's story: the rich man's stealing of a poor man's ewe-lamb is, on the face of it, further removed from David's adultery than the woman's situation of mourning is from David's. She has two sons, one of whom killed the other; so also does David. Her remaining son is the heir of her father's house; so, it seems, is Absalom of David's house. Her son is in exile; so is David's. Her situation involves not just the people of God (v. 13) who have terrified her (v. 15) but even the hand of a specific man who would destroy her and her son from the heritage of God (v. 16); so also, Joab once again may be threatening David. In 2 Samuel 3, David ended the murderous affairs there with his assessment of Joab and his brother: "And I am this day weak, though anointed king; these men, the sons of Zeruiah are too hard for me. The LORD requite the evildoer according to his wickedness" (2 Sam. 3:39). It may be that David now recognizes Joab's threat in the person of the widow of Tekoa, and decides to return Absalom to the court—where the son will begin his revolt in the next chapter. In 2 Samuel 20, Joab will murder Amasa, his replacement, and only on David's deathbed will the king feel secure enough to issue instructions about Joab to Solomon, instructions that in David's words, "requite the evildoer according to his wickedness."

It seems likely, therefore, that the woman's story in 2 Samuel 14 is deliberately couched in such a way that there is no obvious need for David to possess the kind of angelic wisdom that "discerns good and evil" (v. 17) or that knows "all things that are on the earth" (v. 20) in order for him to discover the hand of Joab in her story. On the other hand, the contrast between the transparency of Joab's ploy and the tragedy of David's decision could not be greater. The woman's words about David's wisdom, whether put in her mouth by Joab or uttered on her own account, may be flattering to David but they are surely ironic to the reader, who is supposed to remember them from now on in the story, whenever disaster strikes the house of David.

The Narrator as Messenger: The Social Dimensions of 2 Samuel 14

The Tekoite woman, whom Joab engaged to influence David as God engaged Nathan in 2 Samuel 12, calls herself David's "maidservant" many times in 2 Samuel 14. The two words she uses for this, *'āmāh* in verses 15 and 16 and *šiphāh* in verses 6, 7, 12, 15, 17, and 19, are—here as elsewhere—synonyms, and precisely the terms that an Israelite woman would use to characterize herself in the presence of the king. Nevertheless, there are interesting narrative associations that each of these words for "handmaid" establishes, in reference both to the story that Joab has the woman tell David, as well as to the larger story that the narrator is telling the reader.

David's *'āmāh*

Consider the woman's designation of herself as David's maidservant in verses 15 and 16. The word she uses is *'āmāh,* and in this first variation on servility she is the maidservant of the larger narrative, which puts words in her mouth for the reader's ears just as Joab put words in her mouth for

David's. Both before and after David is led to discover that the woman is speaking for Joab, she is, as I have emphasized, effusive in her praise for David and his wisdom (vv. 17, 20). Speaking perhaps for herself, but more likely still for Joab, she honors David for being God's king (*melek*) and also for being like God's messenger or angel (*mal'āk*). Yet if she is the king's *'āmāh*, she is Joab's also, and who is Joab but David's servant? "Today, your *servant* knows," Joab tells David, "that I have found favor in your sight, my lord the king, in that the king has granted the request of his *servant*" (v. 22).

Such considerations allow us to view the Tekoite woman (who has so honored David) as the handmaid (*'āmāh*) of David's servant (*ʿebed*), and this triangular relationship immediately indicates the larger purposes of the narrative. In 2 Samuel 6, David's frenzied dancing before the ark caused Michal to say in derision, "How the king of Israel honored himself today, uncovering himself before the eyes of his servants' maids (*'amhôt 'abādāyw*: v. 20)." David responded, "I shall make myself yet more contemptible than this, but by the maids (*'ᵃmāhôt*) of whom you have spoken, by them I shall be held in honor" (v. 22). Just as the rape of Tamar in 2 Samuel 13 is merely the first in a series of narrative fulfillments of God's dire prophecy about what is to happen to David's *women*, so the narrative of the Tekoite woman's story, and of David's reaction to it, is merely the first in a series of incidents in David's life which illustrate his prediction in 2 Samuel 6, that there will continue to be handmaidens of his who flatter and honor him, no matter how contemptible he shows himself to be. Here as elsewhere, such maids of honor come upon the scene paradoxically to proclaim and to deny the greatness of David and his house. Is the Deuteronomist telling us that the heart of the narrator is as ambiguously for (*ʿal*) and against (*ʿal*) David as "the heart of David was *ʿal* (for or against?) Absalom" (14:1)?

As I suggested above, the exclusive use of *'āmāh* in Samuel and Kings to designate handmaidens of David or his servants—used of Abigail (1 Sam. 25:24, 25, 28, 31, and 41), of the women referred to by Michal and David (2 Sam. 6:20, 22), of the woman from Tekoa (here in 2 Sam. 14:15, 16), of the wise woman of Maacah (2 Sam. 20:17), of Bathsheba (1 Kings 1:13, 17), and of one of the mothers before Solomon (1 Kings 3:20)—recalls the opening story in 1 Samuel 1. Here Hannah, requesting a son of God as Israel will request a king in 1 Samuel 8, calls herself the handmaid of Eli (*'āmāh*: 1 Sam. 1:11, 16), the royal figure in 1 Samuel 1–4.[17] Despite the ambiguities in 2 Samuel 14, it is noteworthy that *'āmāh* only occurs in Samuel/Kings to designate a woman who by word or work appears to support the cause of kingship in general and the glory of David's house in particular—even while David and his house are in the process of making themselves more and more contemptible. As with the specific use of ^cal in 2 Samuel 14, so with the generalized use of *'āmāh* throughout David's life and beyond: the account of his long career may be said to be $^cal\ dāwid$, somehow both for and against the house of David.

David's *Šiphāh*

The second term that the woman uses to call herself David's handmaid is *šiphāh*. Recall the words that Joab put in the mouth of this woman, "Behold, the whole family (*mišpehāh*) has risen up against (^cal) your handmaid (*šiphāh*)" (v. 7). This play on the root, *šph*, helps to explain why the Tekoite calls herself David's *šiphāh* so many times in her conversation with the king (vv. 6, 7, 12, 15, 17, and 19). David's maidservant (*šiphāh*) comes from a family (*mišpehāh*) that wants to destroy her and her son from the heritage of God, that is, from Israel (v. 16). This family, in the story that Joab has the woman tell David, functions very much like the rich man in Nathan's story. When Nathan told his story, David took sides against the man and incriminates himself; now the Tekoite tells her story, and David appears to take sides against her whole family—once again incriminating himself. More than David's maidservant, the woman, by illustrating David's foolishness for allowing Absalom, his heir, to remain in exile, is, as I have suggested, Joab's maidservant as well. There is obvious irony, therefore, in the woman's depiction of David as wise. Nevertheless, in comparing David's wisdom to that of God's messenger, the narrator is adding a social dimension to such irony. A look at the destructive activities of God's messenger in Samuel/Kings suggests a number of social dimensions to the woman's double comparison of David to a messenger of God.

In contrast to Judges, which is filled with appearances of the messenger of God or the LORD (*mal'āk 'elohîm/YHWH*), 1–2 Samuel has only one story in which the messenger of God performs some emissary function: the account of God's punishment of Israel and sparing of Jerusalem in 2 Samuel 24. It is true, as I have mentioned, that reference to this figure does appear four other times in the Books of Samuel, but in all these instances a character in the story simply compares David to a messenger of God: first Achish (1 Sam. 29:9), then the woman of Tekoa (2 Sam. 14:17, 20), and finally Mephibosheth (2 Sam. 19:27). When we add to the activity of God's messenger in 2 Samuel 24 those actions occurring in 1–2 Kings (1 Kings 19:7; 2 Kings 1:3, 15; 19:35), it is especially clear that God's messenger in Samuel/Kings is always sent in behalf of, or in response to the pleas of, God's special servants—his prophets and kings—just as he is sent in behalf of his judges most of the time in the Book of Judges.

The two acts of destruction wrought by God's messenger in 2 Samuel 24 and 2 Kings 19, against Israel and Assyria respectively, illustrate this stable connection of God's messenger to his *servants*.

In 2 Samuel 24, after seventy thousand Israelites have died from pestilence, "when the messenger stretched forth his hand toward Jerusalem to destroy it, the LORD repented of the evil, and said to the angel who was working destruction among the people, 'It is enough; now stay your hand'" (v. 16). Here God is apparently responding to David's admission of guilt, immediately revealed by the narrator in the very next verse, "When [David] saw the angel who was smiting the people, he said, 'Lo, I have sinned, and I have done wickedly. Let thy hand, I pray thee, be against me'" (v. 17).

In 2 Kings 19, God's messenger again saves Jerusalem, and again he acts in response to the pleas of the king (here Hezekiah) quoted in verses 15–19. Whereas in 2 Samuel 24, God's angel had killed seventy thousand Israelites before sparing Jerusalem, in 2 Kings 19 he slays 185,000 Assyrians in order to protect Jerusalem. And in 2 Kings 19, the narrator quotes God's own words in explanation of the activity of his messenger, "For I will defend this city to save it, for my own sake, *and for the sake of my servant David*" (v. 34).

When we compare the account of David acting in behalf of Absalom in 2 Samuel 14 to the two accounts of God's messenger protecting Jerusalem in 2 Samuel 24 and 2 Kings 19, the social dimensions surrounding the story of how Absalom returned to Jerusalem from exile start to appear.[18] In 2 Samuel 14, the woman interrupts David with, "On me be the guilt, my lord the king, and on my father's house; let the king and his throne be guiltless" (v. 9). Commentators have written at length on this verse, which, as McCarter writes, is "a difficult verse, both with regard to its meaning and to its relationship to the verses that precede and follow it."[19] It may not be accidental that in 2 Samuel 24 David's response to the destruction wrought by God's messenger (*mal'āk*) will be very much like the woman's response to the one whom she compares to God's messenger: David will speak to the LORD and his messenger, "Let thy hand, I pray thee, be against me and against my father's house" (24:17).

In her fabricated story in chapter 14, the woman proclaims herself and her father's house guilty, and pronounces the king, whom she regards as a person like God's messenger, guiltless if only he protect the remnant of her house. In the narrator's story in 2 Samuel 24, it is David who declares himself and his house guilty, at the same time suggesting that the lord and his angel will act justly in sparing the innocent sheep of Jerusalem.

The second story about the messenger of God protecting Jerusalem (2 Kings 19) sheds further light on the national dimensions of David's protection of Absalom in 2 Samuel 14. The preservation of David's house in spite of the acknowledged *guilt* of that house is the paradoxical and unavoidable historical truth that motivates the entire story of the Davidic monarchy. The Tekoite woman' strange request to David that he spare the remnant of her father's house despite her subsequent proclamation of the *guilt* of her father's house is no more paradoxical than David subsequently returning the supposed heir of his house to Jerusalem in spite of Absalom's guilt; or than God graciously sparing Jerusalem despite David's proclamation of his guilt and that of his father's house in 2 Samuel 24; or, for that matter, than God's openly calling David his servant in 2 Kings 19:34 and promising to preserve David's father's house, despite the king's grievous sin in 2 Samuel 11 and his open admission in 2 Samuel 24 that both he and his father's house were guilty.

So the story of God defending Jerusalem "to save it, for my own sake and for the sake of my servant David" (2 Kings 19:34) allows us to reflect back on 2 Samuel 14 and hear the social or national overtones within it. Faced with the siege of Jerusalem by Sennacherib, Hezekiah prays to the Lord, "Save us (*hôšîᶜēnû*) from his hand" (19:19), just as the Tekoite woman falls on her face before David and prays, "Save [me] (*hôšîᶜāh*), O King" (14:4). David's house, the city of Jerusalem, and the tribe of Judah are all intertwined in the story which the Tekoite woman tells David. Her family has risen up "to destroy the heir also, and leave neither name nor remnant (*šeʾērît*) upon the face of the earth" (14:7). We already know, in the immediate application of the story, that her son represents the heir to the house of David, Absalom, who is portrayed here as the remnant of David's house. We recall, in this regard, that David himself was introduced into the larger narrative as the remnant of Jesse's house, the one son who has not yet been rejected by Samuel: "There remains (*šāʾar*) yet the youngest," Jesse tells Samuel in 1 Sam. 16:11 just before we get our first glimpse of David. Like father like son.

On the other hand, the social implications of the Tekoite's plea for David to save her son, the heir and remnant, rest with the larger story's designation of *the tribe of Judah* as the remnant of Israel. When northern Israel will be "torn from the house of David" (2 Kings 17:21), the narrator will explain why, and then focus upon Judah as the remnant: "Therefore, the LORD was very angry with Israel, and removed them out of his sight; none was left (*nišʾar*) but the tribe of Judah only" (2 Kings 17:18). When even *this* remnant is threatened in the siege of Jerusalem by Sennacherib, Hezekiah will send men covered with sackcloth to Isaiah (2 Kings 19:2), as Joab sends the woman with mourning garments to David, and will plead, "Therefore, lift up your prayer for the remnant (*šeʾērît*) that is left" (2 Kings 19:4), just as the woman pleads with David, "Thus [the whole family] would quench my coal which is left (*niš'ārāh*) and leave to my husband neither name nor remnant (*šᵉ'ērît*)" (2 Sam. 14:7).

Described by the woman as "like a messenger of God," David goes on to save his heir just as in 2 Kings 19 the real messenger of God will save Judah and Jerusalem, "the remnant that is left" (v. 4). David indeed returns Absalom from exile. What would happen to the house of Israel were God to return the remnant of Judah from exile in Babylon? This is the unspoken question, the remnant that remains, after reading the last chapter of the Deuteronomic History, 2 Kings 25. For now, the immediate question that occupies the reader at the end of 2 Samuel 14 and the beginning of 2 Samuel 15 is what will happen to the house of David once Absalom returns from exile?[20]

·7·

CURSES
(15:1–16:23)

Curses are like young chickens, they always come home to roost.
(Robert Southey)

At Play in the Fields of the LORD: Paronomasia in 2 Samuel 15

Chapters 15–18 describe the rebellion of Absalom that ends with his death. Four years after David had allowed Absalom to return to Jerusalem, his son's revolt forces David himself to flee the city. That revolt and that flight constitute the main events of chapter 15, which exhibits the interplay of aesthetic brilliance and ideological complexity that has characterized the History from the beginning. Attention to a few apparently minor details in chapter 15 will help to introduce us to the more important issues driving the narrative along.

First notice how verses 1–6 form a neat exposition of the four years preceding Absalom's revolt. In its frequent use of at least seven imperfective verb forms to indicate habitual, repeated, or condensed action, this introductory section of the chapter recalls 1 Sam. 1:1–8, expository verses preparing the reader for the events surrounding the birth of Samuel.[1] Here in 2 Samuel 15, the narrator describes what Absalom *used to do* or *continued to do,* over the four years during which he "stole the hearts of the men of Israel" (v. 6).[2] The importance of recognizing verses 1–6 as exposition that introduces the revolt of Absalom lies in the efficiency with which these verses characterize Absalom, and highlight important issues.

In the exposition, the narrator quotes Absalom, "O that I were judge in the land! Then every man with a suit (*rîb*) or cause (*mišpāṭ*) might come to me, and I would justify him (*wᵉhiṣdaqtîw*)" (v. 4). The significance of this reported speech of Absalom in the expository material introducing his revolt can hardly be exaggerated.[3] By exposing the abiding motivation of Absalom as he played the politician before every Israelite who came to Jerusalem for a suit ("See, your claims are good and right" [v. 3]), verses

149

1–6 move us to wonder on one hand how Absalom's behavior corresponds to the Deuteronomic law code concerning such matters, and, on the other, how such behavior compares to that of other characters in the story.

The relevant legislation in Deuteronomy is straightforward: "When there is a dispute (*rîb*) between men and they come into court, then they shall judge them. They shall justify (*wᵉhiṣdîqû*) the righteous (*haṣṣaddîq*) and condemn the guilty" (Deut. 25:1). The contrast between this law and Absalom's behavior is clear and simple: Absalom ought to distinguish between the innocent and guilty, yet his practice, over many years, of declaring "good and righteous" the claims of everyone coming to Jerusalem for judgement appears to contravene the law code and to constitute a flagrant attempt to steal the hearts of his fellow Israelites in preparation for usurping the throne of his father.

With respect to the legislation of Deut. 25:1–3, Solomon's words in 1 Kings 8 contrast sharply with Absalom's. During the dedication of the temple, Solomon beseeches the LORD to judge those who come before the altar of the temple: "Then hear thou in heaven, and act, and judge thy servants, condemning the guilty by bringing his conduct upon his own head, and vindicating the righteous (*ûlhaṣdîq ṣaddîq*) by rewarding him according to his righteousness (*ṣidqātô*)" (1 Kings 8:32).

What makes the language of justification in Moses's law and Solomon's prayer so important, as a context for Absalom's behavior here in 2 Samuel 15, is its distinctiveness within the History: Deuteronomy 25, 2 Samuel 15, and 1 Kings 8 are the only places in the History where the root *ṣdq* is used in a verbal form (whether *qal, nifal, hifil, or hitpael*). Absalom's habit of declaring innocent *everyone* bringing a suit to Jerusalem appears, then, to focus upon and contravene the law of Moses, even as it stands in sharp contrast to the concept of divine justice voiced, if not practiced, by his half-brother Solomon later on in the story. This aspect of Absalom's preparations for revolt succeeds in surrounding his *character zone* with a negative evaluation from the very beginning. Rather than being shown as trying to take over responsibilities somehow neglected by his father, Absalom is indirectly portrayed here as subverting Israelite law in order to curry favor with those whose support he will need if his revolt is to succeed. We see here how legal and literary context can transform an apparently innocent statement into an implicit condemnation of its speaker.

The chapter's tendency to play with language highlights a second aspect of Absalom's promiscuous justification of fellow Israelites during the period preceding his revolt. When David hears that "the hearts of the men of Israel have gone after Absalom" (v. 13), the king quickly flees the city, and immediately meets three individuals, Ittai the Gittite (vv. 19–22), Zadok the priest (vv. 24–29), and Hushai the Archite (vv. 32–37). Wordplay immediately surrounds David's meeting with Ittai. The account of the meeting comprises only four verses, yet Ittai's name is connected to the circumstances surrounding David's flight in a number of interesting ways. The meeting begins with "Then the king said to Ittai (*'ittay*) the Gittite, 'Why will you also go with us (*'ittānû*)?'" (v. 19), and ends with "So Ittai (*'ittay*) the Gittite passed on, with all his men and all the little ones who were with him (*'ittô*)" (v. 22). In between, Ittai's own oath indicates the thematic function that his name plays in the story itself, "But Ittai answered the king, 'As the LORD lives, and as my lord the king lives, wherever my lord the king shall be, whether for death or for life, there also will your servant be'" (v. 21). The narrative role of Ittai, therefore, whose very name suggests "loyalty" or "companion," is *to be with David wherever he goes*.[4]

Lest we assume that there is something haphazard about the appearance of Ittai in conjunction with the repeated usage of *'et* in verses 19–22, a broader perspective suggests that paronomasia is a widespread feature of the story at this point. As one of the two principal words meaning "with" in Hebrew (*ᶜim* is the other word), *'et* occurs ten times in chapter 15 alone—more often than in any other chapter of 2 Samuel.[5] Moreover, if we look at the larger story of Absalom's revolt, we notice that the occurrences of *'et*, "with," in these five chapters are much more frequent than anywhere else in the book.[6] It is safe to suggest, therefore, that wordplay involving the meeting of David and Ittai in 15:19–22 points to aspects of the narrative that transcend a merely aesthetic connection of the name of Ittai to his abiding desire to be *with* David. A number of paronomastic details within the chapter not only structure its narrative events, but also indicate some authorial perspectives that shape the larger story of Absalom's revolt.

If we return to the expository material in verses 1–6, we will see how wordplay can indicate something about the authorial motivation behind the three meetings recounted in this chapter. I have already remarked how rarely the History uses the language of justification employed by Absalom in verse 4 ("Then *every man* with a suit or cause might come to me, and *I would declare him righteous* [my translation of *wᵉhiṣdaqtîw*]"). Besides providing the initial basis for a negative evaluation of Absalom in the story, his language also serves as aesthetic play preceding further play on the name of the *second* person David will meet in chapter 15, Zadok the priest. Like Ittai, Zadok starts out with David, but unlike Ittai, whom David keeps with him, Zadok must return to Jerusalem. The one whose very name denotes "companion" accompanies David as he flees Jerusalem. On the other hand, Zadok, whose name denotes "justice or righteousness," returns to the royal pretender, who for four years had unscrupulously justified or declared righteous every claimant he met at the gate of Jerusalem. There is something deliciously playful, yet intensely serious, about such verbal and narrative insinuations.

A third, albeit less direct, example of wordplay in chapter 15 involves the name of the last person David meets in the chapter, Hushai the Archite.[7] David's departure from Jerusalem is accomplished *in haste*: "Then David said to all his servants who were with him at Jerusalem, 'Arise, and let us flee; or else there will be no escape for us from Absalom; *go in haste* (*mah^{a}rû*) lest he overtake us *quickly* (*y^{e}mahēr*)'" (v. 14). It is more than accidental that Hushai, whose role in the History is confined to 2 Samuel 15–17, turns up in a story that emphasizes the dangerous haste surrounding David. *Mhr* and *hûš* are synonyms,[8] so that there is an obvious correlation between the presence of Hushai and the increased usage of *mhr* in 2 Samuel 15–19.[9] The man whom we could call in English, "Hasty the Archite," now comes upon the scene, because the semantic wordplay between *mhr* and *hûšay*, like that surrounding the names of Ittai and Zadok, indicates something more than simply the aesthetic pleasure that comes from etymologizing. In such wordplay we encounter a recurring signal about authorial motivations for shaping the story of Absalom's revolt in its present form. David keeps with him Ittai, his loyal companion from Gath, but returns the righteous one, Zadok, to Absalom, the one who had unrighteously declared all Israelites righteous. Then David returns Hushai, his hasty friend, to the royal pretender whose contemplated haste, David declared, would force the king to leave Jerusalem in haste (v. 14).

The names of those with whom David meets and speaks in 2 Samuel 15 tell us something about the ideological dimensions of the story: What does it mean to be *with* David—or *with* Absalom for that matter? Whose side is the side of *justice*, David's or Absalom's? And what evaluative accents surround the *hasty* comings and goings that constitute this part of David's story? Before I can attend to these important questions, further artful aspects within the story need discussing.

Between Mimesis and Artifice: Crossing Boundaries

So much has been written about how the author(s) of 2 Samuel 9–20 wrote from direct personal knowledge and with a wealth of realistic particulars, that I have been at pains to complement this picture by describing some signals of literary composition within it that highlight a central aspect of the story. The account of the succession to the throne of David, at this point at least, appears to possess two opposed stylistic characteristics: a narrative edifice exhibiting an elaborate facade of mimetic detail, and in addition, a well crafted and highly stylized—even ritualized—account of Absalom's abortive attempt to succeed to the throne of David. In connection with the extensive wordplay that I am suggesting characterizes this part of David's story, the profoundly ritualized nature of David's hasty retreat from Jerusalem, and of his painful return, is an important signal of the extent of literary artifice that has gone into the final composition of this story. We can begin to cross over from mimesis to artifice by examining the many ways in which characters cross over (*ᶜābar*) boundaries—in this chapter and in those to come.[10]

We already know from the ritual procession in Josh. 3:1–5:1 that those in the History who cross the Jordan usually carry with them heavy ideological baggage.[11] To cross over (*ᶜābar*) into or out of the land is an especially appropriate action for Hebrews (*ᶜibrîm*), yet there are four sections within the History where occurrences of *ᶜābar*, "to cross over," are particularly frequent: Deuteronomy 2–4; Josh. 3:1–5:1; Joshua 24; and here in 2 Samuel 15–20.[12] One ought not to be surprised, therefore, that the frequent use of *ᶜābar* in 2 Samuel 15–20 carries with it a number of important implications for our understanding of the story. If we concentrate on the choreography of "crossing over" in the account of David's flight from Jerusalem in chapter 15, we can illustrate how the larger complex in chapters 15–20 uses highly stylized language to convey highly ritualized action.[13]

To begin with the *stylistic facade* of 2 Samuel 15, countless readers have commented on the general impression they have when reading 2 Samuel 9–20 that it is based upon an eyewitness account of the events unfolding within it. However, when such commentators give reasons for their impression, they rarely discuss those features that directly and obviously suggest that the narrator may be writing from direct personal knowledge. Chapter 15's extensive use of imperfective verb forms in the reporting speech of the narrator is perhaps the most immediate, yet largely unrecognized, compositional reason for the eyewitness flavor of this portion of the story of Absalom's revolt. There may be no pericope within the Books of Samuel that so abundantly employs verb forms whose function is to bring readers into the center of the action by presenting that action as if it were taking place before their eyes—in a manner similar to the temporal point of view of the characters themselves within the story world. David's flight from Jerusalem, from the conspiracy of Absalom mentioned in verse 12 to Absalom's subsequent taking over of the city in verse 37, is narrated from a predominantly *synchronic viewpoint* that succeeds in slowing the action down and giving readers the impression that they too are present as events unfold.

This obvious feature of the chapter's narrative style says absolutely nothing about anyone's actual knowledge of, or physical presence at, the events described therein. All we can really say is that the function of these imperfective verb forms is to convey an impression of such knowledge. Like the narrator's obvious omniscience, the text's synchronic perspective is simply a conventional literary feature that establishes for us, as Sternberg might say, the truth claim, but not the truth value, of the reliable, or eyewitness, flavor of this chapter's happenings. And, as previous readers have so often remarked, what happens before our eyes in chapter 15 is as much a ritual performance as it is a strategic retreat.[14]

Besides, then, the imperfective verb forms that indicate habitual or condensed action in the exposition in verses 1–6, an unusual number of other imperfective verb forms function in the chapter to draw the reader into the center of action and to represent the temporal perspective of characters rather than that of the narrator. The following narrative statements are synchronic rather than retrospective:

> v. 12: and the people with Absalom *continued to increase* (*hôlēk wārāb*);
>
> v. 18: and all his servants *were passing by him* (*coberîm cal yādô*) and all the Cherethites, and all the Pelethites, and all the six hundred Gittites *were passing in front of the king* (*coberîm cal penê hammelek*);
>
> v. 23: and all the land *was weeping* (*bôkîm*) with a loud voice and all the people *were crossing* (*coberîm*) and the king *was crossing over* (*cobēr*) the brook Kidron and all the people *were crossing over* (*coberîm*) in front of the road to (?) the wilderness;
>
> v. 24: And lo (*wehinnēh*) Zadok and the priests with him *were carrying* (*nośe'îm*) the ark;
>
> v. 30: David *was going up* (*coleh*) the ascent, *going up* (*coleh*) and *weeping* (*bôkeh*), and his head *is covered* (*hāpûy*) and he *was walking* (*holēk*) barefoot, and they *were going up* (*wecālû*) *crying continually* (*cāloh ûbākoh*);
>
> v. 32: Behold (*wehinnēh*) Hushai the Archite to meet him: his coat *is torn* (*qārû'ac*);
>
> v. 37: And just when Hushai, David's friend, came to the city, Absalom *was coming* (*yābo'*) to Jerusalem.

Notice that these synchronic imperfectives are complemented by two *hinnēh*'s, ("behold": vv. 24, 32), by which the narrator further describes action from the various points of view of the characters themselves.

When one relates the distribution of these synchronic verbs to their specific content, it is clear that what is conveyed to readers as happening before their very eyes, as it were, is the series of events that begins with the *continuing increase* of Israelites who side with Absalom in verse 15 and ends with Absalom's *entering Jerusalem* in verse 37. In between these verses, the employment of at least fourteen additional imperfective verb forms succeeds in making the action especially vivid and present to the reader. And yet, paradoxically, this recurring feature of the chapter is the clearest indication we have that such synchronicity is but a stylistic facade indicating the complex artifice that shapes the narrative at this point.

Listen to David after he hears that the hearts of the men of Israel have gone after Absalom: "Arise, and let us flee; or else there will be no escape for us from Absalom; *go in haste,* lest he overtake us *quickly*" (v. 14). Yet, as the events of verses 15–37 unfold, the synchronic, slow motion effect of all the imperfectives employed in these verses combines with the repetitive choreography of David's procession, and with his series of meetings, to turn the narrative into an account of a choreographed withdrawal rather than a hurried flight. What happens before our very eyes is a highly stylized account of the highly ritualized flight of David from Jerusalem.

Three features especially illustrate the stylization of language that pervades chapter 15 and foreshadows further details of the story to come. First, there are a couple of processional reversals using the verb, *ʿābar,* "to cross over." These reversals emphasize the ritualistic nature of the flight itself and prepare us for interesting and unexpected uses of *ʿābar* later on in the story. Second, David's hasty journey out of Jerusalem in chapter 15 is interrupted by ideologically important conversations with Ittai, Zadok, and Hushai, just as chapter 16 will narrate his meeting with Ziba and Shimei near the high point of his flight (16:1), and just as chapter 19 will describe David's meetings with Shimei, Mephibosheth, and Barzillai before he crosses the Jordan back into the land in verse 39. This 3-2-3 configuration of meetings, as David goes up away from and down toward Jerusalem, intensifies the impression of choreography. And, third, there is a definite protocol involved in "crossing over with the king" (*ʿābar ʾet* or *ʿim*) or "making him cross over, escorting him over" (*ʿābar* in the *hifil*). Definite but complicated rewards or penalties await those who manage, or fail, to accompany the king on his processional journey.

Each of these three aspects of David's ritual procession out of and back into Jerusalem offer important ideological indications of what the text is saying at this point in the story.

First, the initial reversal in chapter 15 takes place in verses 17–18, where, at first, the king is in front of the people, but then the procession halts and "all his servants were passing by him (*ʿobeʿrîm ʿal yādô*) and all the Cherethites, and all the Pelethites, and all the six hundred Gittites who had followed him from Gath were passing on before the king (*cobᵉrîm cal pᵉnê hammelek*)." A second processional switch occurs in verse 24, "And behold, there were Zadok and all the Levites with him, who were carrying the ark of the covenant of God, and Abiathar also; they set down the ark of God until the people had all passed out (*cad tom lacabôr*) from the city." The king and the ark precede, but at a crucial point in the journey, that is, at the last house in verse 17 and at the outskirts of the city in verse 24, the leaders stop and allow those behind them to cross over before them, as if following a rubric according to which king and ark are to precede *before* the crucial crossing, but then follow *after* it takes place.

Such ritual moves remind us immediately of the account of Israel crossing the Jordan into the land in Josh. 3:1–5:1. One has only to compare the following sets of verses to see that something similar is going on—whatever its ritual and ideological significance:

> And while all Israel were passing over (*cobᵉrîm*) on dry ground, the priests who bore the ark of the covenant of the LORD stood (*wayyacamdû*). (Josh. 3:17)
> And they stood (*wayyacamdû*) at the last house and all his servants were passing by (*cobᵉrîm*) and all the Cherethites and Pelethites and Gittites were passing over (*cobᵉrîm*) in front of the king. (2 Sam. 15:17–8)
>
> . . . until all the nation finished passing over. (*cad 'ašer tammû lacabor*) (Josh. 3:17)
> . . . until all the people had passed out of (*cad tom lacabor*) the city. (2 Sam. 15:24)

This comparison of Joshua 3–5 and 2 Samuel 15–20 is especially relevant because both complexes center around crossing the Jordan. What 2 Samuel 15–20 adds, however, is a more ritualized and detailed procession and protocol, a stylized series of *crossover points* during the revolt of Absalom. In Joshua 3–5, the procession of Israelites crosses over the Jordan in only one direction (into the land), whereas here in 2 Samuel 15–20 David's crossing the Jordan is in both directions, out of the land in 17:22 and back into it in 19:40. Nevertheless, the journey in Joshua 3–5 is still described from two spatial points of view.[15] More importantly, the two features of crossing the Jordan in procession and of doing so according to a definite protocol concerning who leads or follows are both repeated within 2 Samuel 15–20 through a number of wonderful narrative variations that I shall discuss as each occurs in the following chapters.

Second, chapter 15's account of David's meetings with Ittai, Zadok, and Hushai constitute a series of dialogues before the procession crosses over the Jordan, just as chapter 19's account of the king's meetings with

Shimei, Mephibosheth, and Barzillai interrupt his return journey just before the procession crosses over back into the land in 19:40 (English versification: 19:39). And in between these triple meetings in chapters 15 and 19, David's meetings with Ziba and Shimei follow his "crossing over the summit" in 16:1. The 3-2-3 configuration of meetings that I have already indicated, so obviously determined by the procession's location in reference to various crossover points throughout the journey, lends a stylized and ritualized cast to the account—a slant that is in tension with any "realistic" features one may point to in the text.

As I suggested above, David's dialogue with Ittai, whose name suggests "with me," or "my companion," involves deciding whether he is to accompany David or return to Jerusalem; the conversation with Zadok, whose name suggests "righteous" or "just," leads to his and the ark's return to the royal pretender who habitually declared righteous every Israelite whom he met at the gate; and David's meeting with Hushai, whose name suggests "hurry" or "haste," is surrounded by numerous references to the dangerous haste caused by the revolt of Absalom. In short, these three meetings involve a paronomastic staging that makes this section of 2 Samuel a delight to read and a challenge to interpret.

Third, the emphasis in chapters 15–19 on who is *with* or *not with* the king during his flight, on who escorts the king and who does not, and on the protocol that obtains within the procession itself—such emphasis is best understood when one considers that the local wordplay between Ittai's name and David's statement in 15:19 ("Then the king said to *Ittai* (*'ty*), 'Why will you go, you *with us* [*'th 'tnw*]?'") is actually indicative of a much wider stylistic phenomenon within chapters 15–20. Concerning the two Hebrew words meaning "with," *'et* and *ᶜim,* each occurs with much greater frequency in chapters 15–19 than elsewhere in 2 Samuel.[16] This increased usage of "with" obtains partly because the material itself is so much concerned with who is with David or not with him, with Absalom or not. Nevertheless, the lexical profile of chapters 15–19, insofar as wordplay involving *'et* or *ᶜim* is concerned, corresponds to its thematic profile in ways that transcend the normal union of form and content found in everyday speech.

In short, the story that chapter 15 introduces is highly contrived and stylized, whatever its historiographic profile may be.

David's Flight: Ideological Directions

I have already described the emphasis, in chapters 15–19, on the theme of *being with the king* or not, a theme signaled by the marked increase and frequent wordplay of terms indicating "accompaniment" in this section.

The story of Ittai, Zadok, and Hushai is one of being *with David* even though only Ittai physically and etymologically accompanies him across the Jordan into temporary exile; Zadok and Hushai remain with David despite faithfully and hastily returning to Jerusalem. There was also the definite protocol in the chapter concerning *how* one accompanies the king: in the procession out of the city and across the Jordan, those who are with the king are at times in front of him, at times behind him. To pass over with the king (*ᶜābar 'et* or *ᶜim*) requires *following him* up to the boundary, but then *preceding him* across it. Finally, there are important implications in David's proposed return to Jerusalem.

The narrative, even before Absalom rebels, signals its coming preoccupation with matters of return by quoting Absalom's vow in verse 8. Absalom tells David, "For your servant vowed a vow while I dwelt in Geshur in Aram, saying, 'If the LORD will indeed bring me back to Jerusalem (*yāšîb yᵉšîbēnî*), then I will offer worship to the LORD.'" Absalom's vow introduces us to ideological issues of return (*šûb*) that will occupy the narrative until David's actual return to Jerusalem in chapter 19. Almost half of the occurrences of *šûb* in 2 Samuel appear in chapters 15–19, and the importance of "returning to Jerusalem" is signaled by its introduction into the story even before the revolt begins.[17] Absalom is concerned about returning from exile to his own city, Jerusalem, and this is the first and most important function of the use of *šûb* in 2 Samuel 15–19.[18] After Absalom's revolt and David's flight have begun, David counsels Ittai the exile (*goleh*), "*go back* [to Jerusalem], *go back* and take your brothers with you" (15:19–20). David then tells Zadok, "*Take the ark back* to the city; the LORD *may bring me back* to see the ark's habitation; *go back* to the city" (vv. 25, 27). The narrator reports that Zadok and Abiathar *brought the ark back* to Jerusalem (v. 29), and David finally tells Hushai, "*Return* to the city" (v. 34).

A second issue introduced by *šûb* is the restoration of the king(dom). If the eventual loser in the revolt is shown first returning to Jerusalem even before David—the eventual victor—is forced to start planning his own return in 15:19ff, it is Mephibosheth—already a loser—who first voices this second aspect of return: "Today the house of Israel will *restore* to me the kingdom of my father" (16:3).[19] Will David, the supplanter of Saul, be returned to his throne after his exile across the Jordan?

A third function of *šûb* in this section concerns the question of divine recompense for David's actions. Again it is a loser in the story, here Shimei, who introduces us to this aspect of return. Shimei's curse to David states, "May the LORD *return upon you* all the blood of the house of Saul" (16:8). David's response indicates the alternative that he, understandably, prefers: "It may be that the LORD will look upon my affliction, and that the LORD *will return good to me* in place of this cursing of me today" (16:12).

These three facets of *šûb* in the story—returning to Jerusalem, restoring the king(dom), and repaying the king for his actions—help us to see something of the ideological point of view that permeates the story of Absalom's revolt. The various emphases on return in chapters 15–19 seem not so much required by David's flight from Jerusalem, as David's flight appears necessary in order to focus the story on some central issues: exilic return to Jerusalem; return with or without the king; following him across boundaries in deadly pursuit (17:22–24) or preceding him across as his loyal servants; exilic restoration of the kingship; and finally, divine retribution concerning the house of David. Here is a story wherein the hasty flight of David is slowed down in a highly stylized manner so that the central topic of his eventual return to Jerusalem may be addressed in terms that mirror the complex situation of discourse between a Deuteronomic voice and its contemporary audience.

For example, perhaps the ark is not allowed to cross the Jordan with David because it is no longer with Israel in Babylon. David may be stating to Zadok what many Israelites in Babylon hoped in their hearts, "If I find favor in the eyes of the LORD, he will bring me back and let me see both [the ark] and his habitation" (15:25). As we saw indications of the exilic situation of discourse lying behind references to exile or captivity in 1 Sam. 4:21–22, so also the use of *gālāh* here in 2 Sam. 15:19—where Ittai the exile (*goleh*) is allowed to cross the Jordan with David into a kind of double exile—is the only other instance in the Books of Samuel of *gālāh* denoting "exile."[20]

We find a final hint of the ideological dimensions of chapter 15 in David's command to his servants, "Arise, and let us flee; or else there will be no escape (*pelēṭāh*) for us from Absalom" (15:14). The root, *plṭ*, is found infrequently in the History, yet many of its occurrences concern issues of fratricide, whether familial, tribal, or national in nature.[21]

The authorial perspective on survival during Absalom's revolt looks backward to the judicial period in Israel's history when, in the Jephthah story of Judges 12, the Gileadites smote their tribal brothers, the Ephraimites, and where both are called "survivors of Ephraim (*pelîṭê 'eprāyîm*)" (Judg. 12:4, 5). At the end of Judges, warfare between tribal brothers becomes so severe that the tribe of Benjamin nears extinction: "And they said, 'There must be an inheritance for the survivors (*pelēṭāh*) of Benjamin, that a tribe be not blotted out from Israel'" (Judg. 21:17). Here in 2 Samuel 15, during the monarchic period, "survivors" refer to individuals within the house of David who are threatened by another member of the same house. And David himself will thank the LORD in 2 Sam. 22:44, "Thou didst deliver me (*wattepalleṭēnî*) from strife with my people."

Ahead in the story, the conspiracy of Jehu against Joram also recalls Absalom's conspiracy against David. There, as here, the issue of escaping from the city is central to the plot, "So Jehu said, 'If this is your mind, then let no one escape (*pālîṭ*) from the city to go and tell the news in Jezreel'" (2 Kings 9:15). The Deuteronomic issue of tribal and national survival will take one final turn during Assyria's assault on Israel. Isaiah will prophesy, "And the surviving remnant (*pᵉlēṭat*) of the house of Judah shall again take root downward; for *out of Jerusalem* shall go forth a remnant, and out of Mount Zion a band of survivors (*šᵉ'ērit ûplēṭāh*)" (2 Kings 19:30–31). It is almost as if David's flight from Jerusalem in 2 Samuel 15 is a precursor of Isaiah's prophecy in 2 Kings 19, a ritual procession that looks forward to Israel's exile from the land even as it reverses, with similar choreography, Israel's original crossing of the Jordan *into* the land in Josh. 3:1–5:1.

2 Samuel 16: Considerations of Context

We begin with the ways in which the events in this chapter are structured. Verses 1–14 recount what happens after David crosses beyond the summit of the Mount of Olives, and verses 15–23 report what transpires after Absalom comes to Jerusalem. The parallels between these two halves are striking. First David meets Ziba and Shimei, then Absalom meets Hushai and Ahithophel. The chapter begins "just beyond the summit," at the spatial highpoint in David's procession, where David receives a couple of asses laden with food and drink—gifts from the servant of Mephibosheth "for the king's house." The chapter ends on the roof of David's palace, the spatial highpoint of Absalom's revolt, where Absalom went in to the concubines whom David had left "to keep the house." What happens on high to David in the chapter—beyond the summit and upon the roof—are ironic lowpoints in his career: he is cursed by Shimei and dishonored by Absalom. Finally and perhaps most importantly, the chapter characterizes Shimei's cursing of David and Absalom's taking of David's concubines in much the same way: Shimei curses David because, David believes, the LORD said he should (vv. 10, 11); and Absalom humiliates David in the sight of all Israel because Ahithophel said he should. Since David and Absalom consider the counsel of Ahithophel equivalent to the word of God (v. 23), not just the cursing of David in the first half, but even his humiliation in the second, are believed to be happening at the LORD's behest.

We should not forget that the narrator earlier has David saying, "O LORD, I pray thee, turn the counsel of Ahithophel into foolishness" (15:31). Yet now we hear that David considers this counsel to be "as if one consulted the word of God" (16:23). Are we to understand that David hopes to turn the *word of God* into foolishness? At any rate, we know that

David hopes, "Perhaps the LORD will look upon my iniquity and repay me with good for this cursing of me today" (v. 12). If the structural juxtaposing of these two events in chapter 16 has any obvious authorial point, it may be that David's hope in the first part is supposed to be dashed by Absalom's act in the second. It is not just David and Absalom who equate Ahithophel's counsel with the word of God. The narrative also does this here in as obvious a manner as one could expect. We know that David's sin in 2 Samuel 11 provoked God to prophesy in 2 Samuel 12, "Behold I will take your women before your eyes, and give them to your neighbor, and he shall lie with your women *in the sight of the sun*" (v. 11). As countless readers have understood, Absalom's going in to his father's concubines *in the sight of all Israel* is an indication that Absalom's following of at least *this* counsel of Ahithophel is presented by the Deuteronomist as a fulfillment of the word of God.

Besides this looking backward to the divine prophecy of 2 Samuel 12, the events in 2 Samuel 16 also recall matters discussed earlier in connection with 2 Samuel 2 and 2 Samuel 9.

When viewing the curious "seizing of the head" during Israel's ritualized combat at the pool of Gibeon (2:12–17) in a previous chapter, I suggested that David's *character zone,* from the beginning of his career to the end, is intimately connected with the head (*ro'š*) as a locus of guilt and death, and that blood flows upon and from the heads of David's enemies more often than with any other character in the Bible. I also suggested that the semantic fullness of "head" allows it to be a wonderful vehicle for integrating the Deuteronomist's complex story of Israel's *kings.* Even before David appears, Samuel declared that when the LORD anointed Saul king over Israel, he became *head (ro'š)* of the tribes of Israel (1 Sam. 15:17). We now see that the narrator of Absalom's revolt, and its immediate aftermath, continues to handle the various meanings of "head" with great dexterity and creativity.

Look at the varied uses of "head" in chapters 15 and 16. In 15:30 David ascends the Mount of Olives with his *head* covered, as all the people with him covered their *heads.* In 15:32, when David had come to the *head* (or summit) of the mount, Hushai comes to meet him with earth upon his *head.* Then in 16:1, Ziba presents David with gifts of sustenance after the king had passed a little beyond the *head* of the Mount of Olives. And in 16:9 Shimei's cursing of David provokes Abishai to suggest, "Let me cross over and take off his *head.*" We notice that within the space of only four verses the narrator exploits a number of important associations that illustrate the semantic flexibility of *ro'š.* The head is at once a locus of sorrow or penitence when it is covered or besoiled—and of punishment when it is removed. The head is also the physical high point in both a personal and geographic sense, just as earlier in 1 Sam. 15:17 it is the locus of authority in a political sense.

In addition to these suggestive uses of "head" in chapters 15 and 16, we may reach the summit of such associations in chapter 18 where, as we shall see, Shimei's and God's cursing of David rises up to ensnare even his son: "Absalom was riding upon his mule, and the mule went under the thick branches of a great oak, and his *head* caught fast in the oak, and he was left hanging between heaven and earth" (18:9). Another use of "head" as the locale of punishment will occur in chapter 20 (as in 16:9), when the wise woman of Abel convinces her townspeople to cut off the head of the rebellious Sheba and throw it over the wall to Joab (20:21–22). The contrast between how the heads of God's enemies and those of the king's variously embody punishment will be instructive for our understanding of the ideological dimensions of Absalom's royal revolt—and Israel's.

Besides these capital connections to 2 Samuel 2, 2 Samuel 16's account of David's meeting with Ziba also refers back to their earlier meeting in 2 Samuel 9. There, David restored all of Saul's land to Mephibosheth, but here he returns it to Ziba. Further on, in 2 Samuel 19, David will again vary his position by halving the property between Ziba and his master. Taken together, these three occasions help to characterize David in a less than favorable light. The kindness (*ḥesed*) David shows Mephibosheth for Jonathan's sake in 2 Samuel 9, he now retracts in 2 Samuel 16—only to backtrack once more in 2 Samuel 19. Whether the LORD always shows steadfast love to his anointed, as David sings in 22:51, God's anointed is clearly inconstant in demonstrating *his ḥesed* to friend and foe alike.

The first half of chapter 16 continues the preceding chapter's emphasis on synchrony (through the use of imperfectives and *hinnēh*). The passage is filled with action that is presented by the narrator as if it were happening before our eyes, and represented by characters as if it were happening before theirs:

v. 1:   Behold (*wᵉhinnēh*) Ziba to meet him (*liqrā'tô*) with a pair of asses saddled (*ḥᵃbušîm*).

v. 3:   "Behold (*hinnēh*) [Mephibosheth] is residing (*yošēb*) in Jerusalem." (Ziba to David)

v. 5:   Behold (*wᵉhinnēh*) a man coming out (*yôṣē'*), and as he was coming out (*yōṣē' yāṣô'*) he was cursing (*ûmqallēl*).

v. 8:   "Look at you (*wᵉhinnēh*) in your ruin." (Shimei to David)

v. 11: "Behold (*hinnēh*) my son is seeking (*mᵉbaqqēš*) my life." (David to Abishai)

v. 13: And Shimei was going (*hōlēk*) along on the hillside opposite him, cursing and throwing stones (*hālôk wayqallēl waysaqqēl*) and flinging dust (*wᵉⁱppar*).[22]

When the narrative leaves David's "ongoing" procession and returns to events in Jerusalem in the second half of chapter 16, it reverts to the usual *retrospective* presentation of events: in verses 15–23 the narrator no longer employs imperfective verb forms and *hinnēh*. It is as if we are meant to see what happens in David's procession in the wilderness as somehow *still going on before us*, whereas Absalom's machinations in royal Jerusalem *have happened*, and represent a stable past, one that is in contrast to the highly mobile, ongoing, or durative aspects of David's stylized and ritualized procession in the wilderness. The contrast between Israel wandering in the wilderness, while David's kingship is being threatened (verses 1–14), and Israel's residing in Jerusalem (verses 15–23), where Hushai ambiguously says to Absalom, "Long live the king! Long live the king!" (16:16)—such a contrast may represent the Deuteronomist's own perspective on the *synchronic*, ongoing dimension of Israel in exile (with their king in question and their geographic instability emphasized), and the *retrospective* aspect of royal Jerusalem (with its spatial and temporal permanence over with and done for).

One final feature of 2 Samuel 16 continues a concern of 2 Samuel 15: a heavy emphasis on who is with whom during the constitutional crisis inaugurated by Absalom's revolt.[23] The paronomastic implications of *'et* continue in this section. It remains to be seen whether the increased usage of *'et* within 2 Samuel 15–19 has hermeneutic significance as well.

Cursing and Counseling Kings

The heart of 2 Samuel 16 lies in the complex interaction of two related themes concerning the house of David. First, is the house of David really cursed, and if so, in what ways? And second, what role does the king's counsel play in the cursing of the king? Chapter 16's response to these two matters suggests that there is an intimate connection between the LORD's cursing of the king, and the king's reliance on human counselors. So Shimei's cursing of David in the first half of chapter 16 appropriately precedes Ahithophel's counseling of Absalom in the second half.

The significance of Shimei's cursing of David rests upon the affinity that curses and kings have within the larger narrative. The object of curses, whether uttered or actualized in the History, can be nations, tribes, or individuals.[24] When the accursed is a nation, that nation is exclusively Israel—most often the entire nation, but in 2 Sam. 19:44 the northern tribes alone. However, when the accursed are individuals, these unfortunates are almost always *royal figures*—and David turns out to be the History's favorite king to curse.

The narrative scope of Shimei's cursing of David, and its significance within the larger account of Absalom's revolt, is best seen against the backdrop of the History, which establishes an intimate connection between the cursing of individuals and the curse of kingship. Whether the individual instances combining kings and curses are explicit or not, in most cases accursed individuals are narrative stand-ins for an accursed nation.

Look first at the History's practice. The Deuteronomist's favorite objects of curses, *even before the onset of Israel's royal revolt in 1 Samuel 8*, are kings or those individuals who support them. Given the exquisite care with which the History has been fashioned, it is highly significant that the first person actually cursed using a form of the root *qll* (to curse) is Abimelech, Israel's upstart king in the Book of Judges: "And [the men of Shechem] went out into the field, and gathered the grapes from their vineyards, and trod them, and held festival, and went to the house of their god, and ate and drank and cursed (*wayqalᵉlû*) Abimelech" (Judg. 9:27). Later in this chapter, the narrator has God fulfilling the curse of Jotham upon the men of Shechem themselves because of their original support of Abimelech as king: "And God also made all the wickedness of the men of Shechem fall back upon their heads, and upon them came the curse (*qilᵉlat*) of Jotham, the son of Jerubaal" (Judg. 9:57).

If kings are easy to curse, the History shows that David, of all Israel's kings, is the easiest one of all. No sooner is David anointed king in 1 Samuel 16, than Goliath curses him, "And the Philistine cursed David by his gods" (1 Sam. 17:43). When David brings the ark of the LORD to Jerusalem in triumph, Michal's reproach provokes him to respond, "I shall make myself even more accursed than this (*ûnqalotî ᶜôd mizzo't*)" (2 Sam. 6:22). From then on in 2 Samuel, attention to cursing focuses exclusively upon Shimei's cursing of David (2 Sam. 16:5, 7, 9, 10, 11, 12, 13; 19:21). In his confrontation with Shimei, as with Michal in 2 Samuel 6, David gives what appears to be something like an authorial interpretation of such cursing. David rebukes Abishai, "Let [Shimei] alone, and let him curse; for the LORD has bidden him" (2 Sam. 16:11).[25] Clearly, David is no longer the man after God's own heart.[26]

The History's practice of presenting kings as special objects of God's curse, therefore, suggests that the story of Shimei is significant in terms of the authorial perspectives refracted within it. David's statements to Abishai ("If he is cursing because the LORD has said to him, 'Curse David,' who then shall say, 'Why have you done so?' Let him alone, and let him curse; for the LORD has commanded him") and David's hopes for the curse's reversal ("It may be that the LORD will look upon my iniquity, and will repay me with good for this cursing of me today" [16:10–12]) are striking. If the accursed himself admits that such cursing is from God, and if the substance of the curse is that "the LORD has given the kingdom into the hand of your son Absalom" (16:8), then the understandable failure of Absalom to maintain his throne while he hangs from an oak would appear to corroborate David's prescience on both counts: David indeed is cursed by God, but that does not mean that Absalom will not get cursed in turn.

Once again, we see that God's curse upon David differs from that imposed upon Saul. The cursing of David is like the cursing of his house: both involve the *continued existence* of the accursed. Yet within the house of David, the fates of father and son differ: the curse of Absalom involves hanging from a tree; God's particular curse for David, however, requires returning him to the throne.

Since the king, precisely as *royal head* of his people (1 Sam. 15:17; 2 Sam. 22:44), is a special carrier of the divine curse, it is ironically appropriate that the *character zone* of kings within the History is so often filled with heady violence and bloody heads. In fact, the characters within the History whose heads are bloodied or violently handled form something like an exclusive company of the royally damned—those who are unfortunate enough to get too close to the *character zone* of kings. Here is a listing of everyone in the History who literally suffers some kind of capital misfortune.

To be mentioned first are all those whose heads are somehow bloodied (*ro'š* plus *dām*) in the History:

1. The Amalekite who claimed to have slain Saul is executed by David with these words, "Your blood be upon your head" (2 Sam. 1:16).
2. Joab is executed by Benaiah following Solomon's words to the executioner, "The LORD will bring back [Joab's] bloody deeds upon his own head. So shall their blood come upon the head of Joab and upon the head of his descendants forever" (1 Kings 2:32–33).
3. Shimei is executed by Solomon following these words, "For on the day you go forth, and cross the brook Kidron, know for certain that you shall die; your blood shall be upon your own head" (1 Kings 2:37).[27]

Next comes the procession of those in the History who suffer terminal violence to the head, whether by seizing, crushing, piercing, hanging, strangling, or beheading.

1. Sisera, the general of Jabin, king of Canaan (Judg. 4:2), dies at the hand of Jael, "She struck Sisera a blow, she crushed his head, she shattered and pierced his temple" (Judg. 5:26).

2. Abimelech, the upstart king in Israel, dies after "a certain woman threw an upper millstone upon Abimelech's head, and crushed his skull" (Judg. 9:53).
3. Goliath is beheaded by the newly anointed David (1 Sam. 17:51).
4. Saul is beheaded by the Philistines (1 Sam. 31:9).
5. The twenty-four Israelites at the pool of Gibeon act out the conflict between the royal houses of Saul and David by seizing one another's heads and killing each other (2 Sam. 2:16).
6. Ishbosheth is beheaded by the sons of Rimmon (2 Sam. 4:7).
7. The sons of Rimmon are executed by David, and hung beside the pool at Hebron (2 Sam. 4:12).
8. Ahithophel commits suicide by hanging himself, because Absalom did not follow the royal counsel (2 Sam. 17:23).
9. Absalom is executed while hanging by his head from a tree (2 Sam. 18:9, 10, 15).
10. Sheba is beheaded by the townspeople of Abel, with his head thrown over the wall to Joab (2 Sam. 20:22).
11. The seventy sons of Ahab have their heads cut off, put in baskets, and sent to Jehu at Jezreel (2 Kings 10:7).

It takes little imagination to see that there is a notable affinity, in the History, between the character zone of *royal* heads of nations, on one hand, and the graphic language of doing bloody or terminal violence to anyone having the misfortune to come too close to these heads, on the other. Whatever the particular mix of unconscious mindset and aesthetic motivation lying behind these dangerous linkages of physical and royal heads may be, the widespread tendency in the History to write of bloody heads and capital violence within an almost exclusively royal context argues for a good deal of conscious literary deliberation, else we would find such capital violences occurring more often in stories that do not have a royal cast to them. It is almost as if Moses's principle about the punishment fitting the crime—"If any harm follows, then you shall give life for life, eye for eye, tooth for tooth, hand for hand, foot for foot, burn for burn, wound for wound, stripe for stripe" (Exod. 21:23–24)—is taken over and given a literary application and a narrative form: Israel's capital crime is to have chosen a king to be their head; their punishment now is *head for head*. There is a special connection between curses and kings, insofar as heady violence pertains particularly to the *character zone* of royal heads of nations.

This tendency in the History for royal overkill helps to explain why the story of Absalom's revolt is not a simplistic account of the eventual victory of those in the right over those in the wrong, but rather a complex and nuanced story of the doomed struggles of those whose lives are touched by the cursed sphere of kings. Almost all the characters in chapter 16 follow this rule about the dangers of getting too close to kings. Mephibosheth is sadly mistaken if he indeed said, "Today the house of Israel will return the kingdom to me" (16:3). Ziba may receive all of his master's land, but he soon will lose half of it through David's caprice in chapter 19. Shimei's reward for cursing David, apparently at the LORD's behest, will be execution at Solomon's command. And finally, Ahithophel and Absalom, in chapters 17 and 18, will suffer the LORD's special curse by hanging.

The second half of chapter 16 (verses 15–23) concerns the counsel of Ahithophel, and adds a second reason why the character zone of kings is so fraught with danger. If cursing the king eventually brings death to Shimei, counseling the king will do the same for Ahithophel. What is there about the counseling (*yāʿaṣ*) of kings that connects it to the cursing of kings? Chapter 16 provides us with the beginning of an answer. Simply put, when royalty equates such counsel to consulting the oracle of God, as David and Absalom do in 16:23, then the counsel of kings, like kingship itself, is a threat to the rule of Yahweh.[28]

We learn from the two instances in the History where kings seek advice from royal counselors—Absalom in 2 Samuel 15–17, and Rehoboam in 1 Kings 12—that it is dangerous or risky for *kings to seek counsel.* In the story of Absalom's revolt, "the LORD had ordained to defeat the good counsel of Ahithophel, so that the LORD might bring evil upon Absalom" (2 Sam. 17:14). When forced to decide between the counsel of Hushai and that of Ahithophel, Absalom unfortunately chooses Hushai's, and loses the kingdom. Similarly, when faced with the conflicting counsel of his elders and young men, Rehoboam "forsook the counsel which the old men gave him, and took counsel with the young men" (1 Kings 12:8)—and lost the northern kingdom.

Moreover, the History makes it clear that the danger of seeking counsel in a royal context rests upon the practice's opposition to more theocratic means of seeking advice. If prophetic inquiry constitutes a divinely ordained check upon unrestrained royal rule, then the introduction of "the king's counselor" would appear to be a royal attempt to restrict the power of the prophet within the court.[29] When the narrator informs us that "in those days the counsel which Ahithophel gave was as if one consulted the oracle of God; so was all the counsel of Ahithophel esteemed, both by David and by Absalom" (2 Sam. 16:23), then reveals to us that "the LORD had ordained to defeat the *good counsel* of Ahithophel (2 Sam. 17:14), and, finally, shows us this rejected counselor going home to hang himself (2 Sam. 17:23), the lesson is abundantly clear: whether good or bad, wise or foolish, merely human advice lacks the providential status and epistemological guarantees that result from seeking out or inquiring of the LORD.[30]

The story in chapters 17 and 18 will continue to describe how the word of God, rather than the counsel of men, carries out God's curse upon the house of David.

·8·

COUNSELORS
(17:1–28)

In a multitude of counselors there is safety. (Prov. 11:14)

Books will speak plain when counselors blanch.
(Francis Bacon)

The King's Counselor

The matter of overturning the king's counsel is central to chapters 15–17. One may follow or frustrate counsel, be it good or bad, and these three chapters describe how the LORD—and David—succeeded in overturning the advice of the king's counselor. What has the prominence of this theme to do with the ongoing concerns of the story?

Chapter 15 introduced us to Ahithophel, "David's counselor" (v. 12), and reported David's prayer, "O LORD, I pray thee, turn the counsel of Ahithophel into foolishness" (v. 31). David immediately took steps to assist the LORD in this endeavor by instructing Hushai, "But if you return to the city, then you will defeat for me the counsel of Ahithophel" (v. 34). In 16:20–22, Ahithophel advised Absalom to go in to his father's concubines; Absalom does so "in the sight of all Israel." As we saw in the last chapter, this action not only follows Ahithophel's counsel, it also fulfills the LORD's prophecy in 12:11. Chapter 17 now pits the counsel of Ahithophel against that of Hushai, reveals the LORD's decision to defeat the good counsel of Ahithophel, and accompanies Ahithophel back home in disgrace.

The story of Ahithophel's decline, from initial success in 16:20–23 to suicide in 17:23, forms a wonderful Deuteronomic meditation upon an intermittent biblical theme: the divine destruction ($pārar$) of human plans ($yā^cas/^c\bar{e}s\bar{a}h$). When David proposes (15:34) and God disposes (17:14) "to defeat the counsel of Ahithophel," one is reminded of Isaiah's warning to the peoples and far countries: "Take counsel together ($^cu\d{s}\hat{u}\ ^c\bar{e}\d{s}\bar{a}h$), but it

169

shall be defeated (*wᵉtupār*)" (Isa. 8:10). Isaiah later prophesies the breaking of Assyria's stranglehold on Israel, "For the LORD of hosts has given counsel (*yāᶜaṣ*), and who will annul it (*yāpēr*)?" (Isa. 14:27). The Psalmist also declares, "The LORD brings the counsel of nations (*ᶜaṣat goyîm*) to nought (*hēpîr*)" (Ps. 33:10). This declaration takes on narrative form when God supports Nehemiah's efforts to rebuild the wall: "God frustrated (*wayyaper*) the plans [of our enemies] (*ᶜaṣātām*)" (Neh. 4:9 Hebrew).

We may begin to understand something of the authorial motivation lying behind the story of Ahithophel, first by discussing the style of the royal counselor's discourse, second by tracing within the History the distribution of human counsel in relation to that of divine inquiry, third by seeing the various ways in which royal counsel is evaluated within the text, and finally, by comparing the voice of the royal counselor and that of the Deuteronomic narrator.

The Style of the Royal Counselor's Discourse

What is the style of that royal advice termed "counsel" (*ᶜēṣāh*) like? The corpus of directly reported royal counsel is limited, yet its style is sufficiently distinctive to help us understand how such discourse functions at various points within the History.[1]

First, the most obvious characteristic of royal counsel is its predictive thrust: the royal counselor proposes a future course of action, and then predicts what its outcome will be. This prognostic function explains why such a large number of imperfective verb forms fills the counselor's speech. Within only sixteen verses, the counsel of Ahithophel, Hushai, Nathan, and those advising Rehoboam contains at least thirty-three imperfective verbs, indicating what ought to be done and what will result from the activity proposed:

  2 Sam. 16:21:   Go in to your father's concubines
                  and all Israel will hear
                  and you will be strengthened.
  2 Sam. 17:1:   I will choose
                  and set out
                  and pursue.
  2 Sam. 17:2:   I will come upon him
                  and panic him;
                  the people will flee
                  and I will strike down the king.

2 Sam. 17:3:	I will return all the people,
	and the people will be at peace.
2 Sam. 17:8:	he will not spend the night.
2 Sam. 17:9:	Some of the people will fall
	and will hear
	and will say.
2 Sam. 17:10:	even the valiant man will utterly melt with fear.
2 Sam. 17:11:	let all Israel be gathered to you
	go in battle in person.
2 Sam. 17:12:	we shall come upon him
	and we shall light upon him
	and not one will be left.
2 Sam. 17:13:	all Israel will bring ropes
	and we shall drag [the city]
	until not even a pebble will be found there.
1 Kings 1:13:	and you shall say to him.
1 Kings 1:14:	I also will come in
	and confirm your words.
1 Kings 12:7:	and they shall be your servants forever.
1 Kings 12:10:	Thus you shall speak
	and thus you shall say to them.
1 Kings 12:11:	I will add to your yoke;
	I will chastise you with scorpions.

Whereas the form of these imperfectives varies—imperatives, jussives, participles, imperfects, and *waw*-converted perfects—their function remains stable: to propose future actions and to predict their outcome.

A second notable feature of the royal counselor's discourse appears in 2 Samuel 17: a predilection for *simile,* that is to say, an explicit and imaged comparison of one kind or another. The use of simile is certainly widespread throughout almost all levels of discourse in the Bible, but its pointed use within the formal counsel given the king in 2 Samuel 17 will help us say some things that may not be so obvious about the story of Ahithophel.

Ahithophel's brief statement in 17:1–3 and Hushai's longer presentation in 17:7–13 comprise only ten verses, yet contain five similes:

v. 3: as a bride comes home to her husband
v. 8: like a bear robbed of her cubs in the field
v. 10: like the heart of a lion
v. 11: as the sand by the sea for multitude
v. 12: as the dew falls upon the ground

This turn toward similitude in chapter 17 needs explaining because, on one hand, directly reported speech of the royal counselor does not always contain such comparisons, and on the other hand, Ahithophel's and Hushai's tendency toward simile is complemented by the narrator's double use of this trope in 16:23 to tell us what Ahithophel's counsel was like, as well as by the repeated infiltration of the narrator's reporting speech in the reported speech of characters through terms for comparison in verses 6, 15, and 21.[2] Why are so many voices in this chapter—those of the rival kings, their competing counselors, and even the narrator—addicted to comparisons?

A brief look at the patterns emerging from a consideration of the similes that occur in 1–2 Samuel will help us sort out what is significant about the emphasis upon simile here in 2 Samuel 17.

Throughout 1–2 Samuel, there are about ninety instances in which narrator or character employs explicit comparisons using k^e, $ka'^a\check{s}er$, or $k\bar{e}n$. For example, the narrator tells us that Jonathan loved David "as his own soul" (1 Sam. 18:1, 3) and that the people of Israel wanted a king in order to be "like all the nations" (1 Sam. 8:20). Roughly one-third of these explicit comparisons in 1–2 Samuel (about twenty-eight out of ninety occurrences) are temporal or diachronic, like Hushai's words to Absalom, "As I have served your father, so I will serve you" (2 Sam. 16:19), or the narrator's words to the reader, "So the servants of Absalom did to Amnon as Absalom had commanded" (2 Sam. 13:29). Such temporal statements most often relate the past to the present or future in a "as then, so now" comparison, yet lack the graphic imaging that belongs to simile as a figure of speech. About two-thirds of the explicit comparisons in 1–2 Samuel do involve such graphic images, making such comparisons *similes* in the technical sense of the term.

As the shaft of Goliath's spear was "like a weaver's beam" (1 Sam. 17:7), so Hushai will light upon David "as the dew falls on the ground" (2 Sam. 17:12). When we get to such pictorial images, we are indeed in the territory of simile, and the story of Ahithophel makes it clear that both the narrator and the characters in the story are intent upon exploring simile's inner landscape—as it were. If we can understand *what it is like* to counsel the king, we may begin to understand *what it is like* to narrate a story about counseling the king.

Listen to the narrator explaining what the counsel of Ahithophel *was like*: "Now in those days the counsel which Ahithophel gave was as if ($ka'^a\check{s}er$) one consulted the word of God; so ($k\bar{e}n$) was all the counsel of Ahithophel esteemed, both by David and by Absalom" (16:23). What leaps out from these words is the sheer audacity of the comparison, a figure so striking that the narrator is at pains in verse 23b to make it clear that the startling comparison itself represents how David and Absalom see things, rather than how the narrator does. As a matter of equivalence, Ahithophel's counsel is certainly not equal to God's word. Even as a matter of mere similitude, however, the daring comparison, though uttered by the narrator, is made only on behalf of David and Absalom.[3] The simile is the narrator's, but the mistake is David and Absalom's.

It is now necessary to see how language concerning divine inquiry and human counsel is distributed, and how human counsel is evaluated, within the royal history.

Planning for the Future: Word-Patterns

David and Absalom's desire to discover what course of action would insure the success of their plans is nothing new in the History, which is filled with individuals who find themselves in tight situations where decisions about what is to be done must be made.[4] What *is* new, however, is the particular means these characters choose for uncovering the best course of action to pursue. The narrator in 16:23 now indicates two obvious royal options for strategic planning: David and Absalom consider Ahithophel's counsel ($^{c}\bar{e}\d{s}\bar{a}h$) to be like God's response to a sacred inquiry ($\check{s}\bar{a}'al$), a process usually mediated by priest or prophet.

The narrative voice in 16:23 adds an implicit comparison of its own, namely, that this royal comparison of human counsel and divine inquiry obtained "in those days," but to what era are we to compare "those days"? Are the past days of David and Absalom to be compared to the present days of the narrator, when a connection such as David and Absalom made would not have been considered? Or rather are they to be compared to the days preceding David and Absalom's turn toward counselors? Or perhaps "those days" are to be seen in relation to subsequent times, when kings would turn away from the use of such counselors? These questions require a careful examination of lexical patterns in the History involving matters of divine inquiry and human counsel. How does the Deuteronomist distribute references to the royal inquiry of God on one hand, and to a royal turn toward counselors on the other?

The narrator's mention, in 16:23, of changing circumstances with respect to divine inquiry reminds us of a similar comment made earlier in the History. Compare these two narrative statements:

> In those days the counsel which Ahithophel gave was as if one inquired of (*yiš'al*) the word of God. (2 Sam. 16:23)

Formerly in Israel, when a man went to inquire of (*lidroš*) God, he said,
"Come, let us go to the seer"; for he who is now called a prophet was
formerly called a seer. (1 Sam. 9:9)

In 2 Sam. 16:23, the comparison is between seeking the advice of a
counselor and inquiring of God; in 1 Sam. 9:9 it is between an earlier
designation of the intermediary through whom one inquires of God as a
"seer" and a later term for this person, "prophet." Nevertheless, *our* comparing these two verses uncovers an important fact: whereas David and
Absalom compare only two means for strategic planning, narrative references to these practices involve a triple distinction.

Kings may sometimes consult their counselor (*yā‘aṣ*) and other times
inquire of God (*šā’al bᵉ*), but the narrator makes a further distinction with
respect to divine inquiry: in their quest for God's guidance, Israelites may
be said either to seek (*dāraš* [*bᵉ*]) God on one hand, or to inquire of (*šā’al
bᵉ*) Him on the other. How then does the History exploit these three ter-
minological options as it narrates Israel's monarchic past? Is there a lexical
pattern of distribution that may help us understand what the king's counselor is doing here, at the center of the story about Absalom's revolt
against David? What accounts for Ahithophel's prominence in the eyes of
his masters—David and Absalom on one hand, and the Deuteronomist on
the other?

An obvious feature separating royal counsel from divine inquiry involves
the human limitations of the first and the divine promise of the second.
Royal inquiry is divine, because the king not only consults God, he also
approaches God's representative—usually a priest, a prophet/seer, or
simply a "man of God."[5] However, the narrator also introduces into the
story a number of counselors who are not so close to God: besides
Ahithophel and Hushai, we have the elders and young men advising Rehoboam in 1 Kings 12.[6]

Here is an important fact about the History's lexicon concerning how
kings prepare for the future: kings may indeed alternate between inquiring
of God and consulting with humans, but Israelite practice and narrative
style introduce a third dimension in such an alternation, and do so by
using specific language for specific eras.

First, from the beginning of the History through David's establishment
of Jerusalem as his royal capital in 2 Samuel 6, the consistent language for
inquiring of God is "to ask of (*šā’al bᵉ*) God [or the LORD]."[7] Whether
we find ourselves in the premonarchic period or in the monarchic period
up to 2 Samuel 6, and whether Saul or David does the inquiring, *šā’al* is
the verb used. Moreover, within the royal period up to 2 Samuel 6, there is

never a reference to counseling (*yāᶜaṣ*) the king. In other words, from the establishment of kingship in 1 Samuel 10 to the establishment of Jerusalem in 2 Samuel 6, Israel's kings are always said to ask of (*šā'al bᵉ*) God, but never to seek after (*dāraš bᵉ*) him or consult (*yāᶜaṣ*) with humans.

Second, we find a similar consistency in lexical distribution from 2 Samuel 6, when David establishes his kingdom in Jerusalem, through 1 Kings 12, when David's grandson Rehoboam loses the northern half of that kingdom to Jeroboam. Neither David nor the royal pretenders Absalom and Adonijah, nor Solomon and his son Rehoboam, ever ask of (*šā'al bᵉ*) or seek after (*dāraš* [*bᵉ*]) God in their quest for future intelligence. Three generations of the house of David seem to have abandoned the ancient Yahwistic practice of inquiry through priests and prophets, and to have replaced it with merely human consultation.[8] Even when Nathan conspires with Bathsheba to bring Solomon to the throne, the prophet uses language that befits this foreign or rationalistic phase in the monarchic history: "Come, let me give you counsel (*'îᶜāsēk nā' ᶜēṣāh*)" (1 Kings 1:12). The History's lexical usage is clear: Israel may have sought counsel before the coming of kings (Judg. 19:30; 20:7), and was even accused of lacking counsel (Deut. 32:28), but the seeking of counsel is primarily a practice of the first three generations of David's house.

The third phase in this lexicon of royal practice extends from 1 Kings 13 to the end of the History in 2 Kings 25. Once the story of the divided kingdom begins in 1 Kings 13, every king of Israel and Judah who inquires of God does so by seeking him (*dāraš* [*bᵉ*]) rather than by asking of him (*šā'al bᵉ*).[9] Moreover, no king of Israel or Judah after Rehoboam is ever again said to "seek counsel."

Planning for the Future: Narrative Implications

These clearcut word-patterns enable us to recover a number of evaluative accents that surround the royal practice of seeking counsel, especially as it relates to the varied forms of divine inquiry that precede and succeed it. A comparison between the two practices is introduced in 2 Sam. 16:23 to prepare for the story in 2 Samuel 17, and the reader's struggle to evaluate royal counsel thereby takes on a general as well as a specific stamp. Whereas the story line in chapters 15–17 asks us, as it does Absalom, to compare Ahithophel's individual counsel to Hushai's (is one piece of advice better than the other?), 16:23 specifically invites the reader to compare, as David and Absalom did in their day, the *practice* of counseling the king and that of inquiring of God. The reader must now ask what the

ideological status of these two procedures is within the History. But how can
the reader evaluate David and Absalom's comparing of these two prognostic practices?

As far as the particular struggle between two royal counselors is concerned, the picture within the History is straightforward. In both the
pericopes where the king's counsel is a central figure during crucial turns
in the monarchy—2 Samuel 15–17 concerning the revolt of Absalom, and
1 Kings 12 concerning the division of the kingdom—the particular
counsel chosen by the king leads to disaster: Absalom loses the throne and
his life, Rehoboam half of his kingdom.

Here in 2 Samuel 15–17, narrator and character alike offer explicit eval-
uations of the counsel given. Hushai says, "This time the counsel which
Ahithophel has given is not good" (17:7). After hearing Hushai's advice,
Absalom and all the men of Israel said, "The counsel of Hushai the
Archite is better than the counsel of Ahithophel." Even the narrator
makes explicit what the plot line has all along been developing, "For the
LORD had ordained to defeat the good counsel of Ahithophel, so that the
LORD might bring evil upon Absalom" (17:14), so that David's earlier
prayer will be answered, "O LORD I pray thee, turn the counsel of
Ahithophel into foolishness" (15:31). The picture in 1 Kings 12 is similar:
the obviously wise counsel of the elders is pitted against the obviously
foolish counsel of the young men. When the king chooses the foolish
counsel and rejects the good, he courts disaster.

These two incidents raise at least two important questions. If the royal
practice of seeking counsel customarily involves the comparison and evaluation of at least two sets of advice, must not *our* evaluation of the practice
involve comparing it to its divine counterpart, sacred inquiry? And if God,
David, Absalom, Rehoboam, and the narrator all succeed in turning the
counsel of Ahithophel—and of the young men of Rehoboam—into foolishness, does not the Deuteronomist also succeed in turning the royal
practice of seeking human counsel instead of divine direction against the
practitioners themselves? The answer to each of these questions is yes.

Royal Counsel and Divine Inquiry:
The Foolishness of Image and Imaged

My discussion so far suggests that the Deuteronomist has taken care to
indicate that these two practices are *de facto* antithetical: not only did they
not coexist, the first ought not to be considered an appropriate substitute
for the second. The very introduction of the practice of royal counsel, like
the introduction of royalty itself, contaminated Israel and turned its

Yahwistic spirit into foolishness. When Israel requested a king, they argued in simile, by wanting to be *like all the nations* (1 Sam. 8:5, 19). God responded by complaining to Samuel, "They have rejected me from being king over them" (1 Sam. 8:7). Similarly, when David introduced human counsel into the royal scheme of things, he thereby rejected divine inquiry, and foolishly made human counsel a simile for it. What makes the two explicit comparisons in 1 Samuel 8 and 2 Samuel 16 graphic enough to make them *similes* is this: in the eyes of the Deuteronomist, the two practices that David and Absalom compare in 2 Samuel 16 are as mutually exclusive as God and king are in 1 Samuel 8.

Kingship contaminates Israel, royal counsel contaminates divine inquiry, and neither Israel nor its recourse to God can remain the same, once these contaminants have come upon the scene. There is clear indication in the History that the harmful effects of kings putting royal counsel in the place of divine inquiry remain long after the practice itself has been abandoned.

That the practice of royal counsel perverts Yahwistic institutions while it is in force (from 2 Samuel 6 to 1 Kings 12) is best seen in the story about how Solomon takes over the throne of his father. This transition is detailed in 1 Kings 1–2. Since the practice of royal counsel is apparently still in force when David is old and advanced in years, these chapters do not record any moves toward divine inquiry to determine who should succeed the king. Not only does no one take the initiative in approaching God to inquire who David's successor might be, neither does God take any initiative in the matter by, say, sending his prophet Nathan to convey the divine word about who is to take over David's throne.

We read, instead, how Nathan the prophet conspires with Bathsheba to put her son Solomon on the throne. Nathan's last and final prophetic message from God was in 2 Sam. 12:25 (before we have any mention of the king's counselor), wherein God communicated his love for Solomon. But when the process whereby Solomon, the beloved, succeeds David is being described, we find Nathan now using the discourse of the king's counselor rather than the words of God's prophet. Contrast Nathan's invitation to human counsel—with all the negative connotations with which I have been surrounding it—with Josiah's command to seek out Huldah the prophetess after the Book of the Law has been discovered:

1 Kings 1: Nathan: "Come, let me give you counsel (*lᵉkî ʾîᶜāsēk*)."

2 Kings 22: Josiah: "Come, inquire of the LORD for me (*lᵉkû dirᵉšû*)."

In addition to this example of contemporary contamination, the subversive effects of employing the king's counselor endure long after the last mention of the practice in 1 Kings 12. If Nathan the prophet speaks like the king's counselor in 1 Kings 1, by 1 Kings 22 we see the king treating the LORD's prophet like a counselor rather than an intermediary in divine inquiry. As we have just seen, seeking royal counsel involved weighing the recommendations of one advisor against those of another, as Absalom and Rehoboam do in 2 Samuel 17 and 1 Kings 12 respectively— and this is the precise procedure described in 1 Kings 22. In response to Jehoshaphat's words to the king of Israel, "Inquire (d^eraš nā') first the word of the LORD," four hundred prophets are found who say, "Go up, for the LORD will give it into the hand of the king." But Jehoshaphat responds, "Is there not another prophet of the LORD of whom we may inquire (w^enidr^{e}šāh)?" (1 Kings 22:5, 7). Micaiah is then brought forward and prophesies contrarily, as Ahab had foreseen ("I hate him for he never prophesies good concerning me, but only evil" [1 Kings 22:8]).

The message that the Deuteronomist now gives readers is as obvious as that which Micaiah gave the kings of Israel and Judah: just as "the LORD has put a lying spirit in the mouth of all these your prophets" (22:23), so also did David and his descendants, first by substituting the king's counselor for the LORD's prophet, and then by treating the LORD's prophet as if he were the king's counselor.

The story of Ahithophel, then, is one in which bold similes and persuasive comparisons overwhelm almost everything else in it: the competing counselors fill their advice with colorful similes, as if to convince by rhetoric alone; Absalom and Israel mistakenly compare the advice their counselors give (Hushai's is better than Ahithophel's [v. 14]); David and Absalom foolishly consider Ahithophel's counsel comparable to the LORD's word, even as the narrator compares this past comparison to the situation of another time (16:23); and finally, the Deuteronomist uses this story about the seductive power of human counsel to prepare us for a comparable story about the seductive power of prophetic inquiry in 1 Kings 22. God uses Hushai to entice Absalom just as God will use the four hundred prophets to entice Ahab. Royal counsel and prophetic inquiry may indeed be comparable, the Deuteronomist seems to be telling us, not because one is as good as the other, and not only because the second is better than the first, but also because human conduct, however free, can dispose the LORD to turn both into foolishness.

·9·

CROSSINGS
(18:1–20:24)

And in the lighted palace near
Died the sound of royal cheer;
And they cross'd themselves for fear.
(Tennyson, *The Lady of Shalott*)

Preliminaries

For a number of reasons chapter 18 is pivotal in the story of Absalom's revolt. Occurring midway through the story, this chapter contains the account of Absalom's death and David's reaction to it. The details of that death and of its effect upon David prepare us for subsequent events in chapters 19 and 20. Chapter 18 is filled with problematical statements and fascinating details that challenge our understanding and take issue with preconceived notions about what is happening within the story—and thus about what an authorial voice is communicating to readers.

Take the matter of problematical statements. At three important points in the chapter, we are hard put to understand what one character is saying to another. When the man who saw Absalom hanging from a tree tells Joab, what do Joab's four words of response in verse 14a mean?[1] Then, when Ahimaaz keeps importuning Joab to let him carry news to David, the last four words of Joab's response in verse 22b are laconic to say the least.[2] And after Ahimaaz's repeated pleading to be allowed to carry news to David, this messenger's account to David, in verse 29b, of what he saw is puzzling at its center and lacking of information at the end ("but I do not know what it was").[3] We will have to work around these gaps in the dialogue as we discuss the chapter.

The puzzling matter of words and their reference that pervades much of chapter 18 is perhaps more susceptible to readerly suggestions than are the enigmatic statements of the characters just mentioned. Take, for example, the matter of "the people" (*ᶜam*) who are mentioned so often in the first half of the chapter.[4] There are eleven references to "people" in

179

verses 1–18; the term refers variously to David's troops (vv. 1, 2 [twice], 3, 4, 5, 6, 16 [twice]) or Absalom's (v. 7), or even to both of their contingents (v. 8). That *cam* refers to an army, rather than to a people, especially in military contexts such as we have here, is a common enough and well recognized feature of biblical narrative. Yet once we inquire about the makeup of the opposing armies in chapter 18, we run into controversies that separate commentators into opposing camps.[5] Since 18:7 tells us that "the people of Israel (*cam yiśrā'ēl*) were defeated there by the servants of David," and since the story in chapters 15–20 typically refers to Absalom's side in terms that embrace *all of Israel*, it is immensely important for our understanding of what is going on here to determine, so far as we can, the particular reference that each occurrence of *cam* or *yiśrā'ēl* has in the story.[6]

Despite the controversies surrounding this question, the text itself can help us sort out matters in two ways.

First, the story is structured in such a way that the account of bringing news to David, and of his reaction to it, in 18:19–19:9a clearly forms an important and moving interlude that interrupts the flow of the larger story line.[7] Notice how verse 19:9b resumes the story where 18:17 left off:

> 18:17 And all Israel fled everyone to his own home.

> 19:9b Now Israel had fled every man to his own home.

What these verses signal is that the affecting story between them—how David gets the news of his son's death and how, with Joab's help, he succeeds in overcoming his paternal grief and resuming his royal duties— narrates events from a different perspective than does the larger story that surrounds it. Whereas the surrounding account of the revolt uses the words and actions of individuals to bolster its emphasis upon a national and tribal conflict constituting the wider scope of the story, the interlude formed by the last half of chapter 18 and the first nine verses of chapter 19 narrows its focus to such an extent that the words and actions of "Israel" are never mentioned within it, and those of "the people" appear only at its end (vv. 19:3, 4, 9a)—as if to form a bridge back to the communal concerns of the larger story line. Chapters 15–20 are about *the men of Israel,* whose heart Absalom stole (15:6), whereas verses 18:19–19:9a are about *David,* whose heart Absalom broke. Chapters 15–20 are also about the *men of Judah,* who stole David away (19:42), whereas verses 18:19–19:9a are about *David's sorrow* that threatened to steal victory away from his people (19:3–4).

In addition, this basic compositional feature of alternating perspectives—from predominantly social points of view to deeply personal ones, and back again—helps us discriminate between important aspects within the communal concerns of chapters 15–20: on one hand, the story concentrates its considerable resources upon how Absalom's revolt affected *all Israel*: on the other hand various terms used to denote the whole of Israel—like "all Israel," "all the men of Israel," "all the tribes of Israel," "all the people of Israel," and "all the elders of Israel"—exploit the possible ambiguity of the term "Israel" through a remarkable distribution in reference throughout chapters 15–20.[8]

Look at the lengths to which chapters 15–20 go in order to focus our attention upon how the story of Absalom's revolt transcends a conflict that is purely intrinsic to the house of David. For example, not only is there a marked increase in references to "Israel" and "people" (*ᶜam*) in chapters 15–20 in relation to the rest of 2 Samuel; when "Israel" or "people" *does* occur in chapters 15–20, roughly two-thirds of these occurrences use *kol* to indicate "all Israel" or "all the people" or some similar totality.[9] This emphasis on entirety contrasts, for example, with the rest of 2 Samuel, where only about one-third of the verses in which "Israel" occurs (about twenty of sixty-six verses) use *kol*, and only a quarter of the verses in which *ᶜam* occurs (about thirteen of fifty verses) use *kol* with that term. Clearly, the story of Absalom's revolt concentrates on the effect of that revolt upon *the entire people of Israel.*

Nevertheless, if we pay attention to the precise usage of "Israel" throughout chapters 15–20, we notice a further feature that will help discriminate between the communal concerns of the story before the interlude of 18:19–19:9a and those that are apparent after it. Here is a remarkable fact about the reference of "Israel" in these six chapters: whether the term "Israel" or some form of "all Israel" is used, it appears to refer to the whole nation, not just its northern part, up to 18:17, but from 19:9b to the end of chapter 20 it refers almost always to the northern tribes in contrast to Judah. What the story of Absalom's revolt does, then, is exploit in sequential fashion the ambiguity of the word *Israel* in order to describe what the revolt meant, first, in terms of the entire nation (major elements from both northern and southern tribes sided with Absalom against David) and, second, in terms of the rivalry between northern and southern tribes within Israel (each side vies with the other for the glory of "returning David to Jerusalem" in chapter 19).

Under Absalom, Israel seems to have united major portions of North and South in opposition to David. Once David's cause is victorious, however, the divisions between North and South resurface and help to explain the breakup of the kingdom within two generations. Moreover, from the beginning of the revolt up to 19:9b, the implications not only of this constant identification of the entire nation of Israel as David's enemy (this seems to be the case, I repeat, even when *kol* is not used in conjunction with "Israel") but even of the care with which David's faction is never referred to as "Israel" within this section, are profound and will have to be addressed.[10]

In addition to attending to the complicated matter of words and their reference, as seen in the varying usage of "Israel" and "people" throughout chapters 15–20, we also need to return to the intriguing questions of literary style and narrative mimesis that have been occupying our attention ever since 2 Samuel 2, but more recently since the beginning of the revolt in 2 Samuel 15.

Announcing the Death of Absalom: 18:1–17

One of the dividends of a careful sequential reading of the History is the constant realization of the intricate complexity with which its overall speech plan organizes the narrative in ways that have gone unnoticed by generations of literary historical and other biblicists. The ability of the History to direct the reader's gaze either backwards or forwards as "current events" are being narrated is simply extraordinary. Chapter 18's account of the battle between David's and Absalom's armies, ending in Absalom's death and Israel's flight, offers another fine example of long-range connections, for the chapter clearly directs our gaze back to the events of 2 Samuel 2 in order to provide a series of signals about key authorial concerns motivating the present account. Whether these signals are similarity of locale, repetitions in phraseology and choreographed action, or even a similarity of graphic images lying at the center of the connected events, their combined use makes it virtually certain that the account of Absalom's death in 18:1–17 is a narrative development of the authorial statement made earlier in David's career in 2 Samuel 2. The message of the story from 2 Samuel 2 to 2 Samuel 18 is not especially novel: the more things change, the more they remain the same. Nevertheless, how precisely can two passages, so far apart as 2 Samuel 2 and 2 Samuel 18 are, be said to be integrated within the same authorial utterance?

My discussion of 2 Samuel 2 in chapter 2 above centered on its stylized language and ritualized action: the staged contest at the pool of Gibeon, the choreography involved in "crossing over" with all its attendant baggage, the emphasis on numbers that carry great symbolic weight, the centrality of graphic images—all these features combined to both support and threaten the mimetic details in the narrative. My discussion of chapters 15–17 proceeded in terms that recognize the *general* similarity in stylized language and ritualized action between the story of Absalom's revolt and that of the battle of warring houses in 2 Samuel 2. But there is much in 2 Samuel 18 that *specifically* ties its account to that in 2 Samuel 2, as we shall see.

Look first at the geographic detail in chapters 15–20, which settles David in Mahanaim during the revolt (17:24, 27; 19:32; see also 1 Kings 2:8). This move makes some sense, for Absalom has had himself declared king in Hebron (15:10), so that Judah as well as the rest of Israel "from Dan to Beersheba" (17:11) seem unlikely locales for David's temporary domicile. Nevertheless, a proposed historiographic and strategic cogency for Mahanaim offers only a partial explanation for our finding David there at this point in the story. For apart from references to this city in Joshua's distribution of the land (Josh. 13:26, 30; 21:38), Mahanaim appears in the History only in 2 Samuel 2 and 2 Samuel 18; the coincidence is hardly coincidental.

For one thing, the narrative symmetry set up by the repetition of locales in these two passages is striking.[11] After Saul's death, David's first battle as king was against Ishbosheth, whom Abner had brought to Mahanaim and made king over "all Israel" (2:8–9). Now, many years later, we find David occupying the same narrative and geographic space as Saul's son did in the earlier episode: Ishbosheth then, and David now, rule from Mahanaim.

Once we combine the information about Mahanaim with that concerning Hebron, the geographic similarity between the two passages increases. In 2 Samuel 2, David is king in Hebron (2:3, 11, 32) and Ishbosheth king in Mahanaim. Absalom's trip to Hebron in 2 Samuel 15 and David's to Mahanaim in 2 Samuel 17, therefore, represent strategic moves not just of the story's characters but of its author as well.

Whatever the supposed historiographic reasons for these moves, they take place in chapters 15–20 as part of a concerted narrative strategy that will allow the revolt of Absalom to make sense precisely in light of what has already taken place in 2 Samuel 2. In both passages, when the opposition of kings erupts into warfare, their respective bases in Hebron and Mahanaim—together with their respective situations—will allow the narrator to choreograph their moves in a similar way as they enter into battle, and to describe that battle in similar language.

Here are four examples which illustrate how chapters 2 and 18 not only involve similar military situations, but even describe action with almost identical phraseology. Look first at the language that describes the outcome of the two battles:

2 Sam. 2:17: And Abner and the men of Israel (*'anšê yiśrā'ēl*) were beaten (*wayyinnāgep*) before the servants of David.

2 Sam. 8:7: And the people of Israel (*ᶜam yiśrā'ēl*) were beaten (*wayyinnagᵉpû*) before the servants of David.

Nowhere else in the History do we find such language about David's victories.

Second, cessation of hostilities in both passages comes about in precisely the same manner:

2 Sam. 2:28: So Joab blew the trumpet and all the people (*kol hāᶜām*) pursued (*yirdᵉpû*) Israel no more.

2 Sam. 18:16: So Joab blew the trumpet and the people (*hāᶜām*) came back from pursuing (*mirdop*) Israel.

Once again, such precise language is confined to these two passages.

A third phraseological and thematic detail connects these two passages and invites us to read the later event in light of the earlier one. In 2 Samuel 2 it was Abner's question to him that convinced Joab to stop fighting, "How long will it be before you tell your people to turn (*lāšûb*) from the pursuit of their brethren?" (2:26). Now, long after that incident, we hear Joab having to answer that question a second time, "Joab blew the trumpet, and the people came back (*wayyāšob*) from pursuing Israel" (18:16). It is now clear that the problem with which 2 Samuel began, the pursuit of fratricide through the pursuit of kings, is still a central concern in 2 Samuel 18.

A fourth verbal example illustrates the phraseological and narrative interpenetration of these two passages. I have been intent upon showing that graphic comparisons like metaphors and similes are important for an understanding of authorial motivation: we now realize that the same metaphor to describe the situation in which the combatants find themselves occurs in both passages. In 2:26 Abner asks Joab, "Shall the sword devour forever?" indicating how much it had devoured up until then. In 18:8 we find out that, of the twenty thousand who died in battle, "the forest devoured more people that day than the sword."[12]

All these examples of local and phraseological similarities between 2 Samuel 2 and 2 Sam. 18:1–17 would, I think, be sufficient to suggest that the second passage needs to be interpreted against the backdrop of the first. But there is an even stronger reason for suggesting that each account should be interpreted in the light of the other. It is not just that both passages incline—both generally and specifically—toward highly stylized language and ritualized action; what stands out about this similitude is the use of precisely the same graphic image to choreograph a central action in each account. Both accounts center around a ritual action that combines "seizing the head" (*ḥāzaq roʾš*) with "crossing over" (*ʿābar*).

We recall what happened at the pool of Gibeon. The "gladiators" cross over, twelve by twelve; this configuration represents Ishbosheth versus David. Then "each caught his neighbor by the head and thrust his sword in his neighbor's side" (2:16). When the combatants cross over (2:15) into ritual and narrative performance, the contest is about seizing headship over the tribes of Israel.

Like the death of Eli in 1 Samuel 4 and the contest at the pool of Gibeon in 2 Samuel 2, the death of Absalom in 2 Samuel 18 presents us with a powerful image that transcends the historiographic and mimetic dimensions according to which the History has been so often narrowly interpreted. Like others before it, this image manages to integrate the larger narrative.[13] When we view the stylized description of Absalom's capture and death against the background of the slaughter of fellow Israelites at the pool of Gibeon, we realize that each event forms a ritualized picture of the more mimetic action that surrounds it. Notice the highly stylized language with which the capture of Absalom is described:

> Absalom was riding upon his mule, and the mule went under the thick branches of a great oak, and his head (*roʾšô*) got caught (*wayyeḥˀezaq*) in the oak, while the mule that was under him crossed over (*ʿābar*). (18:9)

Since the king is head (*roʾš*) of the tribes in Israel (1 Sam. 15:17) and may even claim to be the head (*roʾš*) of nations (2 Sam. 22:44), the picture in 18:9 represents the head of the head of Israel being seized just before execution. In the ritual within 2 Samuel 2, there was first the crossing over, and then the seizing of the head; here in 2 Samuel 18, there is first the seizing of the head, and then the crossing over.

How does the crossing over of Absalom's mule figure in the moving picture of Absalom hanging from a tree with his head caught fast? I indicated earlier how the heightened use of *ʿābar*, "to cross over," functions in multiple ways in chapters 15–20.[14] The word occurs only twice in chapter 18 (vv. 9 and 23), yet in each case there is a processional reversal that is something like those already encountered in chapter 15. There, the protocol involved a switch in precedence when an important boundary was reached: approaching the boundary, the king or ark leads, but at the boundary point, who or what was led proceeds on ahead by "crossing over"—with the original "forerunner" now placed behind. Whatever may be the internal significance of this protocol within the worldview and practice of the contemporary Israelites, it may be that, as in chapters 15–16, the narrator in chapter 18 is at play in the fields of the LORD and commenting upon the fate of Absalom in terms of an ironic replay of David's ritual procession already described in chapter 15. Absalom, who wanted to replace David as head over Israel, now finds himself "in front of the servants of David (*lipnê ʿabdê dāwid*: 18:9)," then leads his mule under a tree to the point where, as he hangs "between heaven and earth," the mule "crosses over" and leaves the king behind.

One final element completes the stark picture in 18:9 that dominates the entire first half of chapter 18. Absalom is described as hanging from a tree in verses 9 and 10, and this predicament is the primary way in which kings are presented as cursed within the History.[15] In my discussion of 2 Samuel 16 I described how kings are explicitly cursed.[16] Consider now the ways in which the History *indirectly* conveys this intimate bond between curses and kings.

When the Book of Deuteronomy employs the language of cursing, it is almost always in a section on the fate of the nation Israel.[17] Yet there is one passage in Deuteronomy where the language of cursing applies to individuals: Deut. 21:22. This pericope will turn out to be central to our story in 2 Samuel, for the legislation within it forms a basis for the widespread, yet indirect, cursing of kings throughout the History.

The law of Moses commands that Israelites convicted of capital offenses are to be hung upon a tree, but buried before nightfall because "a hanged man (*tālûy*) is cursed by God (*qilᵉlat ʾᵉlohîm*)" (Deut. 21:22–23). According to Moses, therefore, "to hang (*tālāh/tālāʾ*) someone upon a tree" is equivalent to bringing down upon that person the curse of God. When the Deuteronomic narrative gets around to describing who in fact gets hung upon trees, it turns out that *kings* are especially prone to such mistreatment. When Joshua captured the king of Ai, "he hanged [him] on a tree until evening" (Josh. 8:29). When Joshua later found the five Amorite kings hiding in the cave at Makkedah, he "smote them and put them to death, and he hung them on five trees. And they hung upon the trees until evening" (Josh. 10:26).[18] If a man who is hanged, especially if it is upon a tree, is cursed by God, then it is significant that the fates of king Saul and his sons, Jonathan and Ishbosheth, all involve their, or their murderers', being singled out as *cursed* by the very act of hanging them. More importantly for our purposes here, the arboreal fates of the king of Ai and of the five Amorite kings are narrative instances that single them out as royally cursed by God. To be executed is one thing; to be hung up is quite another. According to Moses, the second situation is a fate worse than death.

So the Deuteronomist's practice of indirectly characterizing as divinely cursed those individuals, especially kings, whose fate involves being hung, especially from trees, is particularly relevant in 2 Samuel 18. Absalom's death, while hanging from an oak "between heaven and earth," alerts us to unavoidably negative accents surrounding his revolt against David. The manner of Absalom's capture, then, clearly indicates his evaluative place within the Deuteronomist's story.

The question naturally arises: how does the narrative manage to keep this powerful *image*, so particular in its impact, from overwhelming the predominantly national perspective that I have been maintaining all along permeates the narrative of the revolt (apart from the personal interlude of 18:18–19:9a)? By what narrative means does this tale of the sorry capture and death of Absalom—and the perhaps sorrier survival of David—remain subordinate to the fate of a nation bent on pursuing their kings? Before answering this important question, the second half of the chapter, verses 19–32 (plus 19:1–9a), needs to be put into proper perspective.

Announcing the Announcement: 18:19–19:9a

This section is different from its immediate surroundings, and yet it still displays a number of significant similarities to that context. Its ability to stand out, even as it fits in, may account for the impact it has had upon countless readers. A brief account of its ambidexterity is in order.

The revelatory character of the passage, that is to say, the revelatory character *in* the passage—David himself—is manifest. Perhaps nowhere else in the History since 1 Samuel 16 have we been allowed such a compassionate glimpse into the heart of David. 1 Samuel 16–31 almost never revealed what was going on within the heart of David, and not until 2 Samuel 11 does the darker side of David's character emerge into full view. Nevertheless, despite the largely negative picture of David since the Bathsheba affair, chapters 18 and 19 portray David in an especially sympathetic light. How can the reader not be attracted to this man, who sends forth his whole army against all Israel with the words, "Deal gently for my sake with the young man Absalom" (18:5)? Even after his anxious conversation with the watchman—a dialogue filled with hopeful anticipation about the news being brought by the two men seen running toward him— his questions to them are not about the victory of his troops but rather about the welfare of his son: "Is it well with the young man Absalom?" (18:29, 32). And when told of Absalom's death in 18:32, David reacts in a way that easily elicits the reader's sympathy, "And the king was deeply moved and went up to the chamber over the gate, and wept; and as he went, he said, 'O my son Absalom, my son, my son Absalom!'" (19:1 MT; 18:33 English versification). Who has ever read these lines and not been moved to pity David?

David's paternal concern for Absalom is so central to the interlude in 18:19–19:9a—and its immediate context—that the king's command, question, and cry concerning Absalom are each recounted twice in the story:

David's Command:

Deal gently for my sake with the young man Absalom. (18:5)

Protect for my sake the young man Absalom. (18:12)

David's Question:

Is it well with the young man Absalom? (18:29)

Is it well with the young man Absalom? (18:32)

David's Cry:

O my son Absalom, my son, my son Absalom! (19:1)

O my son Absalom, Absalom, my son, my son! (19:5)

This doubling of David's words about Absalom insures that the reader hears them, just as the narrator makes doubly sure that those around David continually hear the king's words also: "And *all the people heard* when the king gave orders to all the commanders about Absalom" (18:5); "for *in our hearing* the king commanded you and Abishai and Ittai, 'Protect for my sake the young man Absalom'" (18:12); "for *the people heard* that day, 'The king is grieving for his son'" (19:3).

We have sympathy for David not just because the narrator makes doubly sure we know about the king's worry over Absalom, but also because the story manages to make David's double cry of grief (in 19:1, 5) the climax of a steady buildup of tension. At first, David expresses himself with psychological tact and political restraint: up to the sad but triumphant words of the Cushite, David refers to Absalom as "the young man" (*hanna^{c}ar*) in 18:5, 12, 29, 32. The king can hardly designate as "my son" the one who is out to destroy the very people David is addressing. Then, the highly stylized triple communication between David and his watchman in 18:24–27 also builds up for us David's tense expectations. David's three responses, "There are tidings in his mouth; he also brings tidings; he comes with good tidings" (18:26, 27, 28), show his rising hopes about the good news he wants to hear.

But after the sad news from the Cushite, David's tact completely breaks down, as he cries "my son" over and over again—eight times in total (19:1, 5). All pretense of royal restraint and objectivity is impossible now, and Joab's perception surely mirrors that of the people and readers as well: "For today I perceive that if Absalom were alive and all of us were dead today, then you would be pleased" (19:7). The king's grief threatens royal interests, and as we see David turning away from his grief in 19:9a, we know that the interlude begun in 18:19 has come to an end. David's paternal concern gives way to political necessity, and the narrative resumes its national and social emphases. The story of the revolt began when Absalom "stood beside the way of the gate" (15:2) judging "all Israel" (15:6). We now find David "sitting in the gate; and all the people came before the king" (19:9a). The next words, "Now Israel had fled every man to his own home" (19:9b), return the reader to affairs as they were at 18:17, where the story was interrupted by the narrator's comment in 18:18 and the beginning of the interlude in 18:19.

The narrative, however, does not simply rely upon the words in 19:9b repeating those in 18:17 in order to return the reader to the story's overriding social concerns. For a number of stylistic and other verbal details within the interlude itself accomplish the same purpose. The many ways in which 18:19–19:9a is similar to its context, whether immediate or remote, also insure that the story of Israel will not be overwhelmed by this deeply moving account of a father grieving for his son.

Look at the ways in which the interlude doubles back on its immediate context: the runners' announcement of Absalom's fate in 18:19–32 mirrors the narrator's announcement of that fate in 18:1–17 through a number of important connections.

Take the matter of the ritual crossings and reversals that began in chapter 15 and that motivate, as I suggested above, the manner of Absalom's capture in 18:9. We now find that those who will announce the fate of Absalom to David *enact* a kind of processional reversal similar to that which the narrator describes in 18:9. As Absalom is caught and the mule under him passes by (*ᶜābar*), so Ahimaaz, who was behind the Cushite (18:22), passes him by (*wayyaᶜᵃbor 'et hakkûšî*: 18:23).

Not only does the messenger who was "behind" (v. 22) "cross over" (v. 23) to become the one "in front" (v. 27), his reversal of position mirrors a reversal of message attributed to the runners by the narrator. At first it was Ahimaaz who proposed to Joab "Let me run and carry tidings to the king (*wa'ᵃbaśśerāh 'et hammelek*) that the LORD has delivered him (*šᵉpāṭô*) from the hand of his enemies" (18:19). Yet when Ahimaaz arrives before the king, his message of the LORD's deliverance switches from the verb *šāpaṭ* to *siggēr* (18:28), whereas it is the trailing Cushite who actually delivers Ahimaaz's proposed message: "Greetings O king (*yitbaśśēr hammelek*) for the LORD has delivered you (*šᵉpaṭkā*) from the hand of all who rose up against you" (18:31).

Other details within the interlude keep alive the social and national emphases that motivate the larger story, and nothing does this better than the contrast between what David wants to hear from the messengers and what they actually tell him—especially the Cushite.

The Cushite's message works well simply as a verbal transaction between messenger and king. Realizing the king's concern for the young man, and perhaps attempting to avoid—or at least soften—the harshness that is often dealt to those who carry harsh messages, the Cushite tells the truth, but still deflects his answer away from Absalom by making the young man represent all David's enemies: "May the enemies of my lord the king, and all those who rise up against you for evil, be like that young man (*hannaᶜar*)" (18:32). As a statement made by one character to another, the Cushite's words not only suggest his fear of antagonizing David, they also help to explain Ahimaaz's previous failure of nerve in not reporting Absalom's death to the king. Ahimaaz clearly knows about this death (because Joab told him so in verse 20) but, in fear of the consequences, avoids announcing it by claiming "I saw a great tumult, but I do not know what it was" (v. 29).[19] Simply at the level of the story-world itself, the Cushite's precise message in 18:32 reverberates with his fears and those of other messengers preceding him in the story.

Nevertheless, the Cushite's message works just as well in terms of communication between author and reader. For central to the narrator's story has been not only the ritualized actions illustrated by the use of *ᶜābar*, but also the stylized use of those graphic images we call *similes*. I have commented on the text's tendency toward simile in the story of Ahithophel in 2 Samuel 17. The figure now functions here as it did there.

The Cushite's statement reads not only as a jussive but even as a prediction constituted by the two stylistic characteristics of the king's counsel that I discussed in a previous chapter: a penchant for imperfective verb forms and a taste for simile: "The enemies of my lord the king, and all who rise up against you for evil shall be (*yihyû*) *like that young man* (*kannaᶜar*)" (18:32). David asked about the welfare of Absalom, but the Cushite moves the matter from individual to social concern by making Absalom's fate a simile for the fate of a totality, "all who rise up against you for evil."

But who *are* David's enemies in terms of the story before us? In order to answer this question, we now see the importance of the continued designation of Absalom's side as "Israel" or "all Israel," terms that in 15:1–18:17, I have suggested, refer to both North and South. *The entire nation of Israel*, that is to say, a preponderance of those from both the northern and southern tribes, rose up against David. In this respect it is significant that David's loyal troops are never called "Israel" in the section of the Absalom story before the interlude of 18:19–19:9a, where the loyalists are mostly called "the people" (meaning *army*) or David's "servants."

As a communication between author and reader, then, the news of 18:32 is that Absalom's fate is an explicit and graphic image of—that is, a simile for—the fate of *all Israel*, a nation which should now be seen, the Deuteronomist is telling us, as hanging cursed from the tree just as

Absalom was. By means of a remarkable turnaround, the climax of this personalized account of informing the king of his son's death is a message that this death, however much it grieves David, is also a stark image of the fate of a nation.

The Cushite here is like the Amalekite in 2 Samuel 1: each messenger acts as a double for the Deuteronomist. Just as the narrator's account of David's and the Amalekite's meeting formally mirrored the Amalekite's account of his meeting with Saul, so also I have been describing here how the narrator's announcement of Absalom's fate in 18:1–17 has a number of verbal and formal similarities to the announcement of the messenger's announcement of that fate in the interlude section of 18:19ff.

Finally, it is important to mention here how the two images of "seizing the head" in chapters 2 and 18 amount to much the same authorial message, even though the particulars of the two images differ. In 2 Samuel 2, twelve men of Judah oppose twelve men of Israel. They all seize each other by the head, so that *all Israel,* both North and South, can simultaneously and ritually die by the sword. In 2 Samuel 18, on the other hand, *all Israel,* again both North and South, is already "behind"—or even "under"— Absalom as his head is seized by the oak. The Deuteronomist accomplishes this implicit cursing of an entire nation by means of the Cushite's explicit designation of Absalom as a simile for David's enemies here, who just happen to be both the northern and southern tribes of Israel.

Once we see how Absalom hangs for "all Israel," we can begin to understand what the rest of chapter 19 means. For we continue to encounter statements about "all Israel"—the same term as before, but now referring to just the northern tribes—as it vies with Judah for the honor of being the first to restore the kingship to David by accompanying him across the Jordan and returning him to Jerusalem.

The Returning Procession: 19:9b–44

The central topic of 19:9b–44 is this: what do we do now? Who asks this question? First and foremost there is the king, who is the center of attention in the passage. This concentration on royalty is seen even at the superficial level of lexical repetition: the word "king" occurs proportionately more often here than in any other complex in the History.[20] The king is so much a major participant here that all the other key participants in the story only appear in relation to him. They are the ones who come and converse with him: Israel and Judah on one hand, and Shimei, Mephibosheth, and Barzillai on the other.

The three individuals who speak to David on his return nicely balance off the three individuals whom he meets on his flight from Jerusalem in chapter 15. There, the two Israelites he meets do not accompany him in flight (Zadok and Hushai), but a foreigner does (Ittai); here, the two Israelites with whom he speaks come to accompany him in return (Shimei and Mephibosheth), whereas a foreigner does not (Barzillai).

As for the communal participants in the story, "Israel," as I have suggested, represents the northern tribes (19:10, 12, 23, 41, 42, 43, 44) in contrast to Judah from the south (19:12, 15, 16, 17, 41, 42, 43, 44). Once again, it is of paramount importance to realize that the phrases, "all the tribes of Israel" (v. 10), "all Israel" (v. 12), "Israel" (v. 23, twice), "people of Israel" (v. 41), "every man of Israel" (v. 42), and "man of Israel" (vv. 43, 44 [twice]), all refer to the northern tribes alone. We know that "all the tribes of Israel," who raise the matter of the king's return in verse 10, refer just to the northern tribes, because later in the chapter "the men of Israel" answer "the men of Judah" by referring back to this earlier statement: "Were we not the first to speak of bringing back the king?" (v. 44). We know also that David uses "all Israel" in verse 12 to refer just to the northern tribes, for he contrasts their proposal with the inaction of his addressee, Judah, We can even surmise that David is referring simply to the North when he twice talks of Israel in verse 23, for the question here is of putting to death Shimei, who is from the northern tribe of Benjamin, and who even identifies himself as a northern Israelite: "therefore, behold, I have come this day, the first of all the house of Joseph to come down to meet my lord the king" (v. 20). Finally, this geographic distinction in the use of "Israel" is clear in verses 41, 43, and 44 by the term's explicit contrast to Judah.

One reason why the king is so often on people's lips is because the narrator has them all scurrying around the chapter asking numerous questions about the king. As with the king, so with questions about him: nowhere else in the History are so many questions raised by its characters. There are as many as twenty-three questions in 19:9b–44, and over one-half of them concern the king, with eleven of them using the word itself.[21] Manifestly, all these perplexed participants consider the question of the king, and ask themselves, "What do we do, now that the revolt has failed, and king David is "outside of the land?"[22] Chapter 19:9b–44 provides some answers to this question.

Those actions which are most often mentioned in the passage provide some specifics to these answers. Here, we find ourselves very much where we began in chapter 15, viewing a flurry of activity *to join the king in procession,* but this time as he returns to Jerusalem. The highly ritualized portrait of David's return to Jerusalem indicates the ideological dimensions that the Deuteronomist has incorporated into the story. The particulars of the procession signal what is important within the story itself, as well as within the contemporary situation of its author(s).

First, it is crucial in the story for people to meet up with the king. The word here, *qāra'* "to meet or encounter," occurs often in the chapter. Judah comes to meet the king (v. 16); Shimei rushes to meet him (v. 17) and comes down to meet him (v. 21); and Mephibosheth comes (down) to meet him (vv. 25, 26).[23] As the story develops, we realize that this physical meeting up with the king, as he makes his way back to Jerusalem, is a crucial act for all the characters in the story. Notice, for example, how Israel—in contrast to Judah—is shown to ultimate disadvantage in this regard. Even though Israel was "the first *to speak of* bringing back our king" (v. 44), Judah appears to surpass Israel in actual accomplishment: "All the people of Judah brought the king across, but [only?] half of the people of Israel" (v. 41).

Talk is cheap, as Shimei is quick to argue in his own behalf. He admits to having earlier cursed David with words, but now he points to his subsequent deeds as more important for consideration: "Therefore, behold, I have come this day, the first of all the house of Joseph to come down to meet my lord the king" (v. 21). There is an almost irresistible pull exerted on characters to join the king's procession back to Jerusalem. This rush to the king's presence involves characters who were David's fiercest enemies during the revolt, that is to say, practically everyone he meets in the chapter. Like iron filings to a magnet, everyone moves toward David.

Second, the stated purpose of meeting up with the king is "to bring him back."[24] It is not just a question of allowing the king to return, or even of inviting him to do so. One must *be with him* as he returns. When he left Jerusalem, David measured personal loyalty by a person's willingness to accompany him as he fled. He certainly was impressed with Ittai for wanting to go with him ("Why will you also go with us?" [15:19–20]), but now condemns Mephibosheth for not having done so ("Why did you not go with me, Mephibosheth?" [19:26]). In chapters 15–19, this continuing emphasis on being with the king, on accompanying him, provides a wider context for the repeated wordplay concerning Ittai's name, already discussed. This foreigner personifies a central aspect of the story: *being with the king* in a physical sense pictures forth for us larger themes of siding with him in terms of loyalty, devotion, and allegiance. The best way "to return the king" is "to return with him." And like the History's use of blood brothers, bloodied heads, and material houses as graphic representatives of their less tangible counterparts, this emphasis on *physically* accompanying the king in and out of the land stands for larger ideological and historiographic issues involving allegiance to David, his house, and even kingship itself.

Third, the particulars of the procession that returns David to his house (19:12) demand that everyone in the passage seek "to bring the king across [the Jordan]."[25] Just as the king both "returns" (19:15, 16) and "gets brought back" (19:11, 12, 13, 44), so also he both "crosses over" (19:19, 32, 34, 37, 38, 39, 40, 41) and "gets brought across" (19:16, 19, 41, 42). Here again, the immediate emphasis on "bringing the king across [the Jordan]" is not on allowing him to cross over into Jerusalem nor even on inviting him to do so, but rather on being there with him as he crosses over. In other words, ritual or processional accompaniment is paramount in "bringing the king across (*ᶜābar* in the *hifil*)" just as it was in "returning the king (*šûb* in the *hifil*)." This necessary connection between "crossing over with the king" and "bringing the king across" is best seen in verse 41: "The king crossed over, Chimham and all the people of Judah with him, and they brought the king across—even half the people of Israel [did so]."

Fourth, not only is it important to be part of the procession that returns with the king, that returns the king, that crosses over with the king, or that brings him across, it is especially important to be "the first" and not "the last" to do so. David twice asks Judah, "Why should you be the last to bring the king back?" (19:12, 13), Shimei says to David, "I have come this day, the first of all the house of Joseph to come down to meet my lord the king" (19:21), and Israel asks David, "Were we not the first to speak of bringing back our king?" (19:44). Some precede while others follow. This is the rule for processions as well as for the evaluative positions choreographed in the narrative.

The matter of who is first (*riš'ôn*) or last (*'ahᵃrôn*) in chapter 19 connects up not only with the reversal of runners in the previous chapter, wherein Ahimaaz, who was behind (18:22), crosses over (v. 23) and becomes the first runner (v. 27), but more importantly with the processional reversals in chapter 15 that involve some kind of processional protocol.[26] To cross over with the king (or the ark) means changing positions with them at important crossover points in the procession—the last house in 15:17–18, the brook Kidron in 15:23, the city limits in 15:24.

These repetitions of meetings, returnings, and crossings-over, overlaid with concern about who is first or last in the process, illustrate the obviously ritualized perspectives according to which the story is organized at its most obvious level. The narrative about Absalom's revolt may very well be called historiographic. Nevertheless, the narrator employs details of royal protocol as the means whereby historiographic and ideological issues can be graphically presented and, at times, resolved. What then does all this attention to ritual tell us about the larger issues that drive the narrative along?

The Revolt of Absalom: A Crossroad in Kingship

Geographic details are often signals of larger issues, and chapter 19's references to Gilgal are indeed suggestive. When Judah comes to meet the king and bring him over the Jordan, they travel to Gilgal (v. 16). Once David crosses the Jordan, he crosses over to Gilgal with Chimham, all the people of Judah, and half of the people of Israel (v. 41). Why is Gilgal so important a crossing-place in the process of returning the king? The answer lies in the role that this city plays in the History, from the inception of kingship onwards.

Gilgal is where the kingdom was first renewed, and where the people made Saul king (1 Sam. 11:14–15). Gilgal is where Saul precipitously sacrificed, and where he was confronted by an angry Samuel, who prophesied that his kingship would not continue (1 Sam. 10:8; 13). Gilgal is where Saul and the people sinned, and where Samuel confronted Saul a second time to announce to him that God had rejected him as king (1 Samuel 15). At that time, Saul twice asked Samuel, "Return with me (*šûb ᶜimmî*)"; Samuel at first refused, "I will not return with you," but finally relented "Samuel turned back after Saul" (1 Sam. 15:25, 26, 30, 31). We now find that Gilgal is the place to go when Israel's anointed, Absalom, has died, and the matter of returning with the king is once more raised. Gilgal, then, is the place where kingship is born, broken, and renewed, a royal crossing where one makes or breaks kings, and where kingship itself is renewed.[27]

In 19:9b–44, if "to return the king" is to return with him to Gilgal, and thus, to signal the renewal of his kingship, then the ritual procession here also represents the ideological direction Israel freely takes in the constitutional crisis brought about by Absalom's revolt. Will all Israel, both North and South, now direct their allegiance back to David, after having proclaimed and anointed Absalom king (15:10; 19:11)? This appears to be precisely the issue over which all the people were at strife (*nādôn*: 19:10), an issue which both North and South strive to be the first to resolve.

But the concern is not over simply bringing back the king, for as we have seen, the procession is also one of *crossing over* with the king, of bringing him *across* from the place where he has been, for a time, in exile.[28] The entire procession, from its inception in chapter 15 to its conclusion in chapter 19, finds its authorial raison d'être in the strife which Israelites both in the land and in Babylon must have experienced when they considered whether a return should include "crossing over with the king," in other words, restoring the house of David.

What will Israel in exile do, the Israel of the Deuteronomist's time as well as of David's? At Absalom's death, the people, like Israel in 1 Samuel 11 and 12, had an opportunity to retract their allegiance to kingship, but failed to do so.[29] The History may end in ambiguous fashion, with David's descendant released from prison and dining regularly at the king's table, but when biblical narrative *does* recount Israel's return to the land in Ezra-Nehemiah, there is no mention of restoring the royal house of David—or even kingship itself. This indeed may be the good news hoped for by the Deuteronomist. As for the story in 2 Samuel, the bad news continues.

2 Samuel 20: A Crossroad and Culmination

Chapter 20 offers us an ultimate—or at least penultimate—example of how 2 Samuel has used a small number of concrete images to convey its complex historiographic and ideological messages. The key events in the chapter focus upon the care of David's *house,* the murder of Joab's *blood brother,* and the severed *head* of David's enemy, Sheba. At the same time, the chapter somehow manages to resume a constellation of stylistic features and ideological concerns that characterize the more immediate story of Absalom's revolt. There is some basis, therefore, for claiming that chapter 20 constitutes a fitting conclusion to David's reign, and to the original Book of Samuel. How such an effect can be correlated with the material in chapters 21–24 will be the subject of the last chapter of this book. For now, the climactic characteristics of 2 Samuel 20 need to be described.

The previous chapters in 2 Samuel contained many examples illustrating how the fate of a physical house or household can stand for the fate of dynastic, tribal, and national houses; how the fate of familial brothers graphically suggests what can happen to tribal and national brothers; and how violence to the heads of individuals can represent the violence surrounding the head of a nation. For example, God in 2 Samuel 6 blessed the household of the foreigner, Obed-edom, but instead of blessing David's dynastic house, God covers it with a perpetual curse ("Now therefore the sword shall never depart from your house" [12:10]). Similarly, 2 Samuel's continuing concern with the bloody exploits of blood brothers like the three sons of Zeruiah provides a running commentary on a history of fratricide with tribal and national dimensions. Finally, the choreographed seizing of heads in 2 Samuel 2 and the cursed seizing of Absalom's head in 2 Samuel 18 offer the reader unforgettable images of the fate of "all Israel" as they follow their royal head—whether in support or in pursuit—toward eventual catastrophe. Chapter 20 now tells its story by focusing upon domestic, fraternal, and capital concerns. Physical houses, blood brothers, and a severed head give these abstract issues concrete form.

The first thing David does upon returning to Jerusalem is to incarcerate the ten concubines he had left in charge of his house during his flight from Absalom: "And David came to his *house* at Jerusalem; and the king took the ten concubines whom he had left to care for the *house,* and put them in a *house* under guard, and provided for them, but did not go in to them. So they were shut up until the day of their death, living as if in widowhood" (v. 3). The verse's obvious use of paronomasia is an immediate signal that there is more than historiographic interest in the telling of the incident: David, who left his concubines to care for his house (*lišmor habbayit*) as he fled, now confines them to "a house under guard (*bêt mišmeret*)" upon his return. The irony in the wordplay is wonderfully suggestive; the fate of those who guard the king's house is life-long confinement in a guardhouse, a kind of living widowhood.

Furthermore, the language in verse 3 is sufficiently distinctive to indicate wider meanings at the level of the larger story. For the narrator's description of what happens to David's concubines is bound up with Abigail's prophecy about David in 1 Sam. 25:29. When David was still in deadly conflict with his rival Saul—who like Sheba is a Benjaminite—Abigail offered David some words about his future: "If men rise up to pursue you and to seek your life, the life of my lord *shall be bound up* (*ṣᵉrûrāh*) *in the bundle* (*biṣror*) *of the living*; and the lives of your enemies *he shall fling out as from the hollow of a sling*" (1 Sam. 25:29).[30] It was clear that Abigail's language about the sling was a positive allusion to David's defeat of Goliath in 1 Samuel 17; it is now clear that her words about David being "bound up in the bundle of the living" are ominous rather than salutary.[31] The bundle is to constrict David's life rather than expand it, to distress it rather than protect it.

The threatening tones of Abigail's language should be clear simply from the use of the root *ṣrr* throughout the History: towns or cities are besieged (Deut. 28:52; 1 Kings 8:37), concubines are confined (2 Sam. 20:3), and many individuals, even Israel itself, are sorely distressed (Deut. 4:30; Judg. 2:15; 10:14, 19; 1 Sam. 13:6; 30:6; 2 Sam. 13:2). Nowhere in the History are such physical and spiritual constrictions ever considered pleasant, attractive, or hopeful. It is a terrible thing for a city to be besieged and a soul tormented. The very language, then, which Abigail uses confirms that her words foreshadow the distress that awaits not only David's enemies, but even those who are loyal to his house.

But the particular distress which Abigail predicts for David in 1 Sam.

25:29, and which the Deuteronomist narrates for David's concubines in 2 Sam. 20:3, is a torment in life rather than in dying. Look at the unusual language that binds these two verses together:

> Abigail: The life of my lord shall be bound up in the bundle of the living (*ṣᵉ rûrāh biṣror haḥayyîm*).

> Narrator: So they were bound up, a living widowhood (*ṣᵉ rurôt 'almᵉnût ḥayyût*).

The punishment God inflicted on Saul's house, as 1 Samuel prophesied and 2 Samuel fulfills, is its destruction to make way for another. The punishment, however, of David's house, as God prophesied in 2 Samuel 12 and the rest of the History fulfills, is its prolonged existence in a reduced state, full of torment and distress such as the living widowhood of David's concubines pictures forth in 2 Samuel 20—an image of perpetual domestic powerlessness first adumbrated in the prophecy of the man of God to Eli in 1 Sam. 2:35–36, and to be resumed, finally, in the restoration of David's descendant Jehoiachin in 2 Kings 25:27–30.[32]

In terms, then, of the Deuteronomist's authorial communication to the reader by means of the History taken as a whole, the prophecy of Abigail and the initial action of David in 2 Samuel 20 coincide in their graphic imaging of the fate of David's house, on one hand, and that of Israel, the protector of that house, on the other. Protecting David's house placed Israel in the prison house of history.

Just as the abstract claims of a dynastic house find physical shape both in David's house guarded by his concubines as well as in the guardhouse they eventually occupy, so also matters of tribal and national fratricide now take on graphic shape with Joab's murder of his cousin and rival, Amasa. As I suggested earlier in chapter 2, 2 Samuel makes it clear that Joab's smiting of Amasa in the belly looks backward to the murders of Ishbosheth in 4:6, Abner in 3:27, and Asahel in 2:23. Moreover, these instances of "smiting in the belly" occur only here in 2 Samuel, and always in the context of an explicit reference to "brother."[33] As such, therefore, Joab's murder of his familial brother Amasa is an especially clear illustration of how 2 Samuel conveys its authorial messages.

My remarks in chapter 2 are relevant here. During the life and career of David, and beyond, stories of murder and mayhem that are based upon fraternal considerations of a familial nature are frequent vehicles for reinforcing the History's larger tribal and national concerns. The bloody chaos that envelops brothers (and sisters) within a single royal house, or between fraternal defenders of one royal house and those of another, is simply 2 Samuel's reflection, in personal terms, of the History's central social message about the institution of kingship as a major cause of fratricide on the tribal and national level.

Because the murder of Amasa is central to the fraternal emphases of 2 Samuel in general, it is easy to see why stylistic and thematic details in the account of that murder join it to specific events described earlier in the book, especially those in 2 Samuel 2. The fratricidal pursuit of brethren and Asahel's pursuit of Abner now finds narrative reflection in Joab's and Abishai's fraternal pursuit of Sheba (20:6, 7, 10, 13), and in Joab's cold-blooded murder of his blood brother Amasa. It is significant that Gibeon (2:13; 20:8) is the center for tribal fratricide in chapter 2 and familial fratricide here in chapter 20. Even 2 Samuel 2's extensive and complex wordplay involving the root *'aḥar* finds similar emphasis here in 2 Samuel 20, where, significantly, the root occurs eleven times, and where its use may even help to explain why Amasa botches up his commission by "being delayed (*wayyiḥar*) beyond the set time which had been appointed him" (v. 5).[34] The fallen bodies of Asahel and Amasa even provoke similar reactions: "And all who came (*kol habbā'*) to the place where Asahel had fallen and died stood still" (*wayya ͨamodû*: 2:23); "And when [the man] saw that everyone who came (*kol habbā'*) upon [Amasa] would stand still" (*we ͨāmād*: 20:12). Finally, the battle ends in chapter 20 as it did in chapter 2: Joab blows the trumpet to signal the end of the confrontation between Judah and Israel (2:28; 20:23).

The third focal point of the chapter concerns the capital punishment of David's enemies, and here again, Abigail's prophecy in 1 Sam. 25:29 offers the reader a clue to the authorial perspective according to which the revolt of Sheba is narrated. David and those who protect his royal house are confined to a living punishment. Yet God will also sling out (*qāla ͨ*) as from the hollow of a sling the lives of David's enemies. Abigail's words explain how and why not only David's followers but even his opponents are to be punished. For Abigail's pointed reference to the sling, while looking back to David's battle with, and beheading of, Goliath, also looks forward to David's battle with Sheba, who is now beheaded for his opposition to the king in 2 Samuel 20. Sheba's head is then thrown (*hišlîk*) over the wall to Joab—like Abigail's stone from a sling. The story of Sheba's revolt is about how one can lose one's head, in opposing David as well as in following him.

Sheba's revolt is capital in two senses. One one hand, David's *character zone* is intimately connected with the head as a locus of guilt and death, so that blood flows from the heads of David's enemies more often than with any other character in the Bible. In fact, those who oppose David are typically subject to beheading, like Goliath (1 Sam. 17:46, 54, 57), Saul

(1 Sam. 31:9), Ishbosheth (2 Sam. 4:7, 8, 12), Shimei (2 Sam. 16:9), and Sheba (2 Sam. 20:22). And even when opposition to David does not result in literally losing one's head, such opposition is still presented in the History as a capital offense in which the punishment fits the crime. Thus Absalom is caught by Joab after his head is caught up in a tree, while Ahithophel, his counselor, hangs his head—and himself—in defeat. Yet what is the fate of one who opposes David when his enemy is the entire nation, as in Absalom's revolt, or northern Israel, as in Sheba's?

On the other hand, the present story involves not just opposing David but following Sheba instead: "So all the men of Israel withdrew from David and followed Sheba" (2 Sam. 20:2). And since Sheba wants to be king over the ten northern tribes of Israel, as Absalom was over all Israel from Dan to Beersheba, the pursuit of royalty in favor of Sheba will have a fate similar to the pursuit of royalty in favor of David.

Notice first how Sheba's movements are precisely choreographed to put him and his followers in a position similar to that of David's concubines. "And Sheba passed through (*wayya ᶜabor*) all the tribes of Israel to Abel of Beth-maacah, and all the [the Hebrew is unclear at this point] after him (*'aharāyw*: v. 14)." We now have Sheba's band bundled up for a fate that corresponds to that of David's concubines earlier in the chapter. Whether individuals are shut up, as those loyal to David are in verse 3, or cities besieged, as Abel is in verse 15, the language of constriction is the same in both cases (*ṣārar /ṣûr*), and in both cases the strictures look back to Abigail's prophecy:

> 1 Sam. 25:29: The life of my lord shall be bound up (*ṣᵉ rûrāh*) in the bundle (*biṣrôr*) of the living

> 2 Sam. 20:3: So they were shut up (*ṣᵉrurôt*), living as if in widowhood

> 2 Sam. 20:15: They besieged (*wayyāṣurû*) him in Abel

Notice, however, that the story of Sheba raises the question of a distinction between the punishment inflicted upon a royal pretender on one hand, and that given his royal followers on the other. The wise woman of Abel raises the question, and Joab answers it: "'You seek to destroy a city which is a mother in Israel; why will you swallow up the heritage of the LORD?' Joab answered, 'Give up [Sheba] alone, and I will withdraw from the city'" (vv. 19–21). Once we understand that Sheba wants to be what his fellow Benjaminite before him actually was, "head of the tribes of Israel" (1 Sam. 15:17), we understand the particular punishment he receives. The punishment fits the crime, and Sheba's head is cut off and thrown over the wall.

At the same time, if what is at issue here is not just rival claims concerning headship in Israel, but especially concern over royal headship itself, then a climactic feature of the story lies in graphically resolving the problem before our eyes. When Joab's men "besieged [Sheba] in Abel, they cast up a mound against the city, and it stood against the rampart; and they were battering (*mašhîtim*) the wall to throw it down" (v. 15). But now the counsel of the wise woman of Abel insures that the city wall will not come down, "Behold, his head shall be thrown to you over the wall. And they cut off the head of Sheba and threw it out to Joab. So he blew the trumpet, and they dispersed from the city, every man to his home" (vv. 21–22). What ends the siege of Abel is the severing of the head of the head of "all the tribes of Israel" through which Sheba had passed (v. 14).

So Abel, a city which is "a mother in Israel (v. 19)," does not suffer the fate ultimately predicted for Israel itself: "The LORD will bring you and your king whom you set over you to a nation that neither you nor your fathers have known. The LORD will bring a nation against you from afar. They shall besiege (*weḥēṣar*) you in all your towns, until your high and fortified walls, in which you trusted, come down throughout all your land" (Deut. 28:36, 47, 52). By contrast, Abel's walls stay standing because the severed head of Israel's head is cast out over them.

It is not hard to imagine an audience in exile—of which, and to which, Moses speaks in Deuteronomy 28—hearing the events in 2 Samuel 20, and seeing in them the story of a fateful royal crossing that Israel to their sorrow never took. Sheba's supporters followed him into Abel (v. 14), but in contrast to the human counsel that failed Absalom, the divine inquiry for which Abel was famous (v. 18) prevails, Sheba's royal head is cast back outside the wall that Joab's troops were battering, and "a mother in Israel" survives. The difference between the fate of Abel in 2 Samuel 20 and that of Israel in the History is simply the overthrow of "the head of the tribes of Israel" (1 Sam. 15:17; 2 Sam. 20:14) on one hand, and subjection to that head on the other.

·10·

NUMBERS
(21:1–24:25)

God hath numbered thy kingdom. (Dan. 5:25)

2 Samuel 21–24 has been called an appendix, a miscellany, a conglomeration, and any number of other things. Despite such graphic terms, the arrangement of material within these concluding chapters of 2 Samuel is widely recognized: narratives at the outer bounds (21:1–14; 24:1–25), list-like material between them (21:15–22; 23:8–39), and two poems at the center (22:1–51; 23:1–7). Such an obvious configuration should lead us to treat with suspicion the denomination of chapters 21–24 as a miscellaneous conglomeration of appendages.

The Poetry Within: 22:1–23:7

Two things are obvious about the placement of this poetry in the Books of Samuel. First, David's song (22:1–51) and last words (23:1–7) recall Jacob's poem at the end of Genesis (49:1–27) and Moses's song and blessing near the end of Deuteronomy (32:1–43; 33:1–29). At the same time, David's final poems combine with Hannah's song in 1 Samuel 2 and David's elegy in 2 Samuel 1 to form a magnificent poetic triptych that graces the Books of Samuel at the beginning, middle, and end.[1]

We will not be surprised to see that the poetry at the end of 2 Samuel, like its companion pieces at the beginning of 1 Samuel and 2 Samuel, not only offers us a revealing account of the situation of its speaker—triumphant or plaintive as the case may be—but also provides unusually clear indications of the authorial speech plan that structures and integrates the Books of Samuel within the History itself. As it ranges over the expanses of Deuteronomic narrative, the heightened and condensed language of this poetry gives us an indirect but distinct audition of the ideological accents surrounding that authorial voice I have been calling the Deuteronomist.

Given the abundance of scholarly analysis that has gone into the comparison of 2 Samuel 22 and its replication as Psalm 18, and into the literary history of the poems as they were incorporated into the History, it is all the more important to offer some complementary suggestions about how these poems fit into their literary context. At any rate, some effort must be made to restore the literary luster of poetry that has been especially tarnished by the tendency of scholars to consider it as part of what they believe to be an awkward appendage at the end of 2 Samuel.

To understand how this poetry represents the situation of its speaker within the story-world of the narrative, I will first consider both poems together in a kind of sequential reading that will amplify the poetic message that literary historical research has tended to muffle.

Like the Song of Hannah which is its proleptic summary within the History, 2 Samuel 22 is a royal hymn of personal and national thanksgiving.[2] Its recurrent theme, God's salvation of the king, is obvious through the repeated use both of *yāšaᶜ*, "to save or deliver," in verses 3 (three times), 4, 36, 42 (2 times), and 47, and of its many synonyms. Nevertheless, the *effect* of God's salvation upon the person of the king is at the heart of David's gratitude: the song celebrates David not just as king of Israel but even as "head of the nations" (22:44). As we hear David giving credit where credit is due in his exaltation of the LORD's powerful munificence toward his anointed in time of trouble, we sense the transformation of David from someone almost ensnared by death and Sheol (vv. 5–6) to a figure whose stature so mirrors his benefactor's that an appropriate title for this song would be "The Apotheosis of David."

Look first at some of the language with which David characterizes the LORD. David's God is surrounded by "clouds of dust," someone who "has surrounded himself with darkness [like] a canopy" (v. 12). The LORD "reached from on high" (v. 17), and David proclaims, "Exalted be my God" (v. 47). His God is pure (v. 27), loyal, and blameless (v. 26).[3]

When we turn to David's description of himself in the poem, it is scarcely accidental that all this salvific activity on God's part has transformed the king into a figure who is awesome and terrible in his fierce purity—someone just like his benefactor. God is surrounded by darkness, yet brightness is before him (vv. 12–13); similarly, David thanks the LORD because "my God lightens my darkness" (v. 29). Like his God, who thunders forth "in clouds of dust," David refers to himself in similar language, "I beat them to dust (*weʾešḥāqēm*) like the soil of the earth" (v. 43). And David's purity (*brr*), loyalty (*ḥsd*), and blamelessness (*tmm*) in verses 21, 25, 26, and 27 are simply reflections of the LORD's: David addresses God, "You reveal yourself as loyal to the loyal, blameless to the blameless, pure to the pure" (vv. 26–27). By the end of the song, we cannot help but

see the basis for David's gratitude: God has transformed him into a miniature of himself—a quasi-god in royal garb.

It is at this point that the juxtaposition of the Last Words of David in
2 Samuel 23:1–7 continues the apotheosis of David through language even
more daring than that used in the song. The reach of David's self-
description hits us immediately with his opening words, "The oracle
(n^e'um) of David" (23:1). Outside the History, it is true, we find the
prophet Balaam in the same linguistic position as David is in 23:1, yet the
significant point about David's language is that the History elsewhere only
has the LORD where David here audaciously places himself (1 Sam. 2:30;
2 Kings 9:26; 19:33; 22:19).

The effect of David's appropriation of divine language to himself is to
make the king, at one and the same time, a god-like prophet of God. However much we have seen David's predecessor, Saul, maneuvering to neutralize the divine check on royal power that the prophet Samuel
represented, David's speech now makes Saul's actions appear paltry and
timid. David presents himself as a prophet-king whose speech can hardly
be distinguished from God's: "The spirit of the LORD speaks by me, his
word is upon my tongue" (23:2). What Moses's speech may have
embodied in the Book of Deuteronomy, David's speech now claims for his
own speech.[4]

It may be that Moses himself has offered Israel a means by which to
evaluate David's startling assertion in: "And if you say in your heart, 'How
may we know the word which the LORD has spoken?'—when a prophet
speaks in the name of the LORD, if the word does not come to pass or
come true, that is a word which the LORD has not spoken; the prophet
has spoken it presumptuously, you need not be afraid of him"
(Deut. 18:21–22). As we shall see shortly, the literary context of the poetry
in 2 Samuel 22–23 makes these words of Moses immediately useful: however much David sings of the fear of God (22:11, 16), and of himself
"ruling in the fear of God" (23:3), the narrative setting in which these
poems have been placed allows us to hear an authorial voice speaking
about David in unison with Moses's earlier words, "You shall not fear
(*tāgûr*) him" (Deut. 18:22). Saul might make this mistake about David in
1 Sam. 18:15 ("And when Saul saw that [David] had great success, he
stood in awe [*wayyāgor*] of him"). Yet one who reads these final poems in
their present context will not be disposed to fear David as Saul did.

In 2 Sam. 23:1–2, once David announces himself as a prophet king who
carries within himself those reflections of the divine so graphically
described in 2 Samuel 22, he then appropriates to himself, as Israel's king,
solar language that, to my knowledge, is found in only one other place in
the entire Bible—used there, significantly, to describe God himself. Com-

pare, then, what Psalm 84 says about God with what David says about royal rule:

> For the Lord is a sun and shield;
>> he bestows favor and honor. (Ps. 84:12)

> [The ruler] dawns on them like the morning light,
>> like the sun on a cloudless morning
>> with brightness (*nogah*). (2 Sam. 23:4)

David basks in the reflected glory of God's favor. The brightness (*nogah*) he ascribed to God in 22:13, he now openly appropriates to himself in 23:4.

Poetic Reflections of the Surrounding Narrative

Many scholars have noted the presence of "Deuteronomistic language" in 22:21–25, yet few recognize how many allusions there are in the poem to the rest of the story that forms its literary context. Like the Song of Hannah in 1 Samuel 2 and David's own elegy over Saul and Jonathan in 2 Samuel 1, the Song of David casts its melody over the entire career of David, thereby offering readers signals of an authorial point of view. Few sections in the Books of Samuel characterize David so effectively as this poetic interlude. The following is a catalogue of the more obvious ways in which David's song comments on the larger story line—a list of reasons why the poetry in 2 Samuel 21–24 is more than a haphazard appendage to 2 Samuel.

As McCarter has already recognized, David presents himself in 22:4 as one who, when derided, cried out to God for help.[5] "Made a fool of (*meholāl*), I cried, LORD! I called for help from my enemies" (22:4). This verse reminds us of David, the sly fool, who "much afraid of Achish the king of Gath, changed his behavior before them and played the fool (*wayyitholēl*) in their presence" (1 Sam. 21:14).

When David sings, "In my distress (*ṣar lî*) I called upon the LORD" (22:7), we think not only of the particular distress which Abigail predicts for David in 1 Sam. 25:29, but especially of the fact that the words, *ṣar lî,* "in my distress," are used exclusively by David in 2 Samuel: their use in the song points backwards to David's elegy ("I am distressed for you, my brother Jonathan" [2 Sam. 1:26]) and forwards to David's response to God in 24:14 ("I am greatly distressed; let us fall into the hand of the LORD").

In the song, David claims: "[God] delivered me because he delighted in

me (*ḥāpēṣ bî*: 22:20)." Nothing is clearer in the story of David than that he
is the delight of humans. From the beginning, David is an object of delight
to his fellows, first to Saul (1 Sam. 18:22), and then to Jonathan (1 Sam.
19:1). But it is his self-understanding as *God's* special delight that characterizes his boast in the song. Earlier, during Absalom's rebellion, he
appeared confident enough of this to say, "But if [God] says, 'I have no
delight in you,' behold here I am" (2 Sam. 15:26). And God's delight in
him, he believes, ensures the success of his own desires, as his last words
proclaim, "For will [God] not cause to prosper all my help and my
desire?" (2 Sam. 23:5). Later on, Solomon his son will be said to share in
God's delight when the Queen of Sheba prays, "Blessed be the LORD
your God, who has delighted in you!" (1 Kings 10:9).[6]

Essential to David's claim to be the LORD's delight is his claim to be
righteous (*ṣᵉdākāh*: 22:21, 25). David even refers to his obedience as the
basis for his righteousness: "For all his ordinances were before me and
from his statutes I did not depart (*lo' 'āsûr*: 22:23)." Solomon will repeat
this assertion in his prayer to the LORD, "Thou hast shown great and
steadfast love to thy servant David my father, because he walked before
thee in faithfulness and in righteousness (*ûbiṣdākāh*)" (1 Kings 3:6). Nevertheless, the context of David's assertion in 2 Samuel includes his crucial
sin in 2 Samuel 11 and God's response to it in 2 Samuel 12. It is precisely
because David *did* depart from God's statutes that God's sword "shall not
depart (*lo' tāsûr*) from [his] house" (12:10).

In addition, David's boast that God "set me secure on the high places
(*ᶜal bāmôtay*)" (22:34) may look back exultantly to his own elegy over Saul
and Jonathan, wherein, by contrast, these mighty ones have fallen upon
the high places (2 Sam. 1:19, 25). Nevertheless, David's appeal to the high
places in 2 Samuel 22, like that in 2 Samuel 1, contains an ironic allusion
to the exalted venue of those sacrificial and idolatrous abominations that
the History soon will recount. The heights upon which David now glories
will soon become his house's shame.

In the song, David also describes what he did to his enemies: "I pursued
my enemies and destroyed them (*wā'ašmîdēm*: 22:38)." Although the Gibeonites have just claimed that *Saul* had planned to destroy them (21:5),
David, nevertheless, is the destroyer of enemies *par excellence* in the History.
What Saul fears in 1 Sam. 24:1 ("Do not destroy my name out of my
father's house"), what Joab, through the Tekoite woman, fears for
Absalom in 2 Sam. 14:7, 11, and 16, and what the narrative almost everywhere superficially denies David to have done, David himself now admits
with blunt universality. If there is any truth in David's poetic self-
characterizations, it may lie here, where David describes what he did "on

the day when the LORD delivered him from the hand of all his enemies, and from the hand of Saul" (22:1).

David ends his great song with the words, "[God] shows steadfast love to his anointed, to David and his descendants forever (*ᶜad ᶜôlām*)" (22:51), just as his last words proclaim, "For he has made with me an everlasting covenant (*bᵉrît ᶜôlām*)" (23:5). These claims are in line with his earlier petition, "With thy blessing may the house of thy servant be blessed forever" (7:29), yet once again, over both claim and petition, hovers the perpetual punishment of the sword fashioned by God in 12:10.

Finally, two simple statements serve to neutralize the self-exaltation that David exhibits in 22:1–23:7. First, in contrast to the bombastic picture of a warrior-king posturing like his warrior-God, the list of battles just preceding the poetry presents us with a David who grows weary and must be rescued by Abishai, "You shall no more go out with us in battle," David's men adjured him, "lest you quench the lamp of Israel" (21:15–17). How different this narrative David is from his poetic counterpart, who "dawns upon [men] like the morning light, like the sun shining forth upon a cloudless morning" (23:4). The contrast, then, between the reliability of the narrative and the self-promotion of the poetry is like the difference between a flickering lamp and the blazing sun.

Second, nothing serves to deflate David's boasts better than his own statement, buried almost in the middle of the song. After exalting himself all out of proportion to the details of the story in which he appears, and before he continues to sing about how God exalted him above his adversaries (22:49), David manages to speak words that echo Hannah's words in 1 Samuel 2 and that ought to temper his own exaltation: "Thou dost deliver a humble people, but thy eyes are upon the exalted (*rāmîm*) to bring them down" (22:28). David's mistake, foreshadowed by Hannah and documented throughout the History, was to move too quickly from exaltation to exultation.

Prose Preliminaries

The first question, as I have already indicated, is whether chapters 21–24 are intrusive. Scholars' suspicions on this point tend to move in one of two directions. On one hand, source-oriented scholars often find in these chapters a rich preserve in which their literary historical speculations can flourish. On the other hand, discourse-oriented scholars, while recognizing these chapters' limited literary aspects—such as their so-called "ring-composition"—consider them a rather stunted and ill-shapen con-

clusion to the aesthetic and ideological flourishes encountered in the preceding sections of 1–2 Samuel.

It is not difficult to list a number of textual features within chapters
21–24 that encourage both literary historical speculation to grow and aesthetic admiration to wither. Within 2 Samuel 21, for example, disruptive
or intrusive aspects abound. First, in contrast to the complex indirect allusions that we have been suggesting help to explain 1–2 Samuel's aesthetic
beauty and ideological complexity, we now encounter a direct and explicit
reference that seems to imply literary disunity: "Now the Gibeonites were
not of the people of Israel, but of the remnant of the Amorites; and the
sons of Israel had made an oath concerning them" (21:2) refers back to
the Gibeonite trickery in Joshua 9 as though the reader might not be
aware of it.[7] Second, the fragmentary list of exploits in 21:15–22, with the
recurring phrase, "There was again war with the Philistines" (vv. 15, 18,
19, 20), combines with even more list-like material in 23:8–38 to diminish
the impact of the more complex literary prose in 21:1–14 and 24:1–25 and
of the poetry in 22:1–23:7. Finally, the events in chapter 21 and, consequently, their apparent sequel in chapter 24, exhibit those signs of chronological dislocation that literary historians are so adept at exploiting. There
can be little doubt that if readers transplant these chapters to a place
somewhere before chapter 9, they can improve the temporal comprehen-
sibility of the larger story.

As if these three examples of the so-called intrusiveness of chapters
21–24 were not enough to activate the salivary glands of literary historians
and to assault the taste buds of modern aestheticians, other features in the
section tend to disrupt the very process of reading—whatever one's scholarly inclinations may be. For one thing, we would obviously be better prepared to interpret the story of David's execution of the descendants of
Saul in chapter 21, if we only knew how the Gibeonites executed them.
The Hebrew word is *hôqîᵃᶜ*, and since it appears only here (21:6, 9, 13)
and in Num. 25:4, we simply do not know what constituted the precise
method of execution—whether crucifixion, hanging, or dismember-
ment—nor what its evaluative and literary implications might be.[8]

We are also intrigued and bothered by features in this section that seem
to unify or integrate it, but in ways that are difficult to understand, let
alone describe. Earlier scholars, such as S. R. Driver, quickly recognized
that the structure of chapters 21–24 constituted what modern scholars like
M. Sternberg and D. Damrosch would call a "ring-composition," but such
recognition has offered minimal instruction in formulating interpretations from a discourse-oriented perspective.[9]

Another puzzling feature of these chapters is their predilection for the
number three. Three or thirty are glaringly present in the catalogue of

exploits in 23:8–39, and appear in every other prose portion of this section: in the Gibeonite account with its three years of famine (21:1); in the catalogue following it, with Ishbosheth's spear weighing three hundred shekels (21:16); and especially in the concluding story of the census with its three divine options of three months of flight from David's enemies, three days of pestilence, and (perhaps) three years of famine (24:12–13).[10] Only the poetry within chapters 21–24 lacks a reference to the number three.

Yet 2 Samuel 21–24's numerical interests extend to the number seven as well. This heptamerous embrace involves at least the pleasures of wordplay, since the number seven (*šibᶜāh* in 21:6, 9; 24:15 [and perhaps 13]) plays off the mention of oath-taking (*šābaᶜ*) in 21:2, 7, 17 on one hand, and the triple mention of Beer-sheba (*bᵉ'ēr šebaᶜ*) in 24:2, 7, 15 on the other. The seven Saulides who are executed in chapter 21 and the seventy thousand Israelites who die of God's plague in chapter 24 are thus intricately related to one another through aesthetic function, and it is not difficult to extend this connection to the realm of authorial ideology.

Ideological motivation appears central to such wordplay. *Seven* Saulides die in chapter 21 precisely because of the Israelite *oath* broken by Saul, and *only seven* die because of the *oath* with Jonathan kept by David. In complementary fashion in chapter 24, the *extent* of God's punishment is linked paronomastically to a triple mention of "Beer-sheba," and even to the immediate juxtaposition of this place name and a form of the number seven in verse 15: "And there died of those from Dan to Beer-sheba seventy thousand people (*bᵉ'ēr šebaᶜ šibᶜîm 'elep 'îš*)." The place name, "Beer-sheba," and a form of the number "seven" both appear in a phrase that signals totality or completion, in a geographic as well as a numerical sense. Spatially, the extent of God's plague upon Israel could not be greater, and when the tens of thousands of Israelites who perish at God's hands reach the number seven, the punishment is complete.

In this manner, therefore, 2 Samuel 21–24 begins with wordplay involving the strictures of oath-taking—as if to signal why the Gibeonites' execution of Saulides was limited to only seven descendants—and ends with wordplay involving the geographic completeness of all Israel ("from Dan to Beer-sheba") and the numerical completeness of those who die—as if to explain, by contrast to the situation in chapter 21, why God's execution extended to upwards of seventy thousand Israelites.

Finally, the obvious interest in the numbers three and seven is even integrated into chapter 23's roster of warriors, which, while comprising a total of only thirty-six names, ends with the tantalizing phrase, "thirty-seven in all."[11] Thus even in a fragmentary or catalogue-type section like 23:8–39, there is an obvious interest in those textual features we call literary and aesthetic.

Such exemplary hints as these are still perceptible in the text, even though much of the authorial or editorial motivation for such details may no longer be apparent to us. What is important to emphasize in all this uncertainty is that chapters 21–24 are much more than a mere miscellany.

The Story in 21:1–14 and Its Sequel in 24:1–25

Whatever one may think about a crude versus well-crafted conclusion to 2 Samuel, the ways in which the beginning and end of 2 Samuel 21–24 are implicated with each other increase the likelihood of an authorial speech plan behind this section's tangle of lists and fragmentary repetitions.

For one thing, chapter 24 "is evidently the sequel of 21, 1–14" since both the opening words of chapter 24, and the closing words of each story, unite both accounts in an especially clear way.[12] Chapter 24's beginnings, "The anger of the LORD continued to be kindled [or "was again kindled"] against Israel" (24:1), points backwards to the famine God inflicted upon the land in chapter 21.[13] Moreover, the same phrase ends both stories, and is found nowhere else in the History: "And the LORD [or God] heeded supplications for the land" (21:14; 24:25).[14]

I have already indicated another point of contact between the two stories: their integration of the numbers "three" and "seven" through plot and paronomasia. It is hardly haphazard that the famine in chapter 21 lasts three years, and that a threefold option of three (or seven) years of famine, three months of pursuit, or three days of pestilence moves the story along in chapter 24. Nor is it accidental that wordplay involving "seven" and "oath-taking" in chapter 21, and "seven" and "Beer-sheba" in chapter 24, implicates both stories in the web of ideological issues I have been discussing throughout 2 Samuel. This wordplay concerning three and seven both unites chapter 21–24 internally and enables the entire section to form a fitting conclusion to the Books of Samuel.

Still other features combine to strengthen our impression of the literary interconnectedness of chapters 21 and 24. Notice, for example, the similar intercessory roles that David and God have in resolving Israel's difficulties in chapters 21 and 24 respectively. What the king says and does in chapter 21 is pointedly analogous to what God says and does in chapter 24. David speaks to the Gibeonites as God speaks to David:

David: "Whatever you say I will do for you." (21:4)

God: "Choose one of them and I will do it for you." (24:12)

Similarly, royal mercy in chapter 21 is very much like divine mercy in chapter 24: both serve internally to limit the executions that are meant to atone for sin and dissolve divine anger:

> But the king had mercy (*wayyaḥmol*) on Mephibosheth. (21:7)

> And the LORD repented (*wayyinnaḥem*) of the evil. (24:16)

Because of such pity, only seven Saulides die in chapter 21, only (!) seventy thousand Israelites in chapter 24.[15]

Indeed, the explicit scope of the destruction in each chapter—seven versus seventy thousand—illustrates how even differences serve to demonstrate these chapters' intricate connection. Many of the contrastive features in the two stories complement one another, and provide a concluding picture that is impressive in the scope and cohesiveness of its point of view. Here are a few details that give a kind of stereoscopic vision to the concluding chapters of 2 Samuel.

The Books of Samuel concern the history of two royal houses, Saul's and David's, and it is scarcely accidental that the story in chapter 21 and its sequel in chapter 24 deal with the sins of Saul's house and David's respectively. At the beginning of chapter 21, the LORD says, "There is bloodguilt on Saul *and on his house*" (v. 1); toward the end of chapter 24, David prays to God, "Let thy hand, I pray thee, be against me *and against my father's house*" (v. 17).

No matter how temporally displaced 21:1–14 appears to be, it nevertheless provides a powerful concluding image of the fate of Saul's house, especially as personified in the continuing fate of his crippled grandson, Mephibosheth. Saul's house no longer exists as a serious dynastic contender in Israel (Mephibosheth's fantasies, reported by Ziba in 16:3, admirably emphasize this fact). Saul had to fall in violent fashion so that the History's distinction between the divine punishment of Saul's house and the divine punishment of David's might be established. Therefore, however one views the ambiguous testimony of ancient textual witnesses concerning the end of the Books of Samuel, the overall appropriateness of Saul dying in 1 Samuel 31 and of David still alive in 2 Samuel 24 should not be underestimated. Divine punishment for Saul's house is effective extinction, for David's house a perpetual sword.[16]

A second distinction between the two chapters is even more significant. No matter that the land is ravaged by three years of famine in the first case and three days of pestilence in the second; such devastation is clearly the king's fault in chapter 21 (Saul broke the oath Israel made to the Gibeonites), whereas chapter 24 attributes blame ambiguously to Israel on one hand and to David on the other. A significant widening of the scope of authorial evaluation occurs in chapter 24, in contrast to the narrower view on retribution found in chapter 21.

Chapter 21 concentrates on an individual royal decision that brings disaster upon the land. Despite the inference that three years of famine ought to have decimated at least as many Israelites as only three days of pestilence did, the seventy thousand deaths that chapter 24 enumerates have no counterpart in chapter 21, which emphasizes the effects of the *king's* decisions upon Israel's welfare, rather than wider questions of national responsibility.

By contrast, chapter 24 broadens questions relating to national responsibility for disasters by contrasting David's evaluation of the matter with the narrator's in a manner that could hardly be more obvious. On one hand, David is allowed to voice the view that the sins of Israel's kings ought not to be visited upon the flock they lead, "Then David spoke to the LORD when he saw the angel who was smiting the people, and said, 'Lo, I have sinned, and I have done wickedly; but these sheep, what have they done? Let thy hand, I pray thee, be against me and against my father's house'" (24:17). On the other hand, even though God's prophetic word to David through Gad in 24:12–13 clearly delineates the punishment while completely ignoring any mention of the crime, the reliable narrator makes it clear from the beginning that David's sin in numbering Israel and Judah is incited by the LORD: divine anger "continued to be kindled against Israel" (24:1). The reason, therefore, why the deaths by pestilence of seventy thousand Israelites are explicitly mentioned in chapter 24, whereas the deaths of Israelites by famine are never mentioned, let alone enumerated, in chapter 21, is because dynastic sin is the subject of 2 Samuel 21, but national guilt the focus of 2 Samuel 24.

That God's anger continues to be kindled against Israel (24:1) may be explained proximately by the state of affairs initiated by Saul as recounted in 2 Samuel 21. Nevertheless, the ultimate reason for God's continuing anger lies in the events initiated by Israel in 1 Samuel 8, but not to be concluded until 2 Kings 25. Scholars have expended much effort in trying to explain the legal connections between David's numbering and God's punishment in 2 Samuel 24, and in integrating such speculations within a coherent account of the literary history of 1–2 Samuel in general and 2 Samuel 21–24 in particular.[17] However, the ideological and legal issues involved here may be much less complicated and abstruse than scholars have assumed.

Notice that the story itself has Joab ask David the very question that has puzzled readers down through the ages, "May the LORD add to the people a hundred times as many as they are, but why does my lord the king delight in this matter?" (24:4). Whether David's army is an incredible 1,300,000 strong, as verse 9 indicates, or even a preposterous 130 million, as Joab rhetorically suggests in verse 4, David's great foolishness and sin (v. 10) may not be so much the numbering itself, but the implications he derives from the people's multitude. We need only look forward to Solomon's prayer at Gibeon, "And thy servant is in the midst of thy people whom thou hast chosen, *a great people* (*ᶜam rāb*) that cannot be numbered or counted for multitude" (1 Kings 3:8), to see that Solomon considers this multitude a reward for his father's righteousness and obedience (1 Kings 3:6). Solomon's belief is nothing new in the History. During Joshua's allocation of the land amongst the tribes, Joseph asked him, "Why have you given me but one lot and one portion as an inheritance? I am a numerous people (*ᶜam rāb*) for, so far, the LORD has blessed me" (Josh. 17:14).

David's belief about his people's multitude in 2 Samuel 24, like that of Solomon's and tribal Joseph's, may simply represent the worldview that we have described as *authoritarian dogmatism,* a set of beliefs which the Deuteronomist's *critical traditionalism* succeeds in neutralizing all along the way. It is fitting, therefore, that 2 Samuel ends on such a numerical note, for 2 Samuel 24 strikes at the very heart of the ideology that the History continually opposes: the belief that the size and strength of Israel, "this great people," were certain signs of God's blessing.

So the narrator's opening statement in 24:1 is crucial from an authorial perspective. It makes little difference how numerous Israel is in the story (v. 9) nor does it matter that the LORD, at seventy thousand deaths, repented of the evil he was inflicting upon them. (v. 16), or even that "the LORD heeded supplications for the land, and the plague was averted from Israel" (v. 25). The simple fact remains: "the anger of the LORD continued to be kindled against Israel" (v. 1). This situation does not end with the end of the plague, but endures well beyond the life and death of David—indeed, until the very end of the History.

Finally, these concluding chapters of 2 Samuel, despite those features that have inclined scholars to consider them an "appendix" to the book, contain a number of delicious ironies that correspond to that playful seriousness of purpose that we have found throughout the rest of 2 Samuel — and of the History as well. Consider what happened at the beginning of 2 Samuel. The tragedy of Israel's pursuit of kings was captured in a moment during the ceremony at the pool of Gibeon, when the twelve lads of Judah and the twelve lads of Israel "each caught his neighbor by the head and thrust his sword in his neighbor's side; *so they fell down together* (*wayyippᵉlû yaḥdāw*)" (2:16). Now, near the end of the book, because of "the zeal of Saul for the people of Israel and Judah" (21:2), David surrenders the sons of Saul to the Gibeonites for execution, so that "the seven of them *fell down together (wayyippᵉlû yāḥad)*" (21:9). Nowhere else in Israel but at Gibeon, and nowhere else in the History but in 2 Samuel 2 and 21, do Israelites *fall down together* in the pursuit of kings.

Consider also that at the beginning of this pursuit Israel pleaded with Samuel "that our king may go out before us and fight our battles" (1 Sam. 8:20). Now, in a concluding chapter of 2 Samuel, David's men must adjure him, "You shall no more go out with us to battle lest you quench the lamp (*nēr*) of Israel" (21:17). We are still at that point in the History that was foreshadowed by the narrator's words at the beginning of 1 Samuel: "The lamp (*nēr*) of God had not yet gone out" (3:3). Yet even at the very end of the History, with the release from prison of David's descendant Jehoiachin in 2 Kings 25:30, we will see the lamp of Israel still only flickering.

Consider one last irony: David delights in numbering the people just as the Deuteronomist, as I have been suggesting, takes such obvious delight in numbering the narrative. The text may seduce the reader by means of this playfully serious use of numbers, but the bottom line has God inciting David to a deadly delight in the foolishness of numbers. Chapters 21–24, therefore, illustrate a central feature of the History: its inspired fusing of aesthetics and ideology. The end of 2 Samuel mirrors the central concerns of the History because for the people of Israel, whether by narrative seduction or divine incitation, there is little safety in numbers.

NOTES

1. Heroes (1:1–27)

1. See my remarks on this subject in *Samuel and the Deuteronomist* (Bloomington: Indiana University Press, 1993), pp. 147–51.

2. See *Samuel and the Deuteronomist*, pp. 206, 211.

3. 19:10, 11, 12, 17, 18; 20:29; 22:1; 23:13; 27:1 (3 times).

4. This is not to deny that David is more precisely, in C. F. Keppler's terms, the first self and the Amalekite is David's second self. See *The Literature of the Second Self* (Tucson: University of Arizona Press, 1972).

5. See *Samuel and the Deuteronomist*, pp. 221–23.

6. This persistent questioning of and about David, together with its possible narrative functions throughout the books of Samuel, was first emphasized to me by my student, Rachel Paley.

7. See *Samuel and the Deuteronomist*, pp. 102ff.

8. Josh. 2:16; Judg. 8:21; 15:12; 18:25; 1 Sam. 22:17, 18 (twice); 2 Sam. 1:15; 2:25, 29; 1 Kings 2:25, 29, 31, 32, 34, 46. Only 1 Sam. 10:5 appears to describe a neutral encounter between Saul and a band of prophets; but given the negative juxtaposition of king and prophet in 1 Samuel 10 (*Samuel and the Deuteronomist*, pp. 100–108), perhaps their meeting is to be seen as ideologically antagonistic.

9. *Hammaggîd lô/lî*: 2 Sam. 1:5, 6, 13; 4:10; see also 15:13.

10. See *Samuel and the Deuteronomist*, p. 61.

11. Verse 22, alone of all the verses in the poem, describes with graphic singularity what Saul and Jonathan *accomplished* upon the heights. As I will soon describe in some detail, this verse provides an image that is remarkable in its power to condense into a few words what Bakhtin would call the "ultimate conceptual authority" both of the poem and the History as well. I consider verse 22 to be the eye of the emotional and ideological storm swirling around the words of the lament.

12. "The Problem of Speech Genres," in Caryl Emerson and Michael Holquist, eds., *Speech Genres and Other Late Essays* (Austin: University of Texas Press, 1986), pp. 60–102.

13. See, for example, P. K. McCarter, "The Apology of David," *Journal of Biblical Literature* 99 (1980), pp. 489–504.

14. I discuss *ṣᵉbî* here in its well-attested sense of "beauty, splendour, glory," and will return to this matter below when I come to describe the Deuteronomist's voice within the poem.

15. S. Talmon, "The Textual Study of the Bible—A New Outlook," in Frank Cross and Shemaryahu Talmon, eds., *Qumran and the History of the Biblical Text* (Cambridge, Mass.: Harvard University Press, 1975), pp. 364–65.

16. D. N. Freedman offers a different view of David here by translating verse 26 in this way: "You delighted me greatly, you were extraordinary; loving you, for me, was better than loving women." In "The refrain in David's Lament over Saul and Jonathan," in his *Pottery, Poetry, and Prophecy: Studies in Early Hebrew Poetry* (Winona Lake, Ind.: Eisenbrauns, 1980), p. 265.

17. *Speech Genres and Other Late Essays,* p. 87.

18. Alternate translations of *bāmôt* exemplified most recently by P. K. McCarter, *2 Samuel,* vol. 9 of the Anchor Bible (Garden City, N.Y.: Doubleday, 1984), pp. 74–75, are philologically interesting but, in my opinion, too speculative to warrant dismissal of the usual construal of this word.

19. See Deut. 32:13; 1 Sam. 9:12, 13, 14, 19, 25; 10:5, 13; 2 Sam. 22:34; 1 Kings 3:2, 3, 4.

20. 1 Kings 11:7; 12:31, 32; 13:2, 32, 33; 14:23; 15:14; 22:44; 2 Kings 12:4; 14:4; 15:4, 35; 16:4; 17:9, 11, 29, 32; 18:4, 22; 21:3; 23:5, 8, 9, 13, 15, 19, 20.

21. Similarly, verse 20 of the lament, "Declare it not . . . publish it not," is to be read in the light of 1 Sam. 31:9.

22. In addition, there may even be wordplay here based upon the similarity of *ṣᵉbî* with *ṣābā',* "army, military host."

23. As in 2 Sam. 2:18; Prov. 6:5; 1 Chron. 12:9; Song of Sol. 2:9, 17; 8:14.

24. As in Deut. 12:15, 22; 14:5; 15:22.

25. Apart from its usage here in 1 Samuel 1, the term is nowhere used as a sublime epithet for any individual or person except, as mentioned above, the LORD himself. Isaiah uses this term to describe the remnant of Israel (4:2), Babylon (13:19), Tyre (23:9), and Samaria (28:1, 4). Jeremiah uses it to refer to the land of Israel, "a heritage most splendrous of the nations" (3:19). Ezekiel uses it to describe Israel (20:6, 15), Moab's cities (25:9), and the land of Tyre (26:20), while Daniel refers to the splendor of various lands (8:9; 11:16, 41) or the holy mountain (11:45). When Ezekiel refers to "its beautiful ornament" in 7:20, there is good reason to view this phrase as geographic and communal, referring to the land of Israel in general and Jerusalem in particular, as Ezek. 16:11 and 23:40 indicate.

26. On *kābôd,* see *Samuel and the Deuteronomist,* pp. 46–47.

27. *Speech Genres and Other Late Essays,* p. 89.

28. Exod. 23:18; Lev. 3:17; 7:33; 17:6; Num. 18:17; Isa. 1:11; 34:6, 7: Ezek. 39:19; 44:7, 15. Only in Deut. 32:14 is the sacrificial context missing; but here "blood" is used metaphorically in the phrase, "blood of the grape," to signify wine rather than the literal liquid of life. The sacrificial dimensions of this word-pair have already been pointed out by S. Gevirtz in "David's Lament over Saul and Jonathan," in *Patterns in the Early Poetry of Israel* (Chicago: University of Chicago Press, 1963), p. 88. Gevirtz, however, fails to exploit this dimension in his overall interpretation of the lament.

29. Fokkelman mentions Isaiah 34:6–7 in connection with verse 22 of the elegy, but simply to establish a point about the "drunkenness of weapons," an image he finds in both passages: *Narrative Art and Poetry in the Books of Samuel.* Vol. 2: *The Crossing Fates* (Assen: Van Gorcum, 1986), p. 665. It seems to me that the mixing of the sacrificial and the martial in a stark and savage image is what both pericopes are about.

30. Isa. 42:17; 50:5; 59:14; Jer. 38:22; 46:5; Pss. 35:4; 40:15; 44:19; 70:3; 129:5.

31. Jeremiah utters a prophecy about military defeat (here of Babylon) by describing a successful military campaign as "returning not empty": "For behold I am stirring up and bringing against Babylon a company of great nations. . . . Their

arrows are like a skilled warrior (*gibbôr*) who does not return empty-handed" (Jer. 50:9).

32. See other legislation forbidding a ritual appearance before the LORD empty-handed: Exod. 23:15; 34:20.

33. See *Samuel and the Deuteronomist*, pp. 60–64.

34. *Bāśar* in 1 Sam. 4:17; 31:9; 2 Sam. 1:20; 4:10 (twice); see also 18:19, 20, 26, 31.

35. Gale A. Yee has written an article suggesting how Isaiah 14:4b–21 is a parody of David's dirge in 2 Sam. 1:19–27: "The Anatomy of Biblical Parody: The Dirge Form in 2 Samuel 1 and Isaiah 14," *Catholic Biblical Quarterly* 50 (1988), pp. 565–86. It may be, however, that David's dirge is already a parody of an Israelite elegy or dirge, and that it ought to be read as such in order to recover its authorial dimensions. That is to say, there is speech interference between its perspectives as a straight elegy within the story-world and as a parody of this form. By means of David's words about Saul and Jonathan, the Deuteronomist foreshadows the critical elements in the coming History that led to the fall of mighty Israel.

36. McCarter, *2 Samuel*, p. 76. D. N. Freedman translates "*mgn*" as "benefactor, suzerain, chieftan": *Pottery, Poetry, and Prophecy*, p. 270. Even were this correct, a reference to Yahweh would still be appropriate in context.

37. What counts for poetry is not always clear, but the following list is fairly complete. Out of thirty-five poetic occurrences, "shield" refers to the LORD in twenty-one of them: Deut. 33:29; 2 Sam. 22:3, 31, 36; Pss. 3:4; 7:11; 18:3, 31, 36; 28:7; 33:20; 59:12; 84:10, 12; 115:9, 10, 11; 119:114; 144:2; Prov. 2:7; 30:5.

38. William L. Holladay, "Form and Word-play in David's Lament over Saul and Jonathan," *Vetus Testamentum* 20 (1970), p. 154. Another scholar who emphasizes the secular quality of this poem is Masao Sekine, "Lyric Literature in the Davidic-Solomonic Period," in Tomoo Ishida, ed., *Studies in the Period of David and Solomon and Other Essays* (Winona Lake, Ind.: Eisenbrauns, 1982), pp. 1–11.

39. This is the only occurrence in the Bible of *gā͑al* in the *nifal*.

40. David calls Jonathan "my brother" and whether one sees in this verse intimations of a homosexual relationship between them, the I-you form of the statement clearly expresses the personal relationship between grieving speaker and fallen addressee.

41. See *Samuel and the Deuteronomist*, pp. 22ff.

42. The covenantal implications of *'āhēb* in Deuteronomic discourse appear to me to be appropriate to the elegy as spoken by the narrator. See here William Moran, "The Ancient Near Eastern Background of the Love of God in Deuteronomy," *Catholic Biblical Quarterly* 25 (1963), pp. 77–87.

2. Brothers (2:1–4:12)

1. This is McCarter's apt translation for the locale memorialized in the story in verse 16, *2 Samuel*, pp. 93, 96.

2. See McCarter, ibid., pp. 95–99 for a convenient discussion of such suggestions.

3. We have already seen, more than once, the ideological implications possible through the use of *͑ābar* in the History. See my *Moses and the Deuteronomist* (Bloom-

ington: Indiana University Press, 1993), pp. 99–101, and *Samuel and the Deuteronomist*, pp. 62–63.

4. See Deut. 5:32; 17:11, 20; 28:14; Josh. 1:7; 23:6; 1 Sam. 6:12; 2 Kings 22:2. See also 2 Sam. 14:19 where going to the right or left means disobedience to the king. Only in Deut. 2:27 is "not to swerve to the right or left" a literal phrase about a journey rather than a metaphor for obedience, yet even here Moses's statement may also imply that Israel's passage through Amorite territory was accomplished without violation of any local laws. Here in 2 Samuel 2 the verb for "swerve" is *nāṭāh,* whereas most everywhere else in the History it is *sûr.* Nevertheless, even in 2 Samuel 2 *sûr* is explicitly used as a synonym for *nāṭāh* in verse 21. On 1 Sam. 6:12 see *Samuel and the Deuteronomist,* p. 67.

5. Brian McHale, *Postmodernist Fiction* (New York and London: Methuen, 1987), p. 125.

6. For example, see F. H. Cryer, "David's Rise to Power and the Death of Abner: An Analysis of 1 Samuel 26:14–16 and its Redaction-Critical Implications," *Vetus Testamentum* 35 (1985), pp. 385–94; P. Kyle McCarter, "The Apology of David," *Journal of Biblical Literature* 99 (1980), pp. 489–504; James C. Vanderkam, "Davidic Complicity in the Deaths of Abner and Eshbaal: A Historical and Redactional Study," *Journal of Biblical Literature* 99 (1980), pp. 521–39; and Keith W. Whitelam, "The Defence of David," *Journal for the Study of the Old Testament* 29 (1984), pp. 61–87. Cryer and Vanderkam are especially clear in suggesting how some textual details succeed in indicting David for those convenient crimes of which the murder of Abner is but one of a series.

7. *Postmodernist Fiction,* pp. 124–25. Other helpful sources for understanding this phenomenon and critical theory about it are: M. Ron, "The Restricted Abyss: Nine Problems in the Theory of *Mise en Abyme,"* *Poetics Today* 8 (1987), pp. 417–38; L. Dallenbach, "Reflexivity and Reading," *New Literary History* 11 (1980), pp. 435–49; V. Furedy, "A Structural Model of Phenomena with Embedding in Literature and Other Arts," *Poetics Today* 10 (1989), pp. 745–69; and M. Bal, "Mise en abyme et iconicité," *Litterature* 29 (1978), pp. 116–28.

8. So Ron in the article just cited.

9. Since Abner's power over Israel still poses a threat to David in spite of their covenant, Abner's association with Nabal in this chapter remains a narrative possibility. Abner's angry response to Ishbosheth, "Am I the head of Caleb which belongs to Judah?"—if this indeed be a correct translation of *hr'š klb 'nky 'šr lyhwdh* in verse 8—recalls the theme of David's increasing control over Caleb, which culminated in his marriage to the widow of Nabal the Calebite. At the same time, the Deuteronomist may be using David's lamentation over Abner to liken the deceased to Nabal: "Does Abner die as Nabal died?" (v. 33).

10. See on this point *Moses and the Deuteronomist,* pp. 126–34.

11. See 1:26; 2:22, 26, 27; 3:8, 27, 30 (twice); 4:6, 9; 10:10; 13:3, 4, 7, 8, 10, 12, 20 (four times), 26, 32; 14:7 (twice); 15:20; 18:2; 19:13, 42; 20:9, 10; 21:21; 23:18, 24.

12. This general connection of kingship and personal kinship in biblical narrative is one that Joel Rosenberg has explored with great insight in his book *King and Kin: Political Allegory in the Hebrew Bible* (Bloomington: Indiana University Press, 1986).

13. The narrator's apparent interruption of the story here by mentioning Jonathan's lame son may be no more out of place than the reference to Doeg in 1 Sam. 21:7, which seems to interrupt the story of David and Ahimelek at Nob but actually prepares for Doeg's eyewitness account in 1 Sam. 22:9–10. It remains to be seen

whether further details in the History will indicate why Mephibosheth is mentioned at this precise point in the story.

14. Besides discrepancies between the LXX and the Masoretic Text in verse 6, the MT itself appears to indicate that verses 6 and 7 are variant descriptions of the murder itself.

15. For a plausible suggestion that Hebrew *ḥomeš* is linguistically related to Akkadian *ḫumašum* and that these biblical instances refer to a "smiting on the warrior's belt," see Jack M. Sasson, "Reflections on an Unusual Practice Reported in ARM 10:4," *Orientalia* 43 (1974), pp. 404–10.

3. Houses (5:1–7:29)

1. This Hiram is the king of whom the narrator later says, "He loved David always" (1 Kings 5:15). Because of this relationship Hiram helped not only David but also his son Solomon in all the ways described in 1 Kings 5, 7, 9, and 10.

2. This theme is found in 1 Sam. 2:35; 25:28; 2 Sam. 5:11; 7:5, 7, 13, 27; 1 Kings 2:24; 3:2; 5:17, 19; 6:2; 7:40; 8:17, 18, 19, 20, 44, 48; 11:38.

3. *Samuel and the Deuteronomist,* p. 71.

4. Twelve times in chapter 6 and fifteen times in chapter 7.

5. Deut. 25:9; 1 Sam. 2:35; 25:28; 2 Sam. 5:11; 7:5, 7, 11, 13, 27; 1 Kings 2:24; 3:2; 5:17; 6:2; 7:8, 40; 8:17, 18, 19, 20, 44, 48; 11:38.

6. It is not hard to find the LORD blessing all kinds of houses *outside* the History (for example, see Gen. 39:5; Ezek. 44:30; Zech. 8:13; Ps. 115:12) but, so far as I can tell in the History, the LORD blesses a house only here in 2 Samuel 6.

7. *Gālah* in the *nifal.*

8. A valuable and multifaceted collection of essays exploring the role of Michal in the Bible is David J. A. Clines and Tamara C. Eskenazi, eds., *Telling Michal's Story: An Experiment in Comparative Interpretation* (Sheffield: JSOT Supplement Series, 1991).

9. For a relatively early and persuasive discussion of 2 Samuel 7's overall function within the History, see Dennis McCarthy, "2 Samuel 7 and the Structure of the Deuteronomic History," *Journal of Biblical Literature* 84 (1965), pp. 131–38. Within 2 Samuel 7, God's words in verses 13–16 have spawned countless discussions about the literary history of this chapter. See, conveniently, M. Tsevat's "The Steadfast House" in his *The Meaning of the Book of Job and Other Biblical Studies* (New York: KTAV Publishing House, 1980), pp. 101–17.

10. See V. N. Voloshinov, *Marxism and the Philosophy of Language* (Cambridge Mass.: Harvard University Press, 1986 [1929]).

11. *Moses and the Deuteronomist,* chapter 2.

12. I will discuss the summarizing function of verse 11c later, when I look at the content of Nathan's oracle in some detail. For now, I am concentrating on the compositional implication of indirect discourse imbedded within the direct quotation of God, and on a possible function for such imbedding.

13. From a compositional point of view, the utterance of God has two parts (5–7 and 8–16), with the second part being further divided into 8c–11a and 12–16. When we concentrate more on content and length than on composition, it is more convenient to discuss Nathan's oracle according to its three balanced sections: 5c–7; 8c–11a; and 12–16.

14. For a discussion of how God allowed Samuel to lead Saul, see *Samuel and the Deuteronomist*, pp. 99–108.

15. In Hebrew, *mišpaṭ hannābî'* and *mišpaṭ hammelek*.

16. In verse 7, I understand MT *šbṭy* to refer to "judges," irrespective of any emendation to *špṭy*. For the other option, "tribes," and for a thorough discussion of the evidence supporting emendation or not, see C. Begg, "The Reading *sbṭy(km)* in Deut 29,9 and 2 Sam 7,7," *Ephemerides Theologicae Lovanienses* 58 (1982), pp. 87–105.

17. Many scholars, following Rost, see *wᶜšty* in verse 9b, and the first three verbs in verse 10, as perfective (perfect tense with copulative *waw*) instead of imperfective (*waw* consecutive perfect). However, both the structure and content of God's oracle, in my opinion, corroborate the grammatical situation here of "a carefully constructed sequence of consecutive tenses." See on this point, A. Gelston, "A Note on 2 Samuel 7:10," *Zeitschrift für die Alttestamentliche Wissenschaft* 84 (1972), pp. 92–94 and, more recently, McCarter, *2 Samuel*, pp. 202–3.

18. References to "house" occur more often in 2 Samuel 7 than in any other chapter in Samuel/Kings, and eight out of only thirty-three occurrences of "forever" in Samuel/Kings are in 2 Samuel 7.

19. In 2 Samuel 7, in three-fourths of the contexts in which "forever" occurs, there are references to houses (of various kinds). *ᶜôlām* occurs eight times in 2 Samuel 7: vv. 13, 16 (twice), 24, 25, 26, 29 (twice); in six of these eight instances we also find a reference to "house": vv. 13, 16, 25, 26, and 29 (twice).

20. *ᶜôlām* occurs in 1 Sam. 1:22; 2:30; 3:13, 14; 13:13; 20:15, 23, 42; 27:8, 12; 2 Sam. 3:28; 12:10; 22:51; 23:5; 1 Kings 1:31; 2:33 (twice), 45; 9:3, 5; 10:9; 2 Kings 5:27; 21:7.

21. See *Samuel and the Deuteronomist*, chapters 1 and 2.

22. Notice that 1 Kings 11:39 represents a voice that opposes 2 Sam. 12:10.

23. Such distinctions help us understand how the language of building, which permeates God's and David's words, functions in 2 Samuel 7. If we look at the History's employment of *kûn*, "to set up, establish, prepare for building," we can see the distinction between the historiographic fact of permanent houses and the ideological meaning of their permanency.

The root *kûn* denotes stability, permanence, or certainty. Something may be *nākôn*, "certain, firm, or stable," like truth in Deut. 13:15; 17:4; pillars in Judg. 16:26, 29; and thrones, houses, or kingdoms in 2 Sam. 7:16, 26; 1 Kings 2:45, 46. Information is *'el nākôn* "for sure, certain," as in 1 Sam. 23:23; 26:4. Indeed, *mākôn* means a stable, permanent place for dwelling, as in 1 Kings 8:13, 39, 43, 49. One dresses (*hēkîn*) timber and stone in order to prepare it or make it stable for building (1 Kings 5:32). Whether *kûn* is found in the *nifal, hifil,* or *polel* forms, stability and permanence as a result of action is what the verb denotes, whether a word like *ᶜôlām*, "forever," is used in conjunction with it—as in 2 Sam. 7:13, 16, 24, 26; 1 Kings 2:45—or is missing. The difference between *bānah*, "to build," or *kûn*, "to establish," and, say, *ᶜāśāh*, "to make," or *nāṭaᶜ*, "to pitch," is like the difference between a house on one hand and a tent on the other: we build or establish the one, fixing it in time and place; we only make or pitch the other, for a time and for a variety of places. Only rarely do we find references to making (*ᶜāśāh*) a house: see 1 Kings 12:31; 2 Kings 12:12.

24. See 1 Sam. 17:55, 56, 58; 18:18; 22:14; 24:14; 25:10–11; 26:15.

4. Servants (8:1–10:19)

1. Besides the many studies of David cited *passim* in my *Samuel and the Deuteronomist*, a number of recent books and articles that discuss the biblical picture of David are worth mentioning here: David Damrosch, *The Narrative Covenant: Transformations of Genre in the Growth of Biblical Literature* (San Francisco: Harper & Row, 1987); James Flanagan, *David's Social Drama: A Hologram of Israel's Early Iron Age* (Sheffield: Almond Press, 1988); James Ackerman, "Knowing Good and Evil: A Literary Analysis of the Court History in 2 Samuel 9–20 and 1 Kings 1–2," *Journal of Biblical Literature* 109 (1990), pp. 41–64; J. P. Fokkelman, *King David (2 Sam. 9–20 and 1 Kings 1–2)*, vol. 1 of *Narrative Art and Poetry in the Books of Samuel: A Full Interpretation Based on Stylistic and Structural Analyses* (Assen: Van Gorcum, 1981); J. William Whedbee, "On Divine and Human Bonds: The Tragedy of the House of David," in Gene M. Tucker, David L. Petersen, and Robert R. Wilson, eds., *Canon, Theology, and Old Testament Interpretation: Essays in Honor of Brevard S. Childs* (Philadelphia: Fortress Press, 1988), pp. 147–65; David M. Gunn, "In Security: The David of Biblical Narrative," in J. Cheryl Exum, ed., *Signs and Wonders: Biblical Texts in Literary Focus* (Atlanta: Scholars Press, 1989), pp. 133–51; Peter D. Miscall, "For David's Sake: A Response to David M. Gunn," in Exum, ed., *Signs and Wonders*, pp. 154–63.

It is hardly possible to discuss the story of David beginning in 2 Samuel 9 without mentioning the name of Leonhard Rost. His highly influential work, *The Succession to the Throne of David*, trans. M. D. Rutter and D. M. Gunn (Sheffield: Almond, 1982 [1926]) has generated a mountain of scholarly response since its appearance. Rost considered the succession story in 2 Samuel 9–20 and 1 Kings 1–2 to be "the finest work of Hebrew narrative art" (p. 115) and its author "one of the best narrators in the Hebrew language" (p. 106). Nevertheless, I will rarely comment on what Rost wrote and on the scholarly research he provoked, because my compositional approach is so much at odds with his basic redactional perspective: the very idea of the main theme of this material as a "succession narrative" is suspect (see Peter Ackroyd, "The Succession Narrative (So-called)," *Interpretation* 35 [1981], pp. 383–96 and Gillian Keys, "The So-called Succession Narrative: A Reappraisal of Rost's Approach to Theme in 2 Samuel 9–20 and 1 Kings 1–2," *Irish Biblical Studies* 10 [1988], pp. 140–55) and Rost's very exaltation of the art of his supposed document implies an unwarranted denigration of the aesthetic excellence and ideological sophistication of the Deuteronomic narrative that surrounds such a "document."

2. The term is used by the narrator as a designation for prophets in general, or Moses, Ahijah, and Jonah in particular, in Josh. 11:15; 1 Kings 14:18; 15:29; 2 Kings 14:25; 17:23; 21:10; 24:2; and for David in 1 Kings 8:66 and 2 Kings 8:19.

3. For Moses, see Josh. 1:2, 7 and 2 Kings 21:8; for prophets generally, see 2 Kings 9:7; 17:13; and for David, see 2 Sam. 3:18; 7:5, 8; 1 Kings 11:13, 32, 34, 36, 38; 14:8; 2 Kings 19:34; 20:6.

4. By the way, this ratio of references to David's and Moses's servitude to God (13 to 3 respectively) is roughly the same as the ratio of verses in which David and Moses are mentioned in the History: 522 to 104 respectively.

5. See my *Moses and the Deuteronomist*, chapter 4, especially pp. 146–67, for a detailed discussion of this point.

6. This perceptive point comes from my student, Rachel Paley.

7. "Jonathan, the son of Saul, had a son who was crippled in his feet. He was five years old when the news about Saul and Jonathan came from Jezreel; and his nurse took him up and fled; and as she fled in her haste, he fell, and became lame. And his name was Mephibosheth."

8. Vv. 2 (twice), 6, 8, 10 (three times), 11 (twice), 12.

9. Just as "to serve" and "to bring tribute" are associated actions elsewhere in the History, as I have indicated above, so also "to bow down," *hištahwāh*, is an action that occurs between a lord (*'ādôn*), the one "worshiped," and a servant (*ʿebed*), the "worshiper." If we look at the sixty-one or so occurrences of *hištahwāh* in the History, fully thirty-three of them mention servitude or lordship of some kind: (1) verses in which "to worship" and "to serve" are used in association with each other: Deut. 4:19; 5:9; 8:19; 11:16; 17:3; 29:25 (Hebrew); 30:17; Josh. 23:7, 16; Judg. 2:11–13, 19; 1 Kings 9:6, 9; 16:31; 22:54 (Hebrew); 2 Kings 17:16, 35; 21:3, 21; (2) verses in which both the worshiped is called "lord" (*'ādôn*) and the worshiper "servant" (*ʿebed*): Josh. 5:14; 1 Sam. 25:41; 2 Sam. 18:28–29; 24:20–21; (3) verses in which the worshiper is called "servant" (*ʿebed*): 2 Sam. 9:6, 8; 14:22; 2 Kings 2:15–16; and (4) verses in which the worshiped one is called "lord" (*'ādôn*): 1 Sam. 24:9 (Hebrew); 25:23–24; 2 Sam. 16:4; 1 Kings 1:16–17, 23–24, 31.

10. See Deut. 4:19; 5:9; 8:19; 11:16; 17:3; 29:25; 30:17. Only in Deut. 26:10 is *hištahwāh* used without *ʿābad*.

11. Apart from 1 Sam. 2:36, which we will discuss below in connection with its royal associations, humans receive this act of obeisance, in Samuel/Kings, in 1 Sam. 20:41; 24:9; 25:23, 41; 28:14; 2 Sam. 1:2; 9:6, 8; 14:4, 22, 33; 15:5; 16:4; 18:21, 28; 24:20; 1 Kings 1:16, 23, 31, 47, 53; 2:19; 2 Kings 2:15; 4:37. Deities are so honored in 1 Sam. 1:3, 19, 28; 15:25, 30, 31; 2 Sam. 12:20; 15:32; 1 Kings 9:6, 9; 11:33; 16:31; 22:53; 2 Kings 5:18; 17:16, 35, 36; 18:22; 19:37; 21:3, 21.

12. Deut. 4:19; 5:9; 8:19; 11:16; 17:3; 26:10; 29:25; 30:17; Josh. 5:14; 23:7, 16; Judg. 2:12, 17, 19; 7:15.

13. See my *Samuel and the Deuteronomist*, pp. 72–79.

14. The mention of "Mephibosheth" in 2 Sam. 21:8 as one of the seven executed by the Gibeonites makes no sense at all, unless there was another descendant of Saul with the same name.

15. *Samuel and the Deuteronomist*, pp. 18–79.

16. See Josh. 11:11, 22; 1 Sam. 25:34; 2 Sam. 13:30; 17:12; 1 Kings 9:20; 2 Kings 4:7.

17. When the phrase occurs at the beginning of a sentence, it appears mostly to structure the major events within the book according to a general temporal sequence (that is sometimes important but often not), as in 2:1; 8:1; 10:1; 13:1; 15:1; 21:8; otherwise, when it occurs later in a sentence, it simply orders matters within a particular narrative event, as in 3:28; 21:14; 24:10.

5. Messengers (11:1–12:31)

1. I use an apostrophe for *aleph* in my transliterations of the Hebrew text.

2. My student, Rachel Paley, has documented how and why David's successes largely cease, once he stops roaming about freely in the story and confines himself to his house and its affairs.

3. See Deut. 3:1; Josh. 8:14; 1 Sam. 8:20; 24:15; 26:20; 2 Sam. 13:39; 15:16, 17; 18:2, 3; 1 Kings 20:21; 2 Kings 3:6.

4. *Mal'āk(îm)*, "messenger(s)," occurs in at least eighty-nine verses in the History, with the largest clusters in Judges 6 (nine times), 11 (five times), 13 (twelve times), 1 Samuel 19 (eight times), and 2 Samuel 11 (six times).

5. Out of the eighty-nine or so verses in the History in which *mal'āk* occurs, messengers get "sent" in at least forty-four of them.

6. See 11:1, 2, 4, 5, 6 (three times), 12, 14, 18, 22, 27.

7. See *Poetics of Biblical Narrative* (Bloomington: Indiana University Press, 1985), pp. 186–229, and with reference to the original Hebrew article, p. xi; Frank Kermode discusses 2 Samuel 11–12 in light of Sternberg's and others' views in *Poetry, Narrative, History* (Oxford: Blackwell, 1990), pp. 28–48.

Other helpful discourse-oriented studies of 2 Samuel 11 or 11–12 include: Carole Fontaine, "The Bearing of Wisdom on the Shape of 2 Samuel 11–12 and 1 Kings 3," *Journal for the Study of the Old Testament* 34 (1986), pp. 61–77; Stuart Lasine, "Melodrama as Parable: The Story of the Poor Man's Ewe-lamb and the Unmasking of David's Topsy-turvy Emotions," *Hebrew Annual Review* 8 (1984), pp. 101–25; Uriel Simon, "The Poor Man's Ewe-lamb: An Example of a Juridical Parable," *Biblica* 48 (1967), pp. 207–42; Willem S. Vorster, "Reader-Response, Redescription, and Reference: 'You Are the Man' (2 Sam. 12:7)," in Bernard C. Lategan, ed., *Text and Reality: Aspects of Reference in Biblical Texts* (Philadelphia: Fortress, 1985), pp. 95–123; and Gale A. Yee, "'Fraught with Background': Literary Ambiguity in 2 Samuel 11," *Interpretation* 42 (1988), pp. 240–53.

8. *In Search of History* (New Haven and London: Yale University Press, 1983), p. 290.

9. M. Sternberg, *Poetics of Biblical Narrative*, pp. 528–29.

10. In the roughly eighty-nine verses in which "messenger(s)" (*mal'āk[îm]*) occurs in the History, messengers are *sent* about forty-four times, and are said to *speak, say, or declare* a message about fifty times.

11. 2 Sam. 11:1, 2, 4, 5, 6 (three times), 12, 14, 18, 22, 27.

12. See, for example, Josh. 2:1; 5:23; 13:3, 13, 16, 18; 2 Kings 1:3, 15.

13. In chapter 11, verses 3, 5, 6, 15, 19–20, 23, and 25 are directly reported messages conveyed by a messenger from a dispatcher; verses 8 and 12 report David's words sending Uriah home to sleep with Bathsheba (v. 8) and informing Uriah that he will send him back to the front on the morrow (v. 12); only verses 10 and 11 contain reported speech having nothing to do with messengers or their messages. In chapter 12, Nathan's messages from God in verses 1–4 and 7–12 are responded to by David in verses 5–6 and 13, and Joab's message to David is reported in verses 27–28; only the reported speech of David and his servants in verses 18, 19, 21, 22, and 23 is unrelated to messengers or their messages. That is to say, of the thirty-five verses in chapters 11–12 that contain reported speech, twenty-seven verses, or over three-fourths of them, pertain or respond to messengers, or relate the messages themselves.

14. On this point, see my *Samuel and the Deuteronomist*, pp. 88–100.

15. For a perceptive discussion of many of these questions, especially the last, see now M. Bal, "De-disciplining the Eye," *Critical Inquiry* 16 (1990), pp. 506–31; and *Lethal Love: Feminist Literary Readings of Biblical Love Stories* (Bloomington: Indiana University Press, 1987).

16. *Poetics of Biblical Narrative*, p. 529.

17. *Hēlek*, traveler, occurs in the Bible only twice, confusingly in 1 Sam. 14:26 and less so here in verse 4. The root, *'rḥ*, appears only four times in the History (Judg. 5:6; 19:17; 2 Sam. 12:4; 2 Kings 25:30), occurring in its *qal* participial form, *'orēᵃḥ*, "wayfarer or traveler," in Judg. 19:17 and 2 Sam. 12:4.

18. We find the root used here for "poor" only in 1 Sam. 2:7; 18:23; and 2 Samuel 12, and the root for "rich" only in 1 Sam. 2:7; 17:25; 1 Kings 3:11, 13; 10:23; and 2 Samuel 12.

19. *ᶜēqeb 'ašer* and *ᶜal 'ašer* in verse 6; *ᶜeqeb kî, kî,* and *'epes kî* in verses 10, 12, and 14 respectively.

20. In reference to the rich man of verse 4, I read with S. R. Driver, *Notes on the Hebrew Text and the Topography of the Books of Samuel* (Oxford: Clarendon Press, 2nd edition, 1913), p. 291: *lā'iš* for MT *le'iš*.

21. Jer. 14:8 asks God not to be a "sojourner (*gēr*) in the land" or a "wayfarer (*'orēᵃḥ*) who turns aside to tarry for a night."

22. *Yāraš*, "to inherit, possess," used here in the *hifil*, and *rûš*, "to be poor," are roots that are perhaps related formally as well as semantically.

23. See chapter 4 above.

6. Women (13:1–14:33)

1. A couple of discourse-oriented studies involving chapter 13 are worth mentioning here: Burke O. Long, "Wounded Beginnings: David and Two Sons," in Burke O. Long, ed., *Images of Man and God: Old Testament Short Stories in Literary Focus* (Sheffield: Almond Press, 1981), pp. 26–34; and Charles Conroy, *Absalom Absalom!: Narrative and Language in 2 Sam 13–20* (Rome: Biblical Institute Press, 1978).

2. In 2 Sam. 12:11, the form of "companion" is plural (*rēᶜeyka*, your neighbors) whereas its construal is singular (and *he* shall sleep [*wešākab*] with your women).

3. See S. R. Driver, *Notes on the Hebrew Text and the Topography of the Books of Samuel*, p. 305.

4. See my remarks in *Samuel and the Deuteronomist*, pp. 155–61.

5. In 2 Samuel, "brother(s)" is used familially in 1:26; 2:22, 26, 27; 3:8, 27, 30 (twice); 4:6, 9; 10:10; 13:3, 4, 7, 8, 10, 12, 20 (four times), 26, 32; 14:7 (twice); 15:20; 18:2; 19:13, 42; 20:9, 10; 21:21; 23:18, 24. In Deuteronomy, "brother(s)" is familial only in 13:7; 25:5, 6, 7, 9; 28:54; 32:50.

6. In eleven out of eleven verses, "brother(s)" is a familial term.

7. The History's ideological association of familial relationships with the Israelite monarchy concentrates on *fraternal* expressions; further study needs to be done to clarify whether other words that can denote familial, tribal, or national relationships in the History have similar reference points. My work so far on the Deuteronomic History suggests that words like "house," "son," "companion" (*rēᵃᶜ*), and "brother" are multivoiced expressions whose denotations and connotations distribute themselves according to a rough but still discernible ideological pattern. Such multivoicedness allows for familial expressions, themes, and plots to carry within them tribal and national implications, and vice versa, within the History. See Joel Rosenberg's *King and Kin: Political Allegory in the Hebrew Bible* for similar suggestions that, moreover, transcend the Deuteronomic History.

8. *Bᵉne yiśrā'ēl* in Judg. 19:12, 30; 20:1, 3, 7, 13, 14, 18, 19, 23, 24, 25, 26, 27, 30, 32, 35; 21:5, 6, 18, 24; "brothers" in Judg. 19:23; 20:13, 23, 28; 21:6.

9. *Bᵉnê hammelek* in 2 Sam. 13:23, 27, 29, 30, 32, 33, 35, 36; "brother(s)" or "sister" in 2 Sam. 13:1, 2, 3, 4 (two times), 5, 6, 7, 8, 10, 11, 12, 20 (five times), 22, 26, 32 (two times).

10. Deut. 22:21; Judg. 19:23, 24; 20:6, 10; 2 Sam. 13:13.

11. See *Moses and the Deuteronomist,* pp. 200–4.

12. The roots *'mr* and *dbr* occur twenty-eight and twenty-two times respectively in this chapter. Chapter 13 has the next most frequent number of occurrences of these roots, thirty-two times altogether.

13. Among the awkward or unusual expressions in this chapter are: *meharbit go'ēl haddām* (v. 11); *umiddabbēr* (v. 13); all of v. 14b; *wᵉᶜattāh 'ašer bā'tî* (v. 15); *'iš* (for *yēš*?) in verse 19; and the convoluted construction of the narrator's words in verse 26. On this last point, see S. R. Driver, *Notes on the Hebrew Text and the Topography of the Books of Samuel,* pp. 309–10. Most of these difficulties remain, by the way, whether we rearrange verses 15–17 to immediately follow verse 7, as many commentators suggest, or leave the sequence of verses as it is, as I prefer to do.

14. The phrase, *ḥāšab ᶜal,* is not found elsewhere in the History, but we do know from the Book of Jeremiah that this construction can mean "to devise a plan" either for or against someone. Thus, God threatens Israel, "I am devising a plan against (*ḥošēb ᶜal*) you" (Jer. 18:11), but then tells those in exile about his "plans in behalf of (*mahᵃšābôt ᶜal*) you, plans for welfare and not for evil" (Jer. 29:11).

15. This second narrative situation is precisely what generally obtains within the Deuteronomic law code of Deuteronomy 12–28, where God's words and Moses's words are mostly indistinguishable, both to this fellow Israelites and to the reader. See my remarks in *Moses and the Deuteronomist,* pp. 43–69.

16. On the women in 2 Samuel 14 and 20, see Claudia V. Camp, "The Wise Women of 2 Samuel: A Role Model for Women in Early Israel?" *Catholic Biblical Quarterly* 43 (1981), pp. 14–29.

17. See chapter 3 above on 2 Samuel 6.

18. It is important to repeat here that there are especially strong verbal and narrative correspondences between David and the Tekoite woman in 2 Samuel 14. On the dual level of plot (both Joab's and the narrator's), David returns Absalom to Jerusalem just as the woman pleads for the return and protection of her remaining son. Verbal detail also enhances this narrative correspondence. As the narrator calls the woman wise (v. 2), so she calls David wise (v. 20). And if Joab tells the woman to "behave like a woman who has been mourning many days" (v. 2), this deception strengthens our perception of her as corresponding to David, who, the narrator tells us in 13:37, "mourned for his son day after day." But for which son does David mourn? David and the Tekoite woman are, both of them, wise and ambiguous mourners.

19. McCarter, *2 Samuel,* p. 347.

20. These many correspondences between the individual happenings within the house of David and the larger story of Israel are the basis for James Ackerman's insight, "The Court History foreshadows that split [the breakup of the United Kingdom] as originating from a division within David himself" ("Knowing Good and Evil: A Literary Analysis of the Court History in 2 Samuel 9–20 and 1 Kings 1–2," *Journal of Biblical Literature* 109 [1990], p. 48).

7. Curses (15:1–16:23)

1. See *Samuel and the Deuteronomist*, pp. 19–20.

2. S. R. Driver remarks, "Notice the pff. with *waw* conv., indicating what Absalom *used* to do. From 2b to 4, however, the narrator lapses into the tense of simple description, only again bringing the custom into prominence in vv. 5, and 6a (*yb'w*)" (*Notes on the Hebrew Text and the Topography of the Books of Samuel*, p. 310). We now believe that the narrator's "lapse" into perfective verb forms in the MT of verses 2–4 probably reflects more accurately a lapse of textual traditions instead. There is some evidence from LXX[L], 4QSam[a], and 4QSam[c] that even the perfective verbs used by the narrator in verses 2–4 of the MT, like those of verses 1, 5, and 6, were originally imperfectives denoting Absalom's habitual actions. See on this point McCarter, *2 Samuel*, p. 354 and his reference there to Ulrich's work.

3. In *Samuel and the Deuteronomist*, pp. 60–63, I suggested that many details in 2 Samuel 15 look back to the ark account in 1 Sam. 4:1–7:2. Here I am concentrating on how chapter 15 looks forward to aspects of the story to come.

4. See M. Garsiel, *Biblical Names: A Literary Study of Midrashic Derivations and Puns* (Ramat Gan: Bar Ilan, 1991), p. 219, who has independently noted the wordplay between Ittai and *'th/'tnw* in 2 Sam. 15:19. I am suggesting here that such wordplay extends beyond 15:19, and that its narrative functions are closely related to other textual features of chapters 15–20.

5. 15:3, 11, 12, 14, 19, 22, 24, 27, 30, 33. Twenty percent of the occurrences of *'et* in 2 Samuel appear in 2 Samuel 15: *'et* occurs fifty-three times in 2 Samuel and ten times in chapter 15 alone. (In terms of verses, chapter 15 constitutes about only five percent of 2 Samuel).

6. In chapters 15–19, *'et*, "with," occurs twenty-nine times out of the fifty-three times it appears in 2 Samuel.

7. Wordplay involving Hushai has already been pointed out by Garsiel, *Biblical Names*, p. 105. My discussion here widens the scope of his comments.

8. For example, in 1 Sam. 20:38: "Jonathan called after the lad, 'Hurry (*mehērāh*), make haste (*hûšāh*), do not stay (*cal tacamod*).'"

9. *Ḥûš* appears rarely in the History (Deut. 32:35; Judg. 20:37; and 1 Sam. 20:38); the root *mhr* "to hurry," however, appears much more frequently—over forty times. What is important for our purposes is, first, that 1 Sam. 20:38 uses the two words as synonyms and, second, that in the books of 2 Samuel–2 Kings, for example, *mhr* occurs only ten times, yet five of these occurrences are here in 2 Samuel 15–19 (2 Sam. 15:14; 17:16, 18, 21; 19:17), precisely and only where we find Hushai, the hasty one, participating in the story (15:32, 37; 16:16, 17, 18; 17:5, 6, 7, 8, 14, 15). Hushai, as the father of Baaniah, is simply mentioned in 1 Kings 4:16.

10. Ari Cartun has written an important article on topography as a literary template for 2 Samuel 15–19, thus highlighting an important aspect of this section's highly stylized language and composition: "Topography as a Template for David's Fortunes during His Flight before Avshalom," *Journal of Reform Judaism* (Spring 1991), pp. 17–34. See also David Gunn, "From Jerusalem to the Jordan and Back: Symmetry in 2 Samuel 15–20," *Vetus Testamentum* 30 (1980), pp. 109–13.

11. For an account of the ideological implications of crossing the Jordan in Josh. 3:1–5:1, see my remarks in *Moses and the Deuteronomist*, pp. 91–110.

12. In Deuteronomy 2–4, the root *ʿābar* occurs thirty times in 115 verses; in Joshua 3:1–5:1, twenty-five times in only 42 verses; in Joshua 24, eight times in 33 verses; and in 2 Samuel 15–19, thirty-eight times in 165 verses. In 2 Samuel 15–19, a majority of occurrences (twenty-five) appear in the first and last chapters of the section.

13. This combination of stylization and ritualization is similar to the narrative style employed by the narrator to describe the events in 2 Samuel 2. See chapter 2 above.

14. See McCarter, *2 Samuel*, pp. 375–76.

15. See my remarks in *Moses and the Deuteronomist*, pp. 99–101.

16. Simply put, the preposition *ʾet* occurs only 53 times in 2 Samuel, and 29 of these 53 occurrences are in chapters 15–19. Similarly, *ʿim* occurs about 70 times in 2 Samuel, and yet 16 of these occurrences are found in chapters 15–19. Taken together, *ʿim* and *ʾet* occur in chapters 15–19 a total of 45 out of 123 times in the book. And this high proportion does not take into account the 8 occurrences of the name Ittai in chapters 15–19.

17. Some form of *šûb* occurs fifty-seven times in 2 Samuel, and twenty-five of these occur in chapters 15–19: 15:8 (twice), 19, 20 (twice), 25 (twice), 27, 29, 34; 16:3, 8, 12; 17:3 (twice), 20; 18:16; 19:11, 12, 13, 15, 16, 38, 40, 44.

18. Returning to one's city, especially Jerusalem, is the focus of *šûb* in 15:8 (twice), 19, 20 (twice), 25 (twice), 27, 29, 34; 17:20; 19:38, 40.

19. This slant on "return" is found in 16:3; 17:3 (twice); 19:11, 12, 13, 15, 16, 44.

20. See my remarks in *Samuel and the Deuteronomist*, pp. 66, 237.

21. The root, *plṭ*, occurs in Josh. 8:22; Judg. 12:4, 5; 21:17; 2 Sam. 15:14; 22:2, 44; 2 Kings 9:15; 19:30, 31.

22. On the frequentative or imperfective aspect of these verbs in verse 13, see S. R. Driver, *Notes on the Hebrew Text and the Topography of the Books of Samuel*, p. 319, and McCarter, *2 Samuel*, p. 369.

23. *ʾet* meaning "with" occurs proportionately more often in these two chapters (2 Samuel 15–16) taken individually than anywhere else in the book: *ʾet* occurs ten times in the thirty-seven verses of 2 Samuel 15 and seven times in the twenty-three verses of 2 Samuel 16. On average in 2 Samuel, *ʾet*, "with," occurs only about once every thirteen verses, but increases to once every 5.7 verses in 2 Samuel 15–19, and once every 3.5 verses in 2 Samuel 15–16. There are people *with* David in the wilderness (v. 14); Ahithophel is *with* Absalom in Jerusalem (v. 15). Absalom questions Hushai's loyalty *with* David by asking, "Why did you not to *with* your friend?" (v. 17). Hushai ambiguously promises to remain *with* the chosen of God (is this David or Absalom?) (v. 18) and Ahithophel counsels Absalom to make himself odious *with* his father so that the hands of those who are *with* Absalom may be strengthened (v. 21).

24. For nations, see Deut. 11:26, 28, 29; 23:5, 6; 27:13; 28:15, 45; 29:26; 30:1, 19; Josh. 8:34; 24:9; 2 Kings 22:19. For tribes, see 2 Sam. 19:44. And for individuals, see Deut. 21:23; Judg. 9:27, 57; 1 Sam. 2:30; 3:13; 7:43; 2 Sam. 6:22; 16:5, 7, 9, 10, 11, 12, 13; 19:22; 1 Kings 2:8; 2 Kings 2:24.

25. The boys who jeer Elisha, and are roundly cursed by him in 2 Kings 2:24, are the only non-royal figures cursed in the History with the language of *qālal*. The only other accursed characters in the History whom I have not yet mentioned are Eli's sons, whom God curses in 1 Sam. 2:30 and whom the narrator accuses of

cursing God in 1 Sam. 3:13. See *Samuel and the Deuteronomist,* pp. 44–54, for my discussion of the royal dimensions of the cursing found in 1 Samuel 2 and 3.

26. When I discuss the execution of Absalom in chapter 18 below, I will return to the question of royal curses, especially as they are indirectly indicated in the story.

27. Blood is called down upon the heads of God's enemies in Deut. 32:42, and upon those who go against the promise of Joshua's spies in Josh. 2:19, but these threats receive no narrative fulfillment in the story.

28. "To counsel" (*yā ̒as*) appears at least thirty-four times in the History (either in nominal or verbal form), and fully thirty-one of these thirty-four occurrences explicitly concern the giving of advice to or about kings. Most of this royal counsel (twenty-seven of thirty-one occurrences) is found in 2 Samuel 15–17, where Absalom does not follow Ahithophel's counsel and loses the throne he seized from David, and in 1 Kings 12, where Rehoboam refuses to follow his elders' advice and loses the ten northern tribes.

There are two passages that variously compare royal counsel to other kinds of royal consultation. In 2 Sam. 16:23, the narrator has David and Absalom equate the counsel of Ahithophel "in those days" to the oracle of God, and during Hezekiah's reign, the story has the King of Assyria talking about Hezekiah's supposedly disastrous *counsel* in 2 Kings 18:20, but the sequel contrasts this characterization with Isaiah's conveying of the (correct) *word of God* to Hezekiah in 2 Kings 19. Clearly, *giving counsel* in the History is predominantly a *royal affair* (as in 2 Samuel 15–17; 1 Kings 1:12; 12; 2 Kings 6:8; 18:20), but not always (see Deut. 32:28; Judg. 19:30; 20:7).

29. See my discussion in *Samuel and the Deuteronomist,* pp. 99–100. Another attempt to limit the restrictions of the prophet would be to set up the royal prophets one against the other, as recounted in 1 Kings 22.

30. We also see in the History that inquiring of the LORD/God typically involves seeking out a prophet ("Formerly in Israel, when a man went to inquire of God, he said, 'Come, let us go to the seer'; for he who is now called a prophet was formerly called a seer" [1 Sam. 9:9]) or priest (1 Sam. 14:36–37), whether in the presence of the LORD's ark (Judg. 20:27) or ephod (1 Sam. 30:7–8). If both David and his son consider their counselor's advice like an inquiry of God, then it may be helpful to see how these two royal means of consultation, the one human the other divine, are distributed throughout 1–2 Samuel during the reigns of Saul's and David's houses.

8. Counselors (17:1–28)

1. Ahithophel's counsel is directly reported in 16:21 and 17:1–3; Hushai's in 17:7–13; Nathan's in 1 Kings 1:13–14; and that of the elders and young men of Rehoboam in 1 Kings 12:7, 10–11.

2. Neither Ahithophel's initial advice to Absalom (2 Sam. 16:21) nor Nathan's counsel to Bathsheba contains comparisons of any kind. At the same time, the brief advice of the young men around Rehoboam suggests that he speak to the people by means of graphic comparison: "Say, 'My little finger is thicker than my father's loins; my father chastised you with whips, but I shall chastise you with scorpions'" (1 Kings 12:10–11).

3. This distinction in 16:23 between a character's worldview and the narrator's, when we analyze the reported speech of the narrator, is a good example of what Bakhtin means by *pseudo-objective motivation*. See M. Bakhtin, *The Dialogic Imagination: Four Essays by M. M. Bakhtin* (Austin and London: University of Texas Press, 1981), p. 305.

4. We have even seen this attitude about the future take on excessive dimensions in stories within the Book of Judges, especially in the story of Gideon. See my remarks in *Moses and the Deuteronomist*, pp. 168–76.

5. A priest appears to be the case in Judg. 18:5; 1 Sam. 14:37; 22:10, 13, 15; 28:6; a prophet-seer in 1 Sam. 9:9; 28:6; 1 Kings 22:7; 2 Kings 3:11; and a "man of God" in 2 Kings 8:8. The matter is spelled out in further detail in 1 Sam. 28:6: divine inquiry is accomplished through dreams, through Urim—a priestly affair— or through prophets. All three of these are means of *divine* communication.

6. I will discuss shortly the special situation of Nathan in 1 Kings 1:12. What is a prophet doing counseling instead of either prophesying or conveying a response to a divine inquiry?

7. Judg. 1:1; 18:5; 20:18, 23, 27; 1 Sam. 10:22; 14:37; 22:10, 13, 15; 23:2, 4; 28:6; 30:8; 2 Sam. 2:1; 5:19, 23. The one exception to this pattern is 1 Sam. 9:9, which speaks about "seeking (*dāraš*) [the word of] God."

8. During this era, we find the exclusive use of *yāʿaṣ* in 2 Sam. 15:12, 31, 34; 16:20, 23; 17:7, 11, 14, 15, 21, 23; 1 Kings 1:12; 12:6, 8, 9, 13, 14, 28.

9. The following verses represent all the instances between 1 Kings 13 and 2 Kings 25 that refer to divine inquiry, and *dāraš* is used in all of them, with *šāʾal* never mentioned: 1 Kings 14:5; 22:5, 7, 8; 2 Kings 1:2, 3, 6, 16; 3:11; 8:8; 22:13, 18. It is worthwhile to repeat here that this clear-cut lexical distribution of *šāʾal* and *dāraš*, when used to refer to divine inquiry, finds its only exception, throughout the entire History, in the narrative interruption of 1 Sam. 9:9, where we would expect to find *šāʾal*, but find *dāraš* instead. There may be a literary historical dimension to this lexical feature of 1 Sam. 9:9, especially since this verse is a narrative interruption explicitly comparing the former days of Saul with the present day of the narrator. As for the use of *šāʾal* in 2 Sam. 16:23, here again we have a narrative statement comparing one epoch to another, and indicating that the royal practice of asking of (*šāʾal*) God, mentioned many times before this, has fallen into disuse, and been replaced by the king's counselor, who stands in for God in determining royal strategy.

9. Crossings (18:1–20:24)

1. The Hebrew is *loʾ kēn ʾōhîlāh lepānêkā*.

2. The Hebrew is *ûlkāh ʾēn beśôrāh moṣēʾt*.

3. The middle of the messenger's account reads in Hebrew: *lišlōᵃḥ ʾet ʿebed hammelek yôʾab weʾet ʿabdekā*.

4. The chapter is easily divided into two parts: verses 1–17 concerning the defeat and death of Absalom and verses 19–32 concerning the announcement of these events to David, with verse 18 the narrator's interruption concerning what Absalom had done in his lifetime and what Absalom's monument is called "to this day."

5. See P. K. McCarter, *2 Samuel*, pp. 357–58 for a helpful discussion of this question.

6. See the various formulations for all Israel in 15:6, 10; 16:15, 18, 21, 22; 17:4, 10, 11, 13, 14, 24; 18:17; 19:8, 9.

7. P. K. McCarter, *2 Samuel*, p. 419, notices how 19:9b resumes the story back at 18:17. See also S. R. Driver, *Notes on the Hebrew Text and the Topography of the Books of Samuel*, p. 334. This phenomenon is not rare in biblical narrative. S. Talmon has drawn attention to it in "The Presentation of Synchroneity and Simultaneity in Biblical Narrative," in J. Heinemann and S. Werses, eds., *Studies in Hebrew Narrative Art throughout the Ages* (Jerusalem: Magnes Press, 1978), pp. 9–26; his helpful discussion is extended in Burke Long's "Framing Repetitions in Biblical Historiography," *Journal of Biblical Literature* 106 (1987), pp. 385–99.

8. As is well known, depending on the context, "Israel" can refer predominantly to the entire nation or simply to the northern tribes.

9. The term "Israel" occurs in about 18 percent of the verses in 2 Samuel 15–20 (35 out of 191 verses) and in only about 13 percent of the verses in the rest of 2 Samuel (66 out of 504 verses); the term *ᶜam* appears in about 17 percent of the verses in chapters 15–20 (33 of 191 verses), but in only 10 percent of the verses in the rest of 2 Samuel (50 of 504 verses). When one ignores the personal interlude (18:19–19:9a) in chapters 15–20, these figures become even more revealing.

10. For all the reasons suggested by McCarter, *2 Samuel*, pp. 357–58, the specificity of 17:11 describes what is mostly the case throughout 15:1–19:9a: "Israel" or "all Israel" refers to an entity extending from "Dan to Beersheba." Notice that David's troops are never called "Israel" in this section, and that 18:7 seems to express the situation exactly: "And the army (*ᶜam*) of Israel were defeated by the servants of David." The revolt, then, is of an entire nation against their king and his army. Notice also that David's success is attributed not just to the LORD's resolve to frustrate the counsel of Ahithophel, but also to the crucial efforts of foreigners like Hushai the Archite and Ittai the Gittite. And when it comes time to announce the "good news" to David, the messenger with the most is not Ahimaaz, the priest's son, but an anonymous Cushite.

There is no hint in the text, therefore, that the "Israel" mentioned in the following verses is ever to be distinguished from "Judah": 15:2, 6, 10, 13; 16:3, 15, 18, 21, 22; 17:4, 10, 11, 13, 14, 15, 24, 26; 18:6, 7, 16, 17; 19:9. On the other hand, with the possible exception of 19:10, reference in the use of "Israel" from 19:10 to 20:23 is to Israel of the north, in contrast to Judah in the south: 19:12, 23, 41, 42, 43, 44; 20:1, 2, 14, 19, 23.

11. There are, of course, many contrasts or differences between the details of 2 Samuel 2 and those of 2 Samuel 18; such features will be integrated into an interpretation once the connection between the passages is clearly seen.

12. In the History, the sword devours only in Deut. 32:42; 2 Sam. 2:26; 11:25; and 18:18.

13. The power of the account of Absalom's death to integrate the entire History does not at all deny the important insight that the picture presented in 2 Samuel 18 is at the same time an allusion to the binding of Isaac, according to the persuasive suggestion of James Ackerman, "Knowing Good and Evil: A Literary Analysis of the Court History in 2 Samuel 9–20 and 1 Kings 1–2," *Journal of Biblical Literature* 109 (1990), p. 50.

14. See chapter 7 above.

15. 4QSam ᵃ indicates that we should read *wytl* for *wytn* in 18:9.

16. See chapter 7 above.

17. Deut. 11:26, 28, 29; 23:5, 6; 27:13; 28:15, 45; 29:26; 30:1, 19.

18. We read that the Philistines had hung Saul and Jonathan in the public square of Bethshan (2 Sam. 21:12) and that David had the murderers of Ishbosheth killed and hung beside the pool of Hebron (2 Sam. 4:12), but in each case trees are not mentioned.

19. Hovering around these suggestions about the cautious bearing of news concerning the fate of David's enemies is the king's response to the Amalekite who brought news of Saul's death in 2 Samuel 1 (David kills him), and David's subsequent remark in 4:10 about the incident: "When one told me, 'Behold Saul is dead,' and thought he was bringing me [good] news, I seized him and slew him at Ziklag, which was the reward I gave him for his news." In addition, behind the mixed news of the Amalekite and the Cushite, in 2 Samuel 1 and 18, lie the tidings that the messenger brought Eli in 1 Sam. 4:17. The death of Eli that follows in verse 18 embodies the Deuteronomist's graphic evaluation of the kingship that Israel at first thought would bring good news and glad tidings; the news, throughout the History, is about royal death and destruction—however triumphant the story of royalty can appear to be. See my remarks in *Samuel and the Deuteronomist*, pp. 61–63.

20. "The king" is so often on everyone's lips in the passage that it occurs an amazing fifty-five times in only thirty-five verses. Put another way, within these thirty-five verses only two verses, 14 and 22, do not contain the word. The term *melek* occurs most often in the following complexes: 2 Samuel 13–14; 1 Kings 1–2; 1 Kings 22; and here in 19:9b–44, yet even when we compare such royal passages, the last one predominates in its frequent mentioning of the king. Clearly, the king is at the heart of this passage, more so than anywhere else in the History.

21. 19:11, 12, 13, 14, 22, 23 (three times), 26, 29, 30, 35, 36 (four times), 37, 42, 43 (three times), 44 (two times).

22. The Hebrew is *min hā'āreṣ*: 19:10.

23. In biblical Hebrew, *qārā'* more often means "to cry out, call, or invite," centering on an aural semantic field, and less often "to meet, encounter, happen upon." In 2 Samuel 18 and 19, the root appears frequently (seven times in chapter 18 and five times in chapter 19), with each of these two meanings emphasized sequentially: the story of the battle and its announcement to David in 18:1–19:9a emphasizes the aural sense of *qārā'* (18:18 [twice], 25, 26, 28; we encounter an encountering *qārā'* only in 18:6, 9), whereas the story of David's return in 19:9b–44 uses *qārā'* only in its encountering sense (19:16, 17, 21, 25, 26).

24. The Hebrew is *šûb* in the *hifil*: 19:11, 12, 13, 44.

25. The Hebrew is *ᶜābar* in the *hifil*: 19:16, 19, 41, 42.

26. See my discussion above in chapter 7.

27. All the occurrences in 1–2 Samuel, from 1 Samuel 8 onwards, deal with the matter of restoring kings—or even restoring kingship itself. See 1 Sam. 10:8; 11:14, 15; 13:4, 7, 8, 12, 15; 15:12, 21, 33; 2 Sam. 19:16, 41.

28. An unusually high frequency of the root, "to cross over" (*ᶜābar*) occurs in 2 Samuel 15–19 (thirty-eight times), and this root often carries heavy evaluative and ideological baggage in the History—especially whenever it is the Jordan that must be traversed.

29. See my suggestions in this regard in *Samuel and the Deuteronomist*, pp. 108–25.

30. The Hebrew is *ṣᵉrûrāh biṣror hahayyîm* and *yᵉqallᵉᶜennāh bᵉtôk kap haqqālāᶜ*.

31. See *Samuel and the Deuteronomist*, pp. 211–12.

32. See my remarks in *Samuel and the Deuteronomist*, pp. 44–49.

33. The Hebrew words are *nākah* and *ḥomeš*.

34. The verb in the MT, *wayyihar*, is best explained as a form of *'ahar*, "to remain behind, delay, tarry." See S. R. Driver, *Notes on the Hebrew Text and the Topography of the Books of Samuel*, p. 341.

10. Numbers (21:1–24:25)

1. Fokkelman has recognized the strategic positioning of these songs of Hannah and David in 1 Samuel 2, 2 Samuel 1, and 2 Samuel 22–23: *The Crossing Fates (1 Sam. 13–31 and 2 Sam. 1)*, pp. 647–82, vol. 2 of *Narrative Art and Poetry in the Books of Samuel*.

2. See my discussion of the Song of Hannah in *Samuel and the Deuteronomist*, pp. 30–39.

3. The Hebrew for "darkness' is *hošek* and for "dust," *šeḥāqîm*; "on high" is *mārôm*, and "exalted" *yārûm*; "pure" is from the root *bārar*, "loyal" from *ḥāsad*, and "blameless" from *tāmam*.

4. See my suggestions about Moses's speech in *Moses and the Deuteronomist*, pp. 43–69.

5. McCarter, *2 Samuel*, p. 456.

6. Despite all this self-confidence about God's delight over the house of David, 2 Samuel ends with David making the same mistake that Saul made in 1 Samuel 15: placing more emphasis on sacrifice than on obedience. However much such sacrifices may have been responsible for averting the plague from Israel in 2 Samuel 24, David's disobedience in 2 Samuel 11 explains why there continues to exist over David's house not God's delight but his perpetual sword. Too bad even for David that the LORD has greater delight in obedience than in sacrifice (1 Sam. 15:22).

7. On the other hand, two other textual references in 2 Samuel 21 can just as easily be interpreted as tying the chapter to preceding events in 1–2 Samuel: 21:7 is an explicit reference to the events in 1 Samuel 20, and 21:12 refers directly to the closing verses in 1 Samuel 3.

8. For my suggestions about the meaning of this term, see "*HWQY^c and Covenantal Institutions in Early Israel*," *Harvard Theological Review* 62 (1969), pp. 227–40.

9. See S. R. Driver, *Notes on the Hebrew Text and the Topography of the Books of Samuel*, pp. 349–80; M. Sternberg, *Poetics of Biblical Narrative*, pp. 40–41; and D. Damrosch, *Narrative Covenant*, pp. 237–38.

In contrast to the views of Sternberg and Damrosch that the ring composition in 2 Samuel 21–24 "hardly coheres as more than an appendix," (Sternberg, *Poetics*, p. 40), Walter Brueggemann has written a welcome article that suggests more cohesion in these chapters: "2 Samuel 21–24: An Appendix of Deconstruction?" *Catholic Biblical Quarterly* 50 (1988), pp. 383–97.

10. In the prose portion of chapter 23, "three" or "thirty" appears in verses 8, 9, 13, 16, 17, 18 (twice), 19 (twice), 22, 23 (twice), 24, and 39. In the story of the census, the MT of 24:13 has the number "seven," but the LXX and 1 Chron. 21:12 have the more likely "three."

11. The Hebrew is *kol šelošîm wešibᶜāh*.

12. S. R. Driver, *Notes on the Hebrew Text and the Topography of the Books of Samuel*, p. 372.

13. Once again, translators hardly ever exploit the meaning of *hôsîp*, "to continue (to do something)," most of the time favoring this word's equally possible

meaning, "to do (something) again." See my remarks on this misleading practice in *Moses and the Deuteronomist*, p. 177.

14. The Hebrew is *wayyēᶜātēr YHWH la'ares* in 21:14, with *'ᵉlohîm* instead of *YHWH* in 24:25.

15. Notice, however, that this similar *internal* function of numerical limitation works together with the *complementary* functions of limitation in chapter 21, but extension in chapter 24.

16. On the text-critical and literary-historical questions surrounding the end of 2 Samuel and the beginning chapters of 1 Kings, see McCarter, *2 Samuel*, pp. 16–19.

17. See McCarter, *2 Samuel*, pp. 512–18 for a brief account of such speculations.

INDEXES

Subject Index

Scripture Index

Index of Hebrew Forms

(Words beginning with *'aleph* and *'ayin* appear at the beginning of the index.)

'ādôn, 96, 222
'āh, 48, 49, 134, 136
'ah^{a}bāh, 24
'āhar, 199, 232
'āhar/ah^{a}rê, 29-30
'aharāyw, 200
'ah^{a}rê hah^{a}nît, 27
'ah^{a}rê kēn, 107
'ah^{a}rôn, 194
'āhaz b^e, 64
'āhēb, 11, 24, 217
'ahîm, 47
'^{a}huzzāh, 64
'ak, 86
'ākal tāmîd, 103
'ākēn, 86
'al, 135, 138
'āmāh, 66, 143, 144-45
'^{a}māhôt, 144
'āmar, 116, 139
'amhôt '^{a}bādāyw, 144
'anšē yiśrā'ēl, 183
'ap kî, 52
'āsap, 116
'^{a}šer nôtar l^{e}bêt šā'ûl, 102
'bl, 141
'e^{ce}śeh hesed, 107
'ek, 63
'el nākôn, 220
'^{e}lohîm, 233
'epes kî, 224
'ereṣ, 19
'et, 151, 157, 163, 226, 227
'i^{c}āsēk nā' ^{c}ēsāh, 175
'îš, 225
'îš roš, 125
'ittānû, 151
'ittay, 151
'ittô, 151
'mr, 225
'ohel, 77
'orē^{a}h, 121, 124, 224
'rh, 224
'th 'tnw, 157, 226
'ty, 157
^{c}ābad, 92, 96, 97, 99, 222
^{c}ābar, 28, 152-57, 158, 185, 189, 190, 194, 217, 227, 231

^{c}ābar 'et or ^{c}im, 155, 158
^{c}ad '^{a}šer tammû la^{ca}bor, 156
^{c}ad ^{c}ôlām, 81, 207
^{c}ad tom la^{ca}bôr, 156
^{c}al, 139, 140, 144, 145
^{c}al '^{a}šer, 224
^{c}al bāmôtay, 206
^{c}al dāwid, 145
^{c}al š^{e}bu^{c}at YHWH, 105
^{c}al ta^{ca}mod, 226
^{c}ālāh 'ah^{a}rê, 30
^{c}āloh ûbākoh, 154
^{c}am, 179, 180, 181, 230
^{c}am rāb, 213
^{c}am yiśrā'ēl, 180, 184
^{c}ānāh, 137, 138
^{c}āśāh, 220
^{c}āśāh l^e, 121, 124
^{c}āšar, 124, 129
^{ca}sat goyîm, 170
^{ca}sātām, 170
^{c}āšîr, 121
^{c}ebed, 89, 92, 96, 144, 222
^{c}ēqeb '^{a}šer, 224
^{c}ēqeb kî, 224
^{c}ēsāh, 170, 173
^{c}eṣem, 54
^{c}ibrîm, 153
^{c}im, 151, 157, 227
^{c}obēr, 154
^{c}ob^{e}rîm, 154, 156
^{c}ob^{e}rîm ^{c}al p^{e}nê hammelek, 154, 156
^{c}oberîm ^{c}al yādô, 154, 155
^{c}ôd, 98
^{c}ôd '^{a}šer nôtar, 99
^{c}ôlām, 79, 220
^{c}oleh, 154
^{c}uṣû ^{c}ēsāh, 169

bā', 43, 61
bā'û, 35
ba^{ca}bûr, 105
bāmôt, 17, 216
bāmôtêkā , 15
bānāh, 220
bārak, 65
bārar, 232
bāśār, 52, 54, 217
bassātēr, 126
bat šeba^c bat '^{e}lî^{c}am, 123
bayit, 55, 56, 65, 78, 82

ROBERT POLZIN is Director, School of Comparative Literary Studies, and Professor of Religion, Carleton University. He is the author of *Moses and the Deuteronomist* and *Samuel and the Deuteronomist*, both volumes in a series on the Deuteronomic History, as well as *Late Biblical Hebrew*.